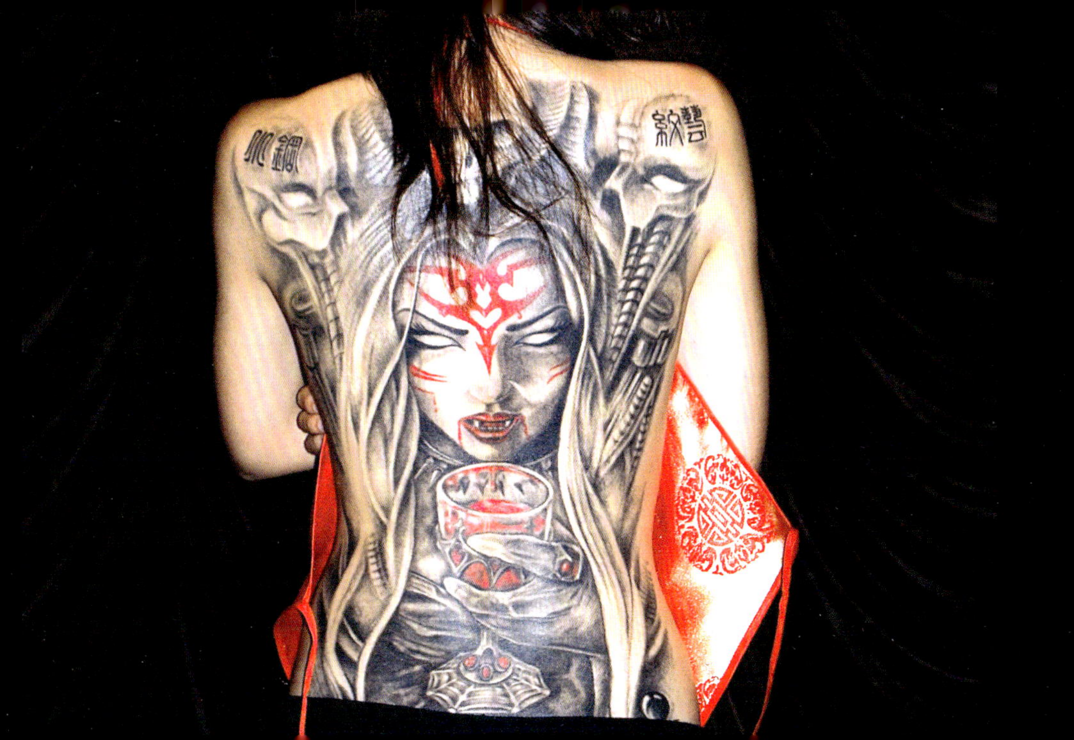

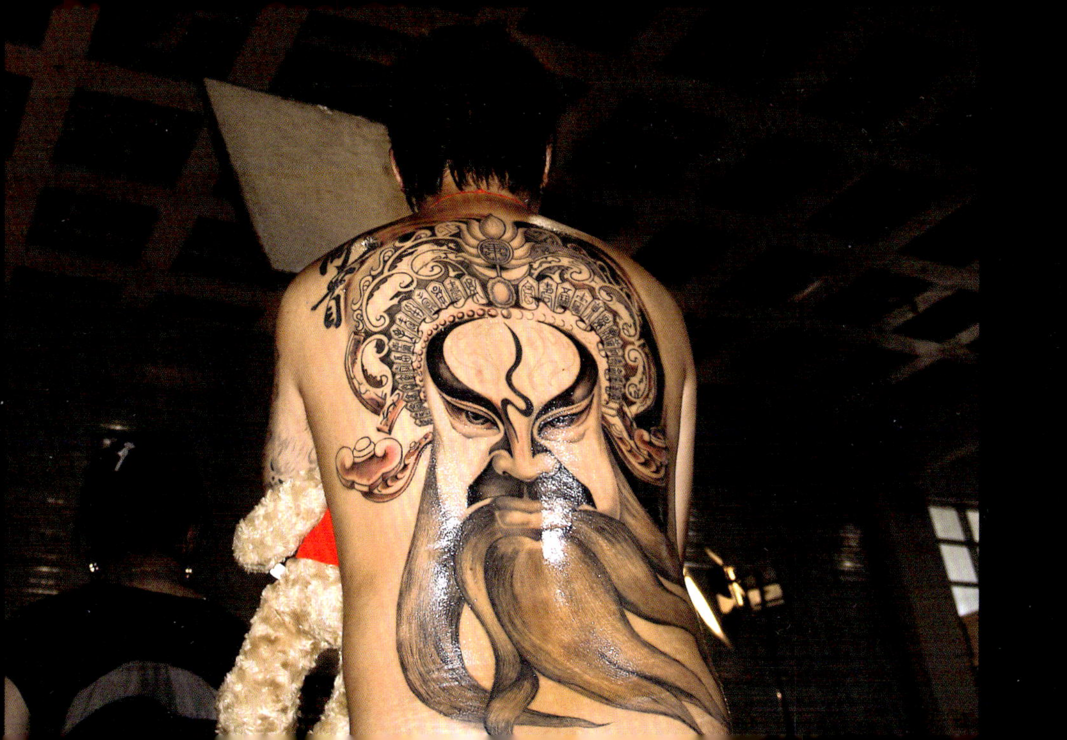

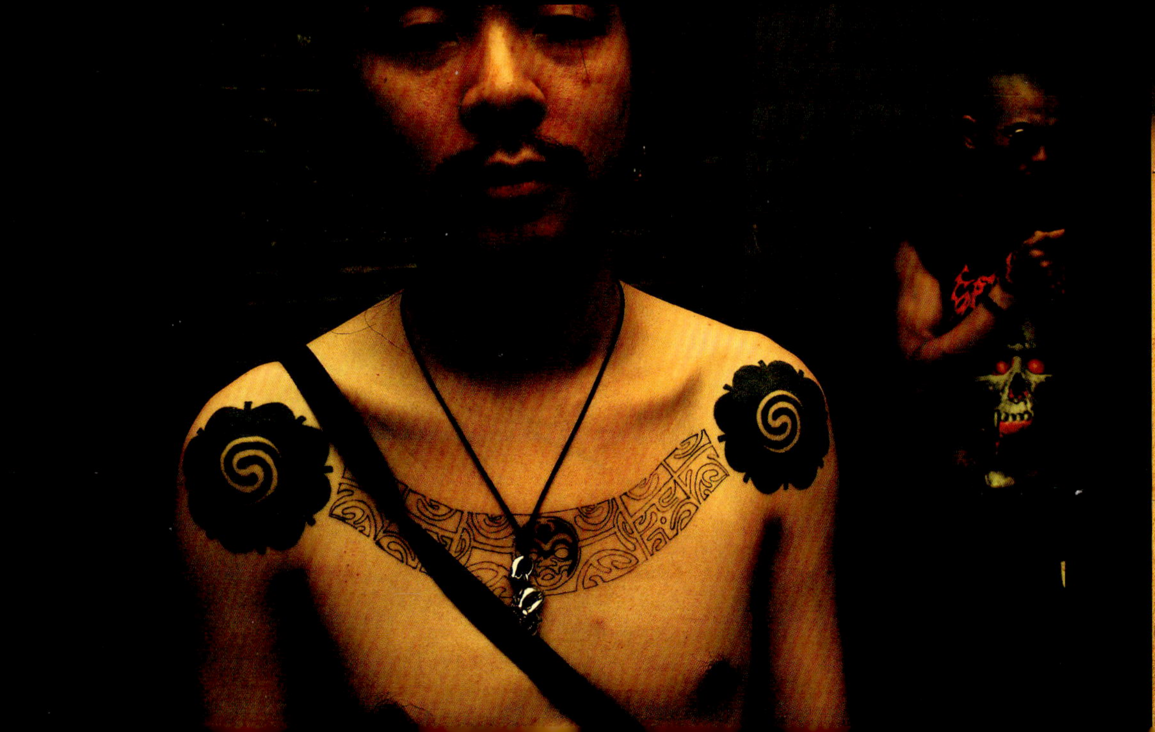

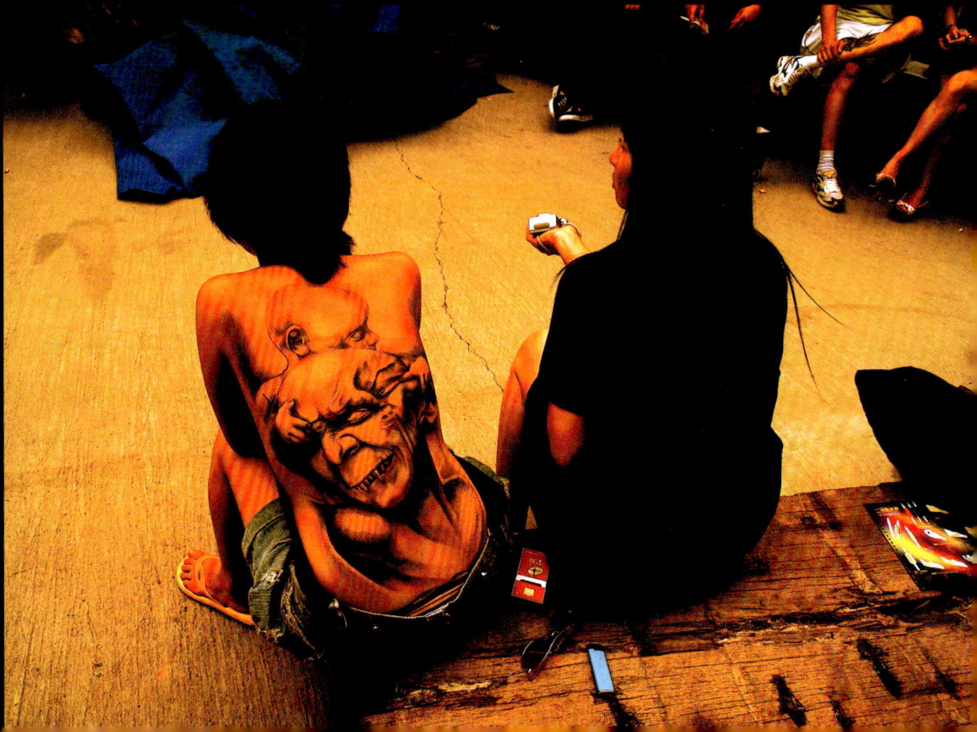

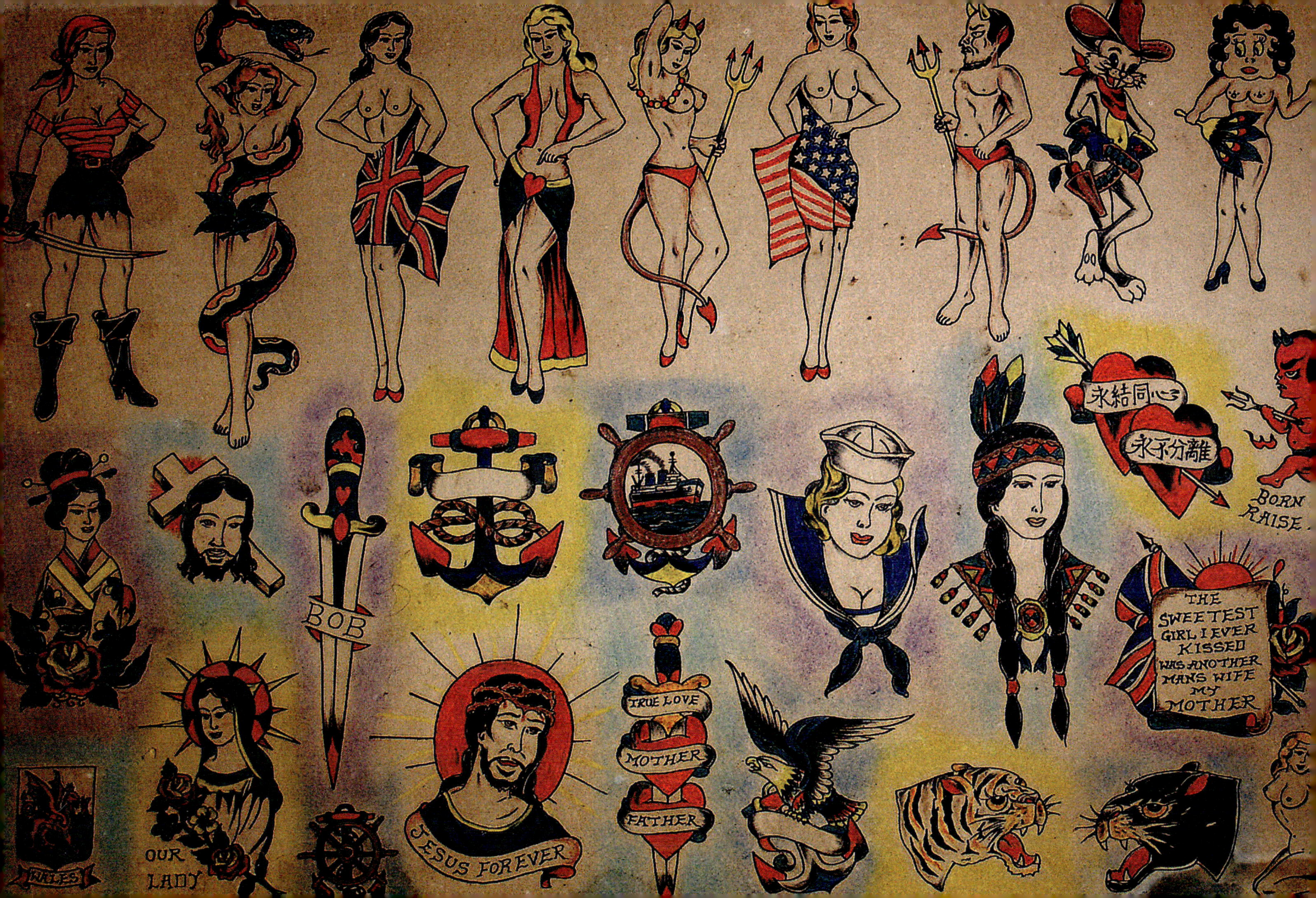

永結同心
永不分離
BORN
RAISE
BOB
THE SWEETEST GIRL I EVER KISSED WAS ANOTHER MANS WIFE MY MOTHER
TRUE LOVE
MOTHER
FATHER
JESUS FOREVER
OUR LADY
WALES

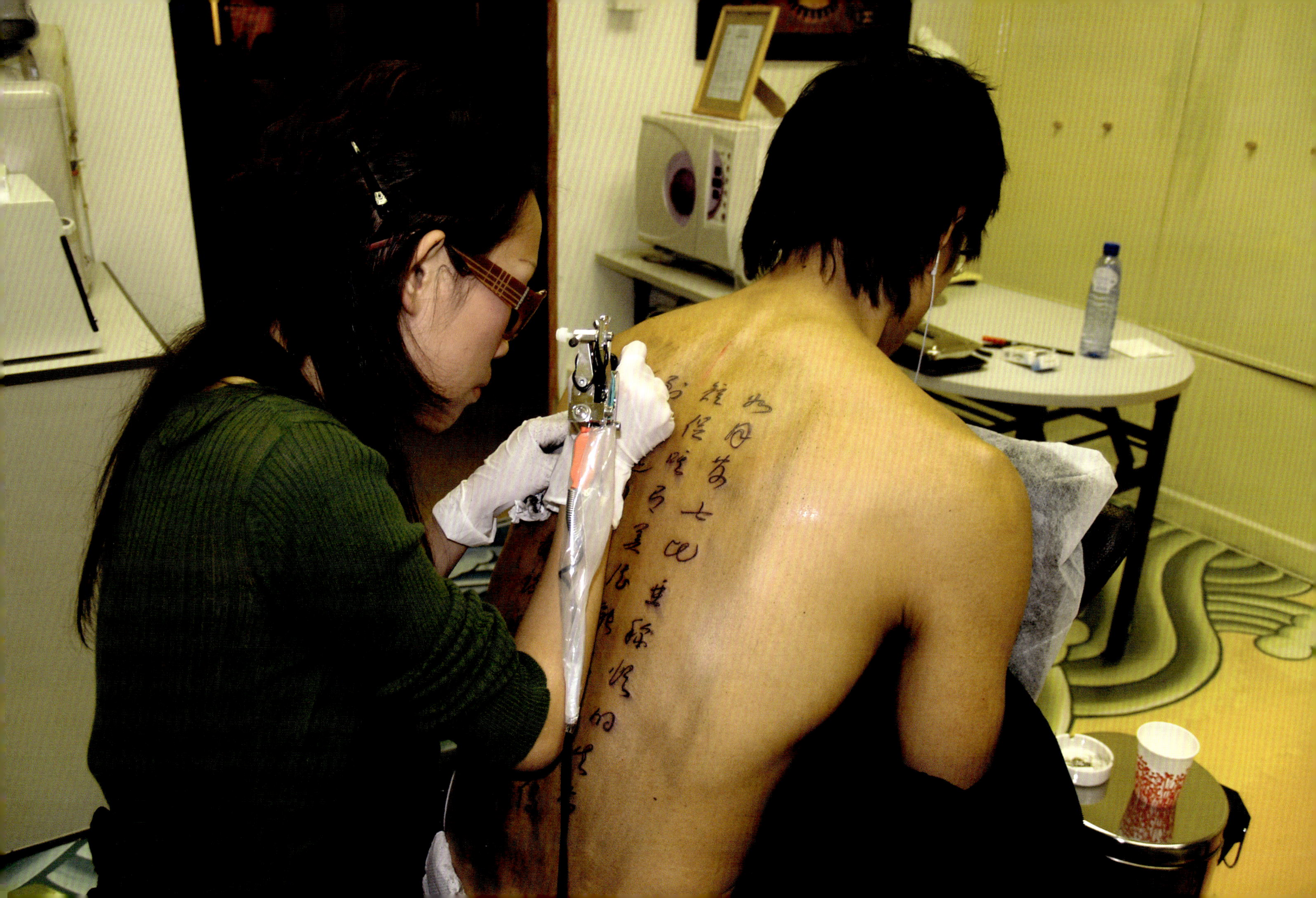

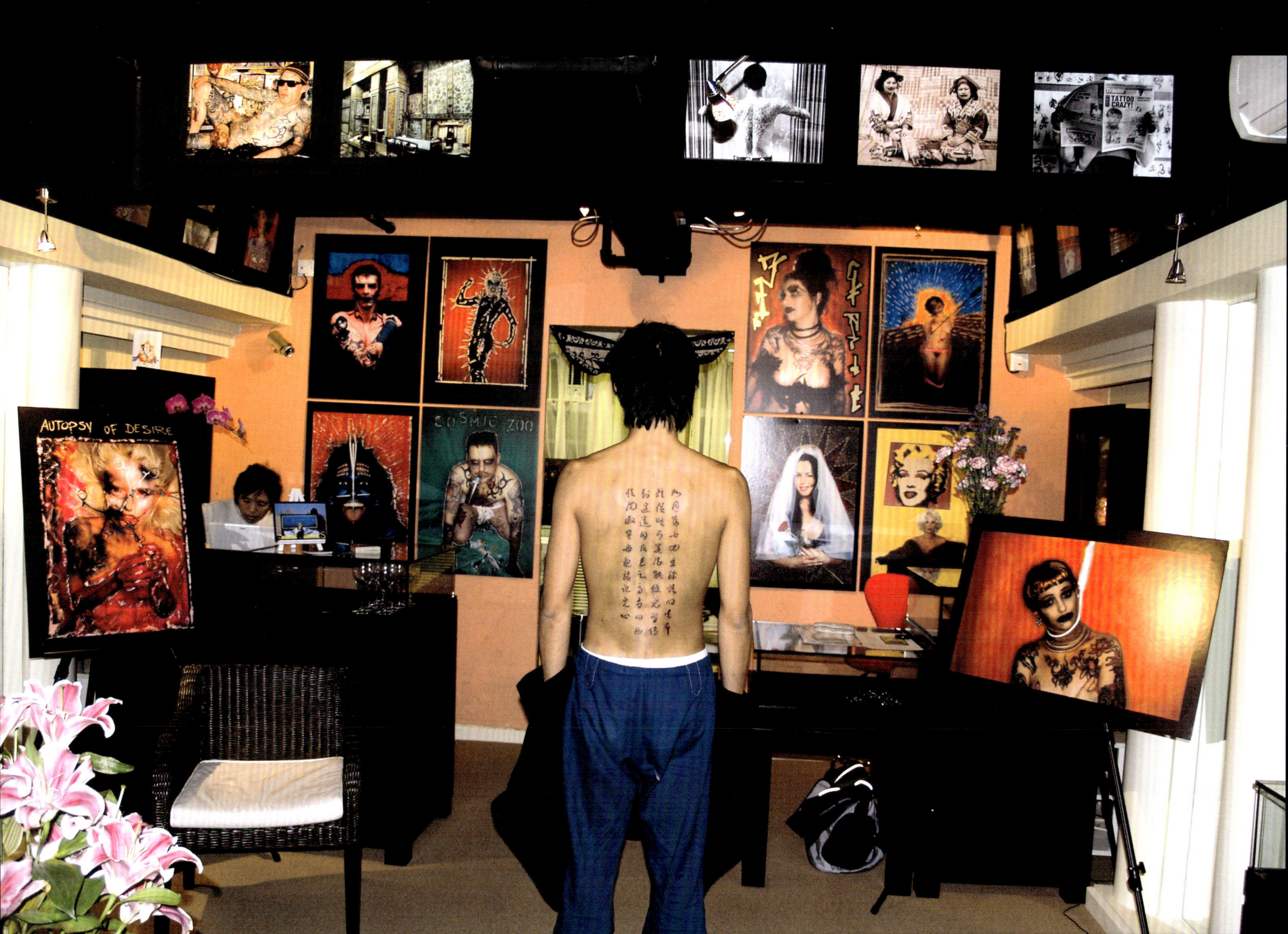
TATTOO CRAZY!
AUTOPSY OF DESIRE
COSMIC ZOO

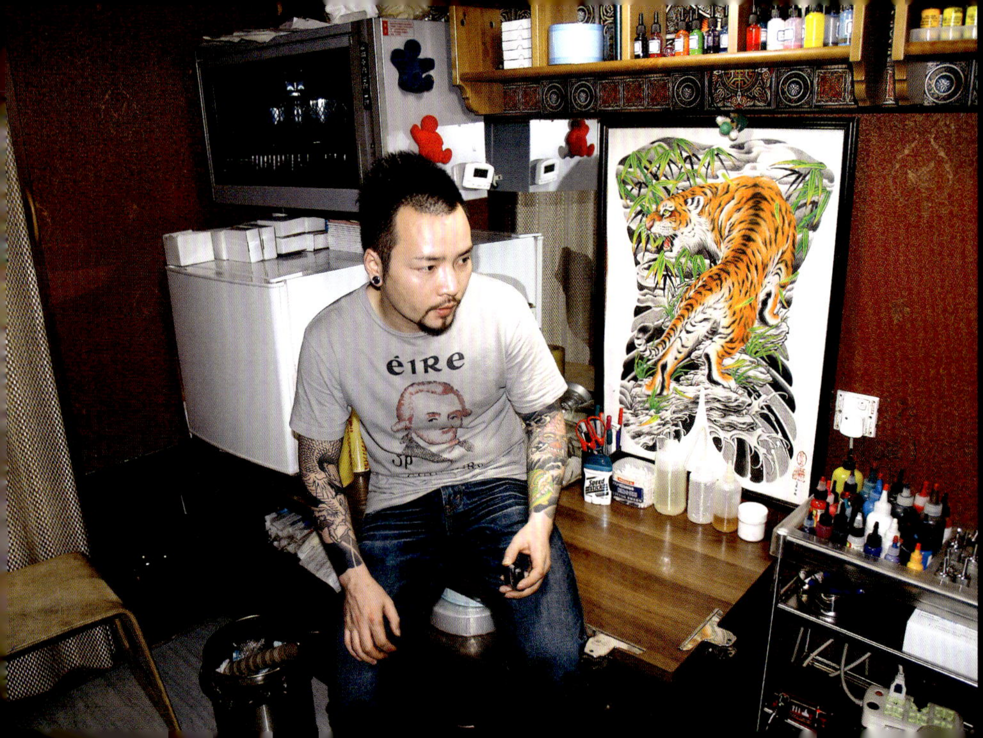
éire

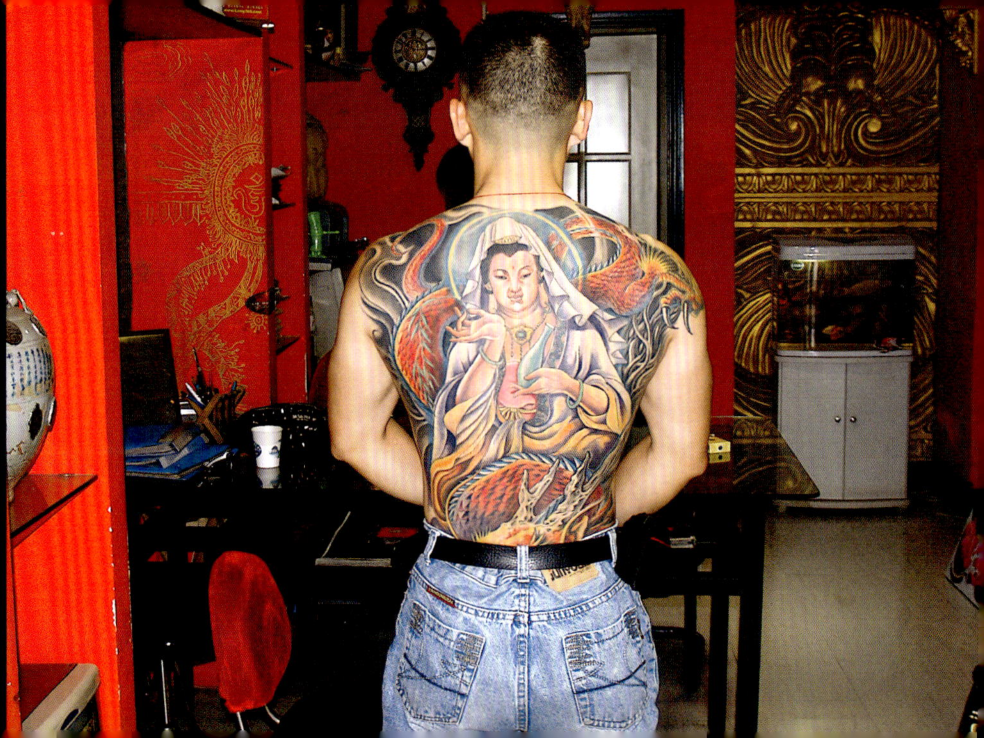

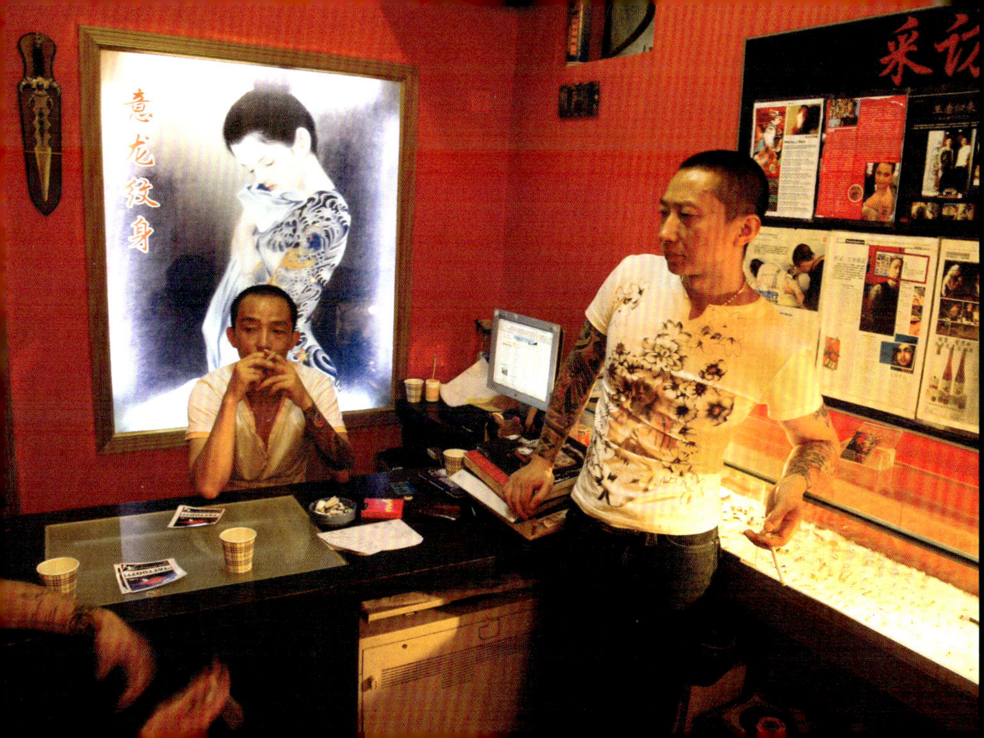
意龙纹身
采访

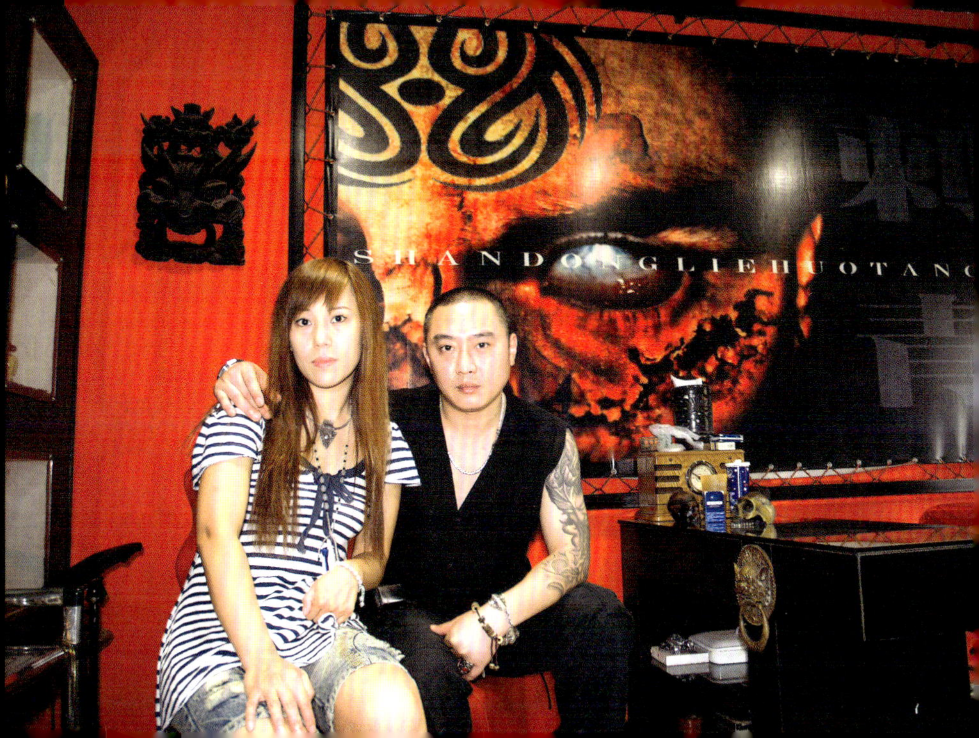
SHANDONGLIEHUOTAN

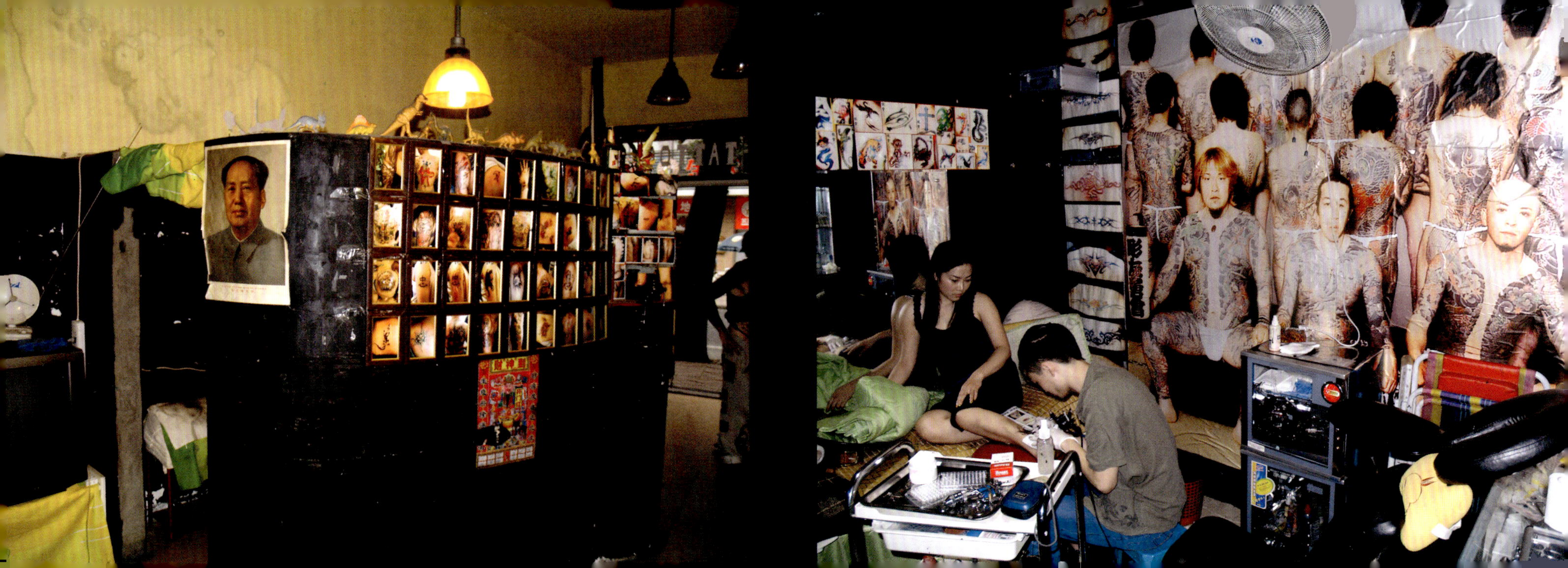
財神到

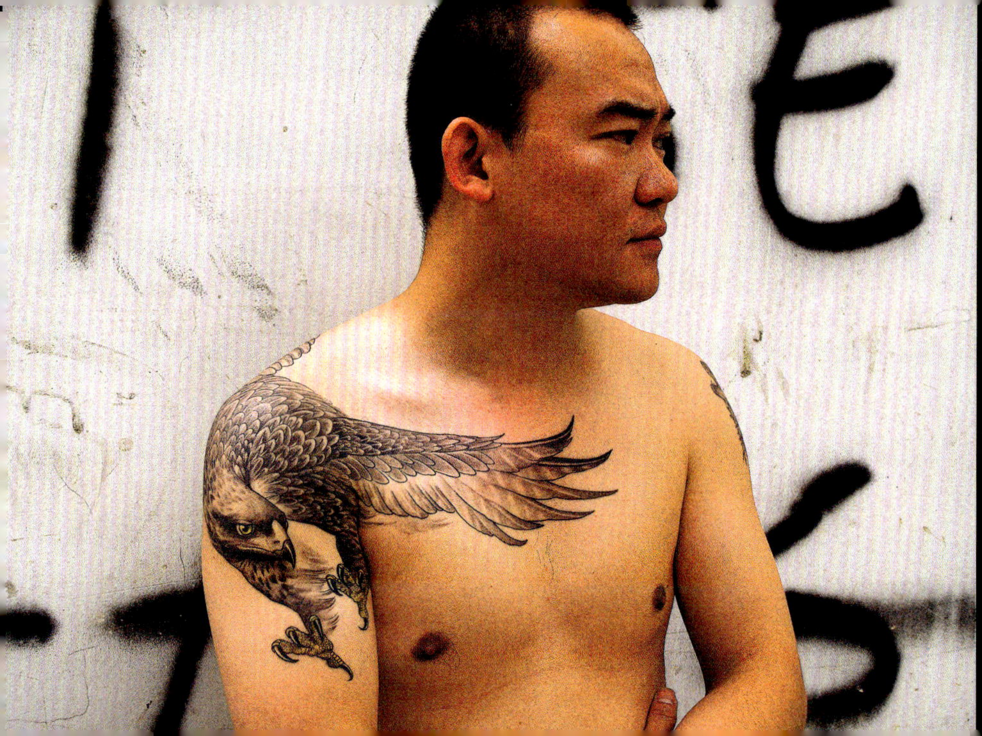

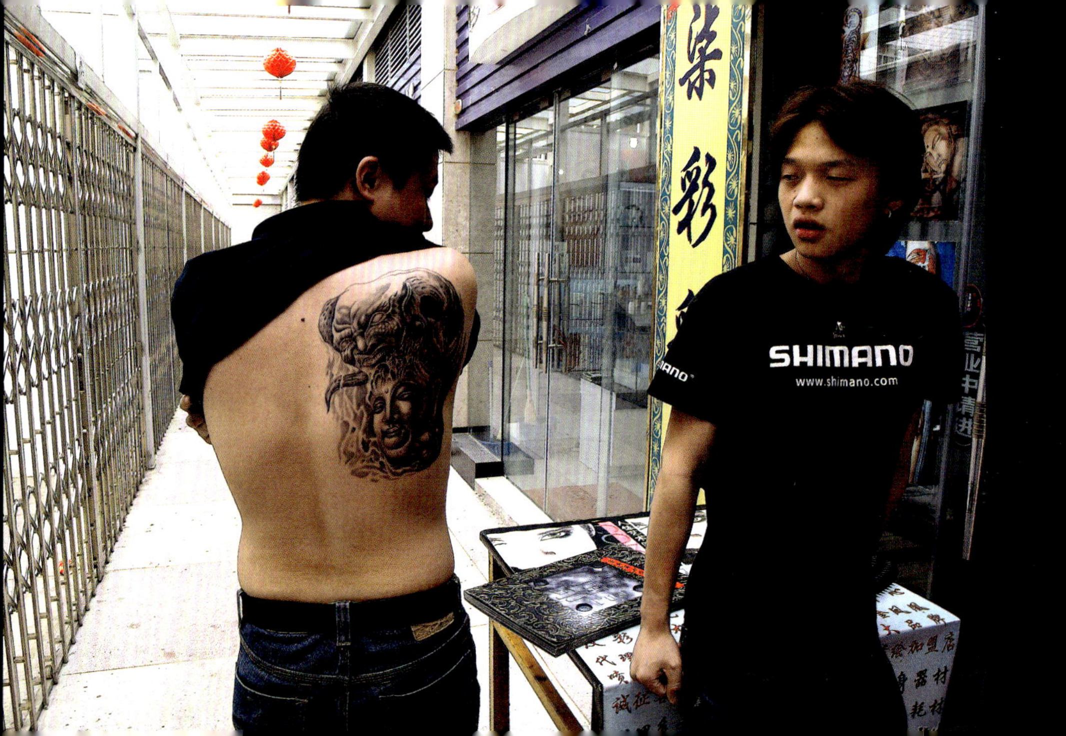
SHIMANO
www.shimano.com

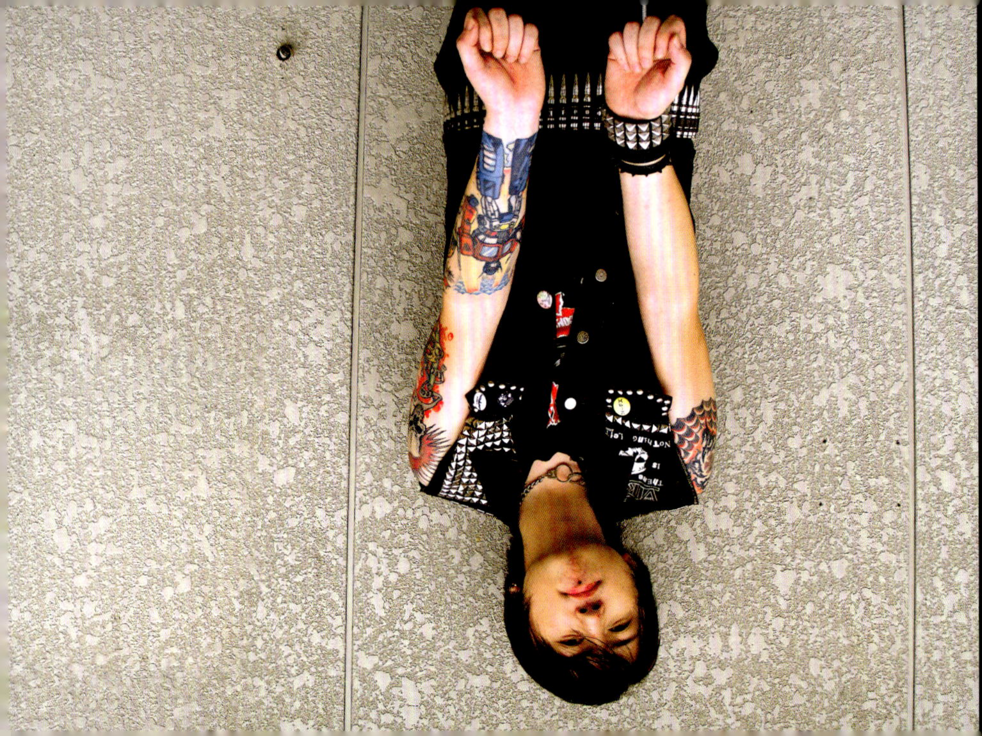

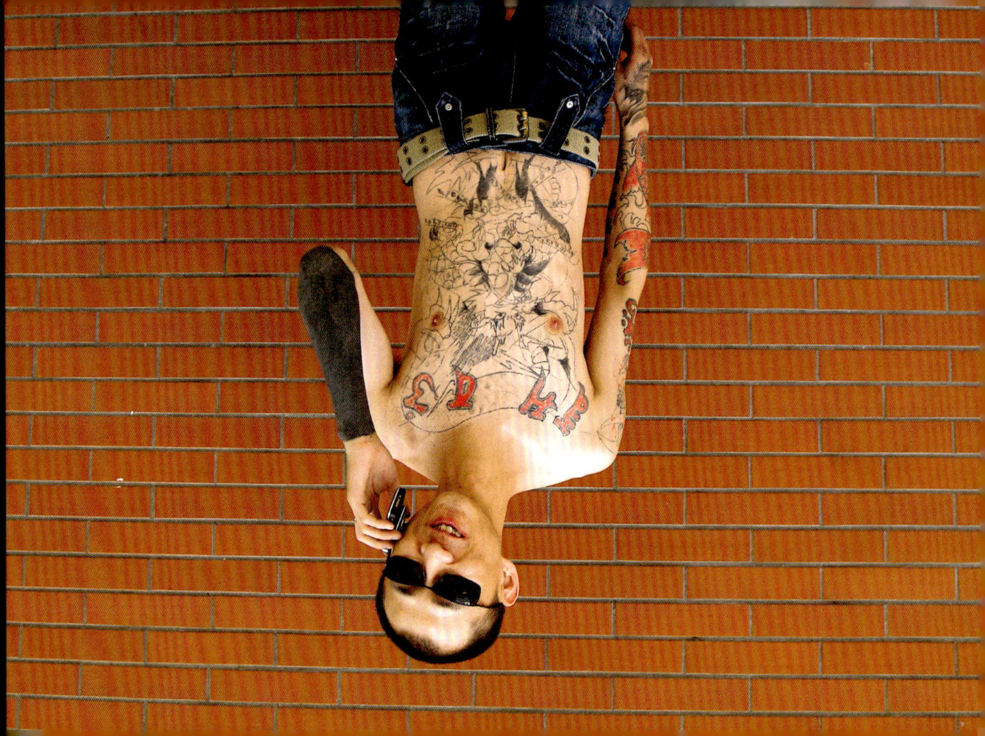

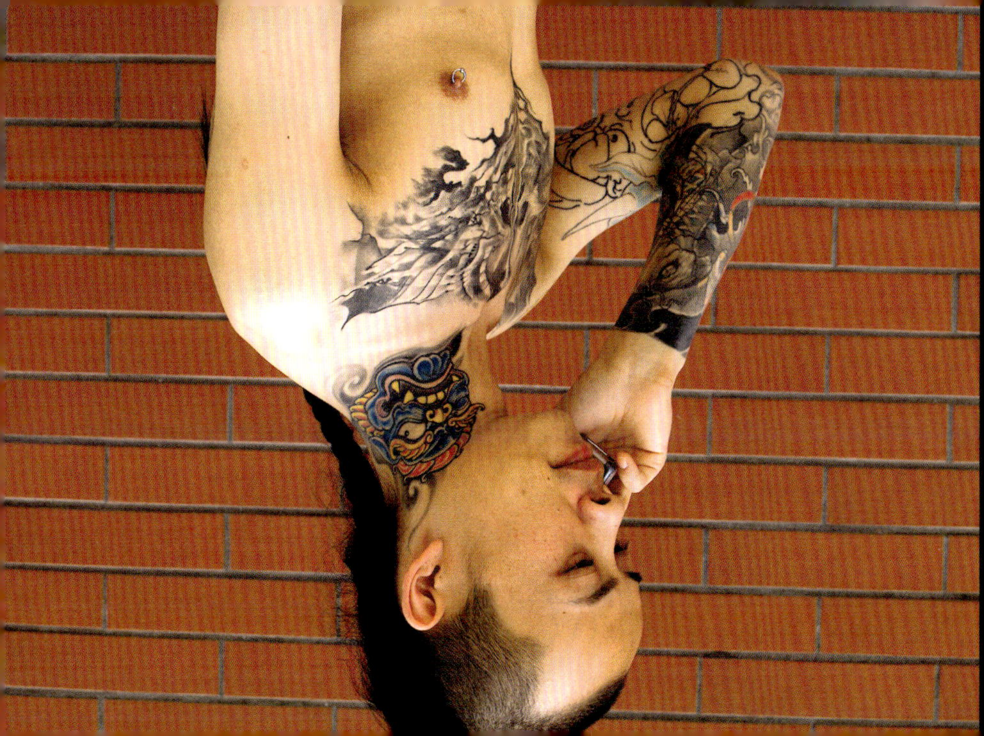

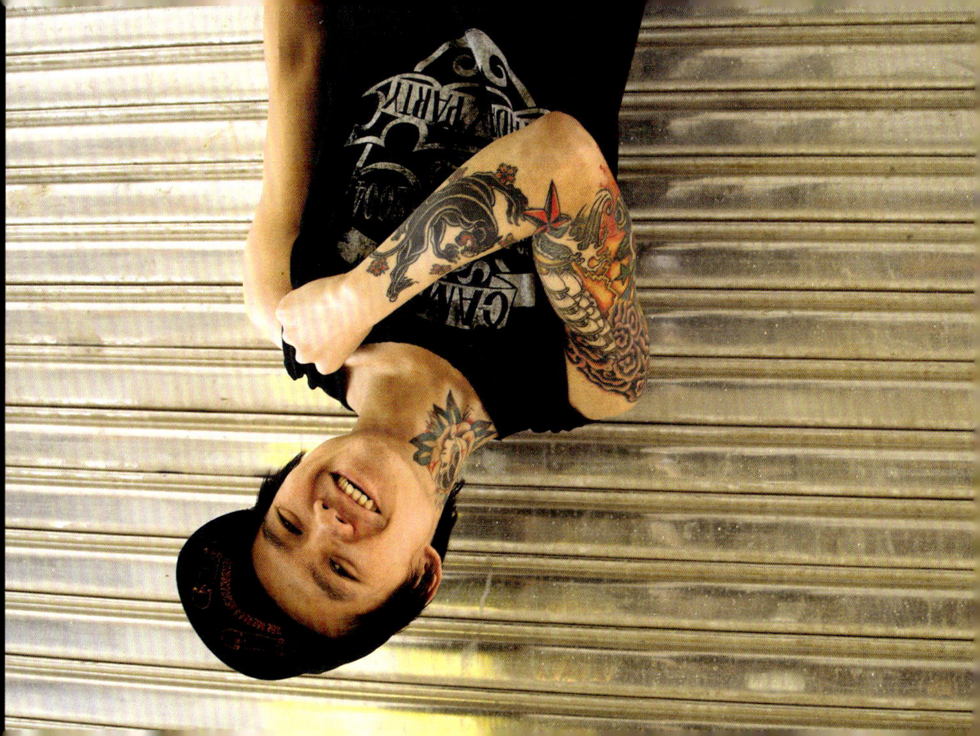

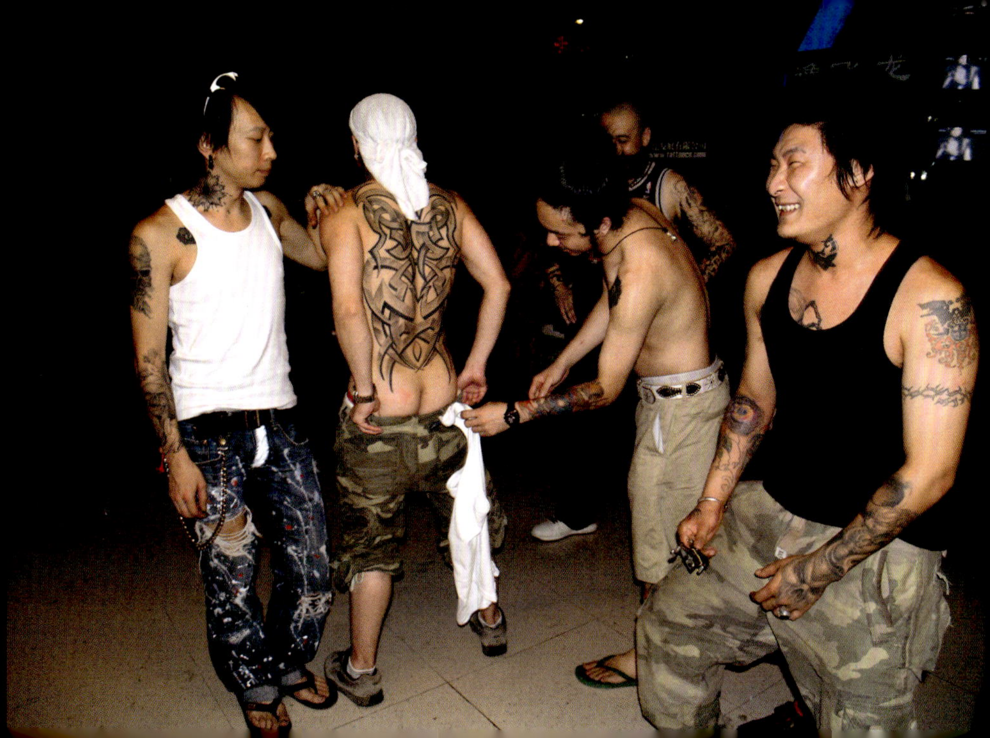
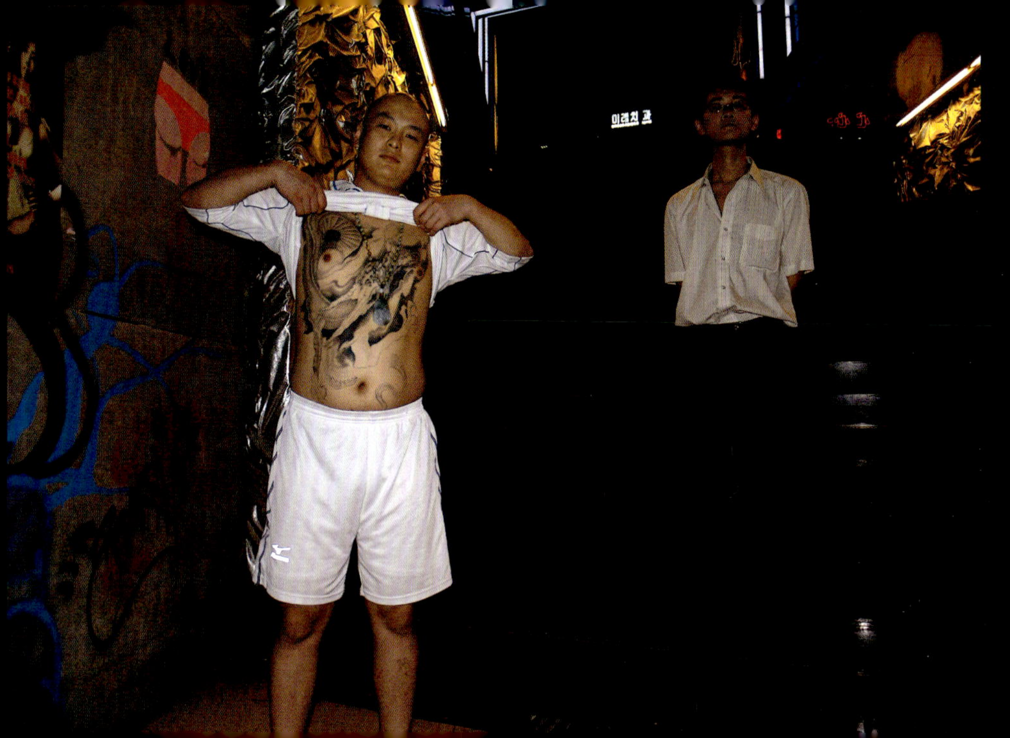

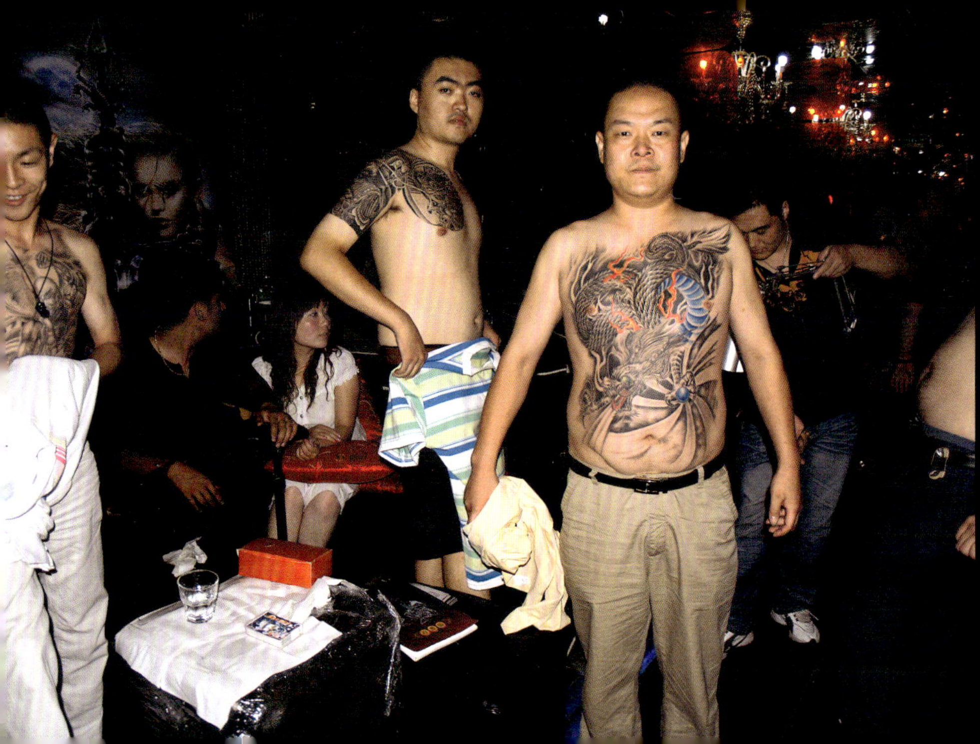

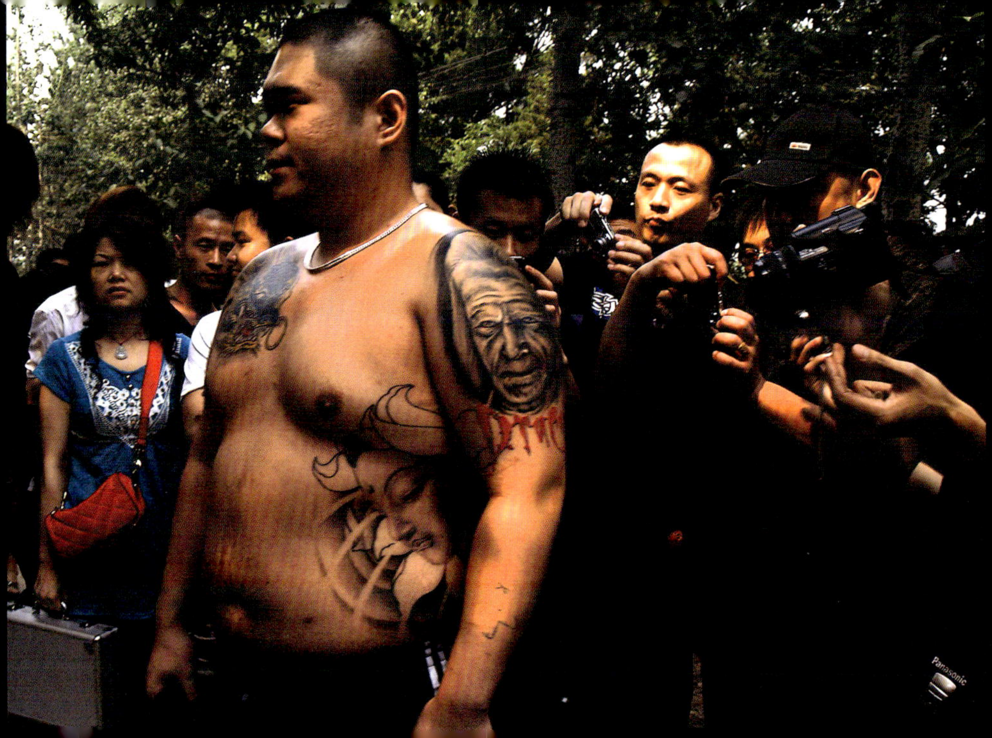
Panasonic

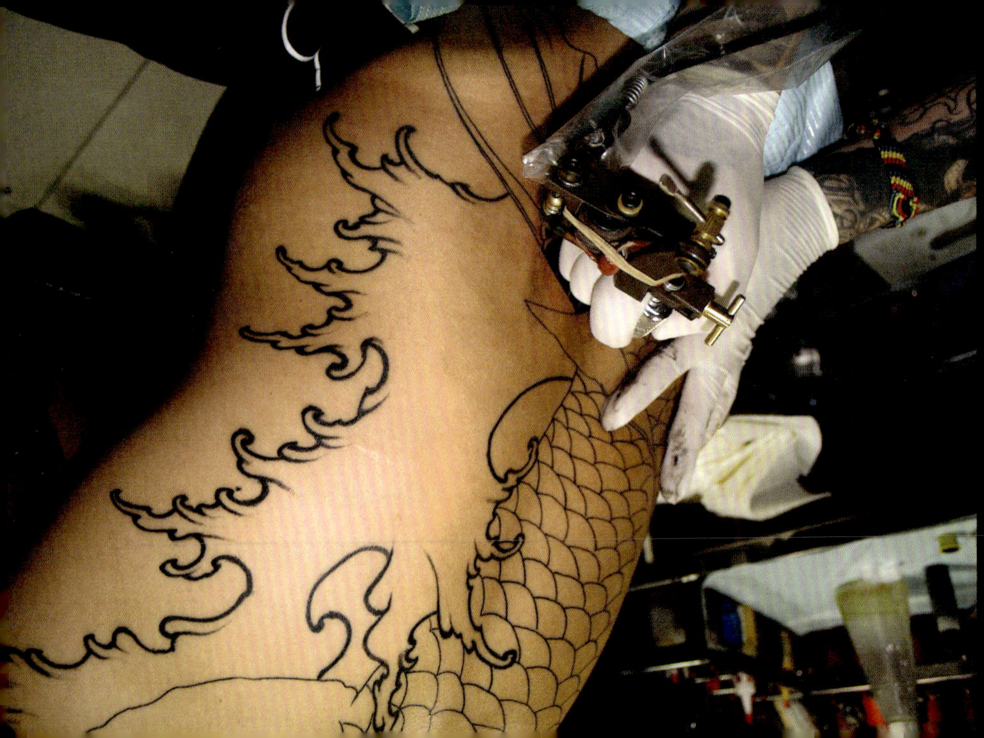

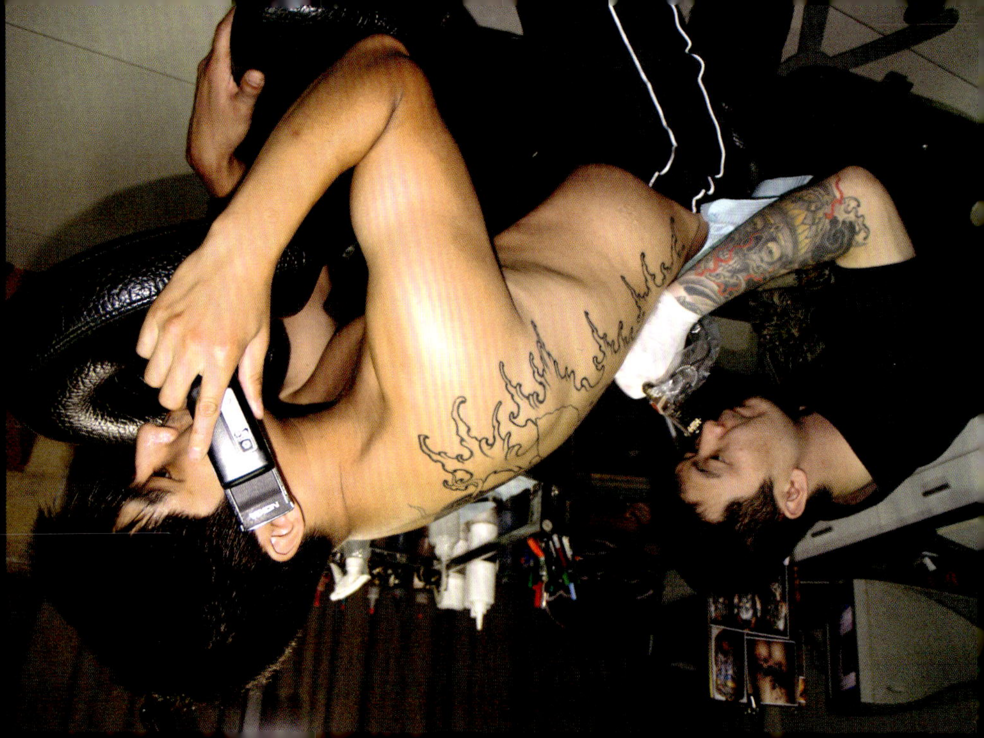

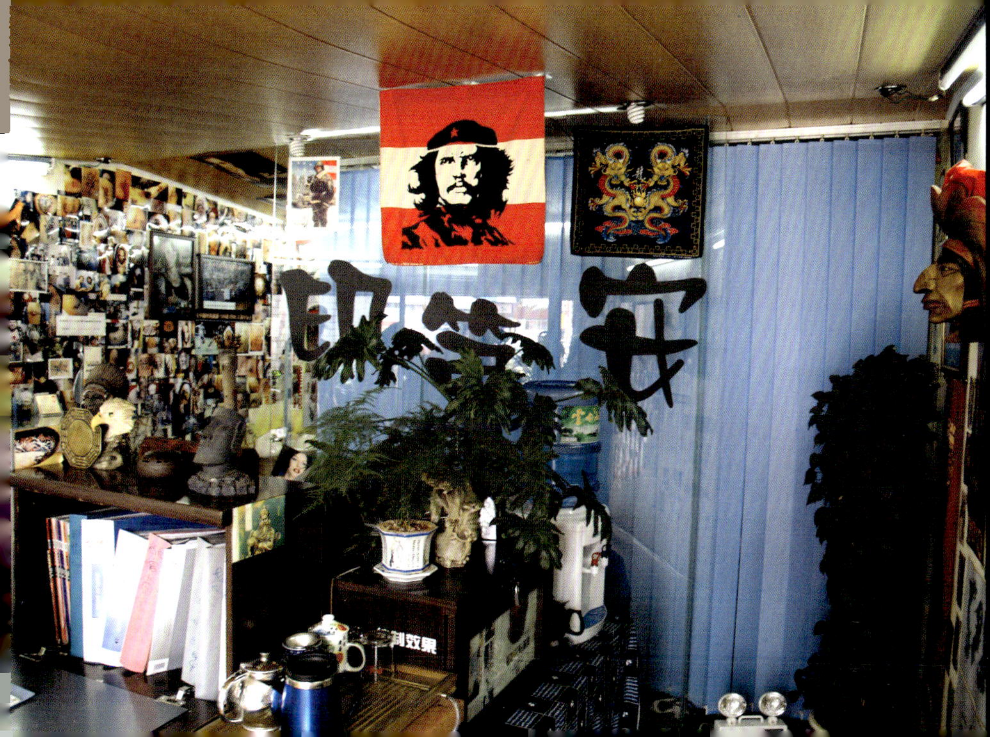

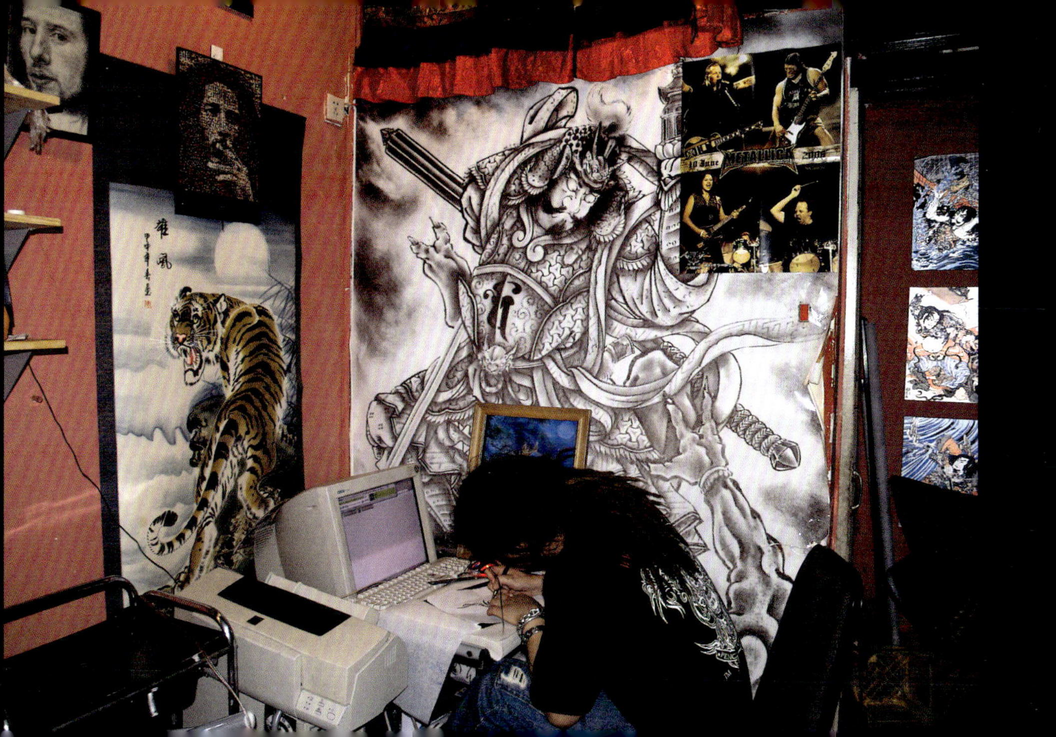
METALLICA

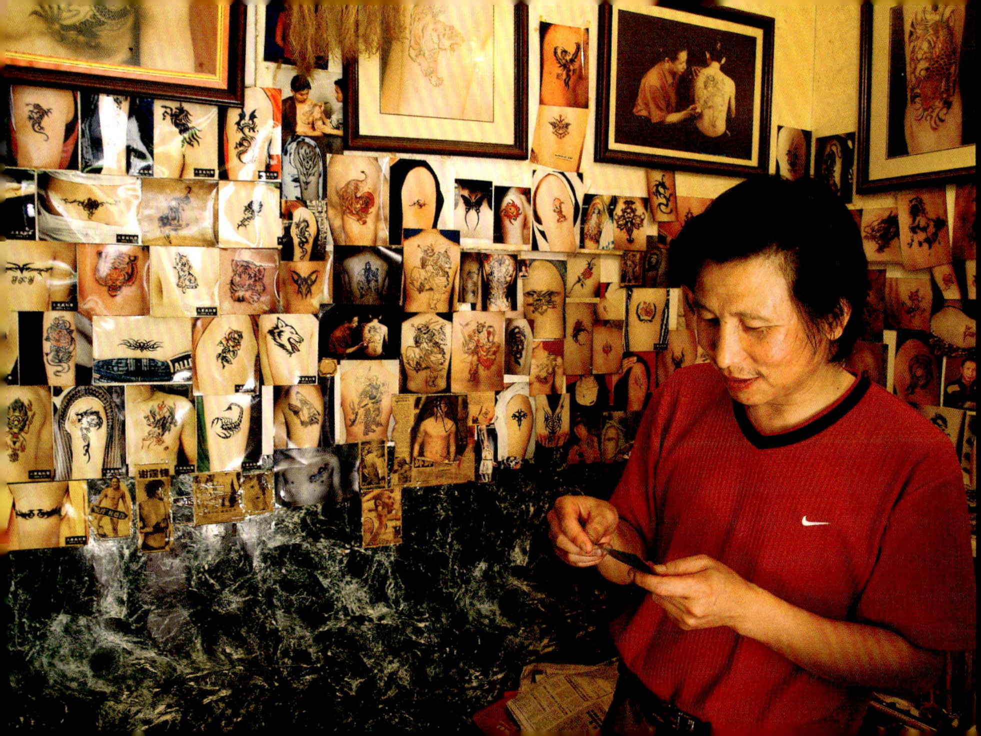

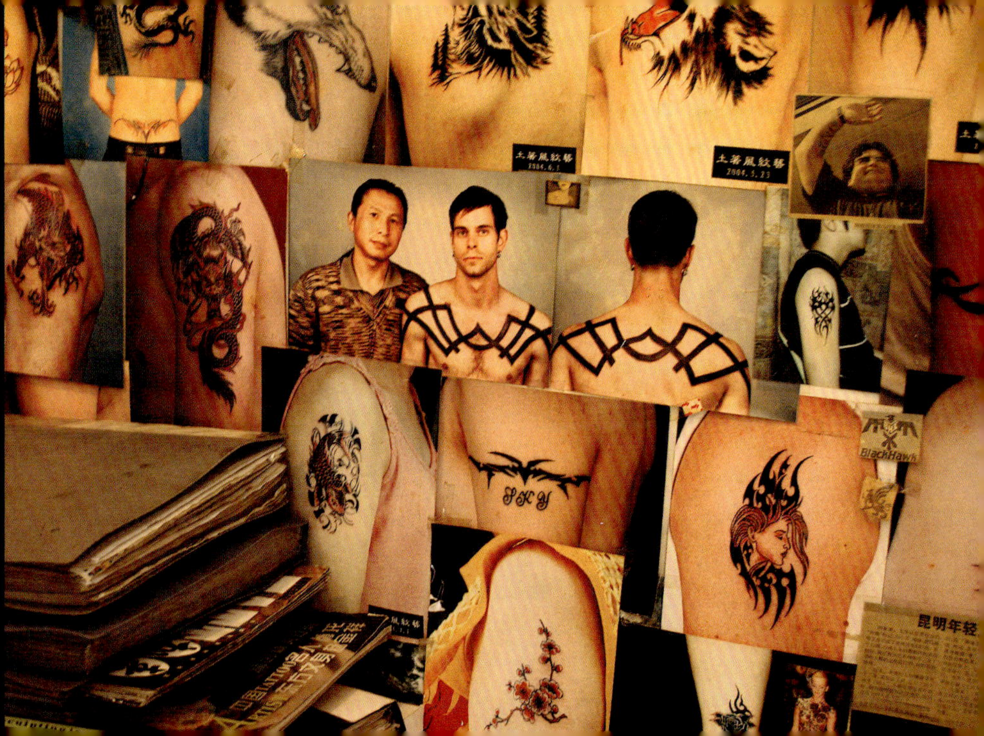
BlackHawk
昆明年轻

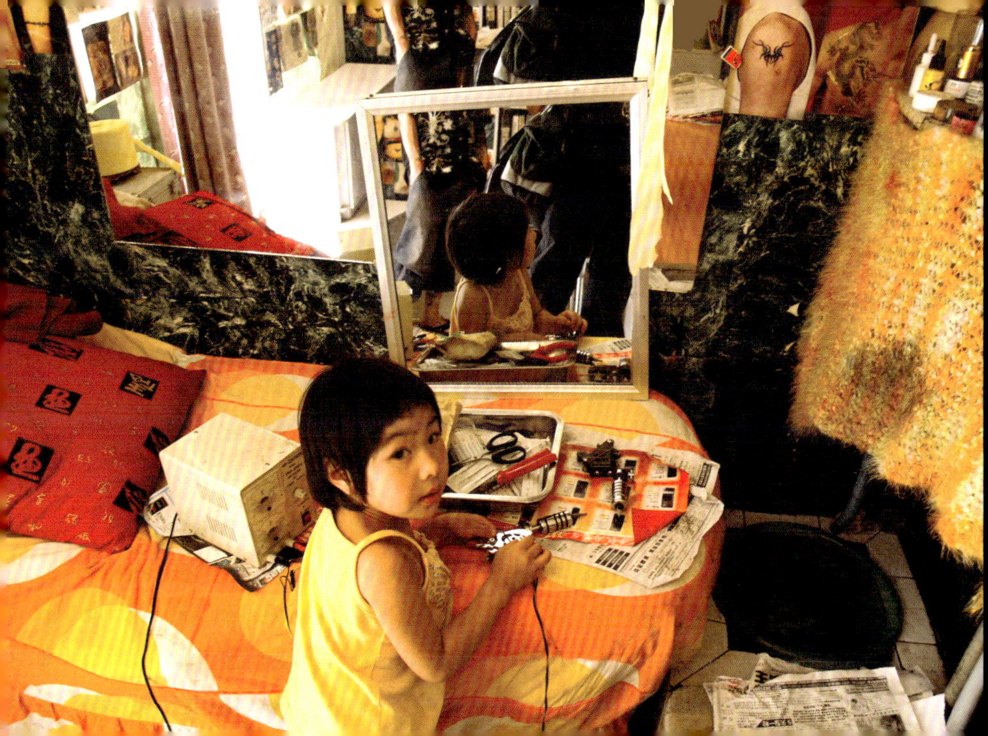

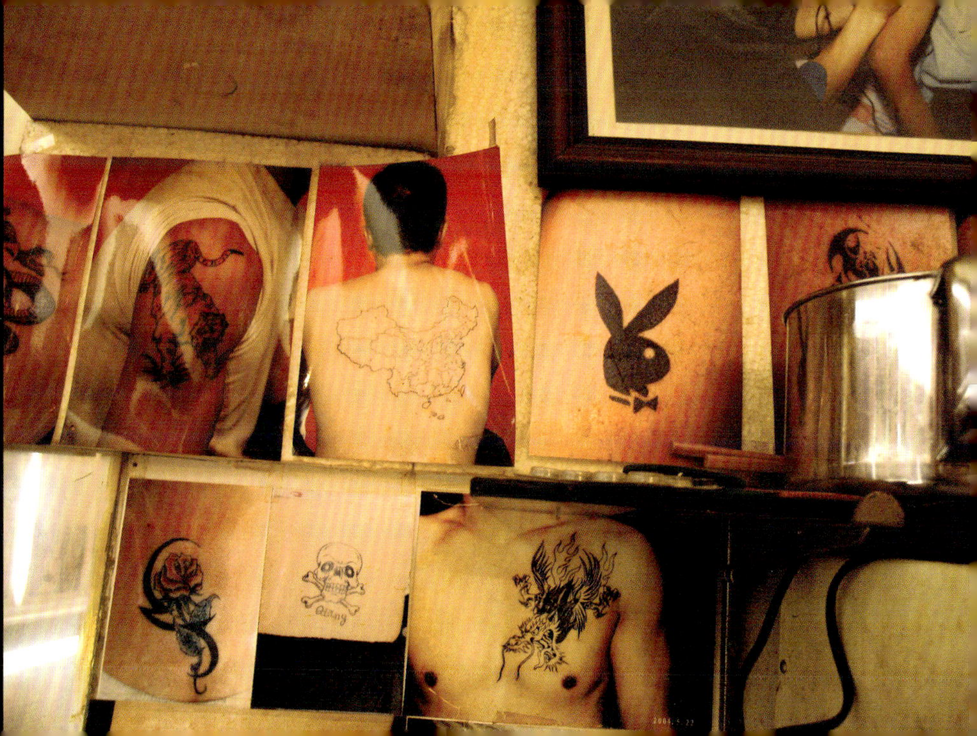

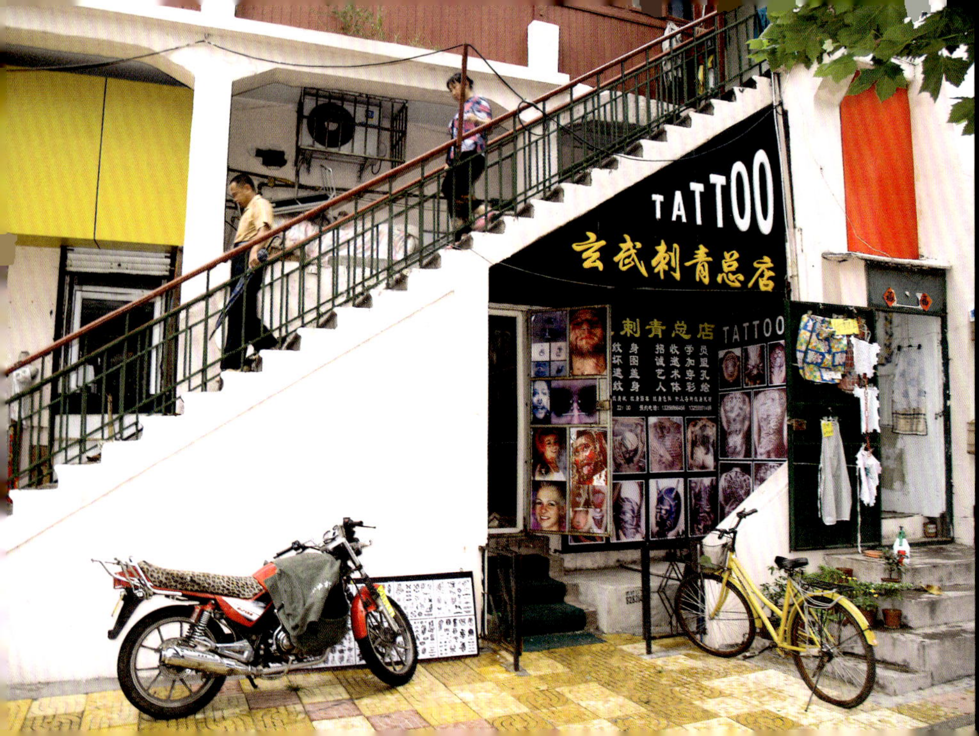
TATTOO
玄武刺青总店
TATTOO

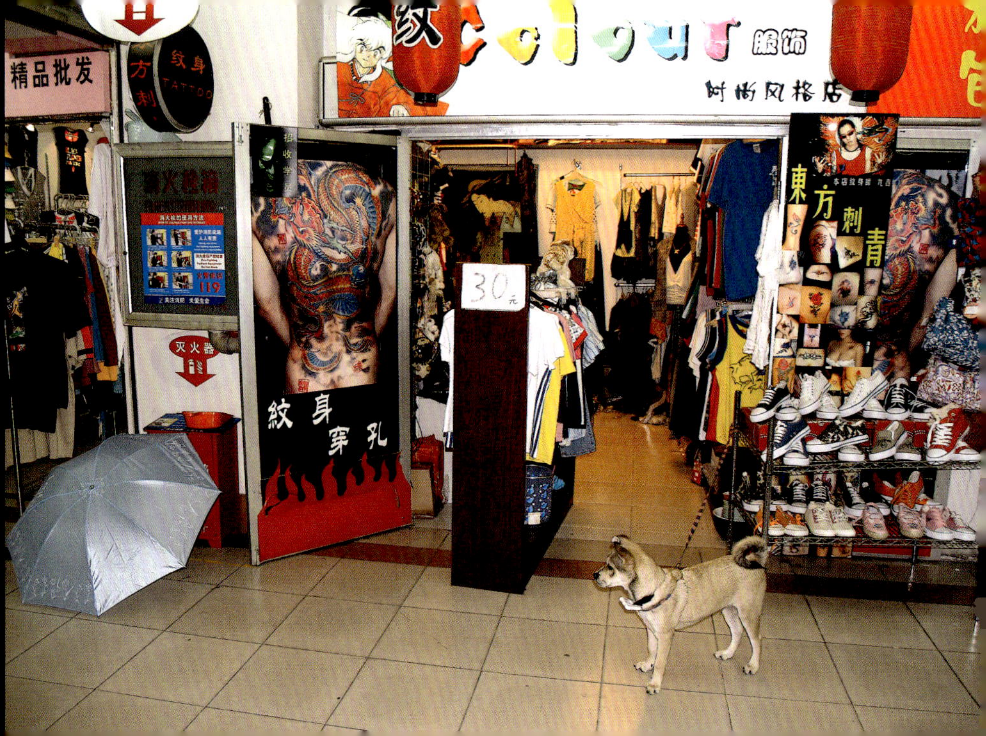
精品批发
纹身
TATTOO
服饰
时尚风格店
灭火器
紋身
穿孔
30元
東方刺青

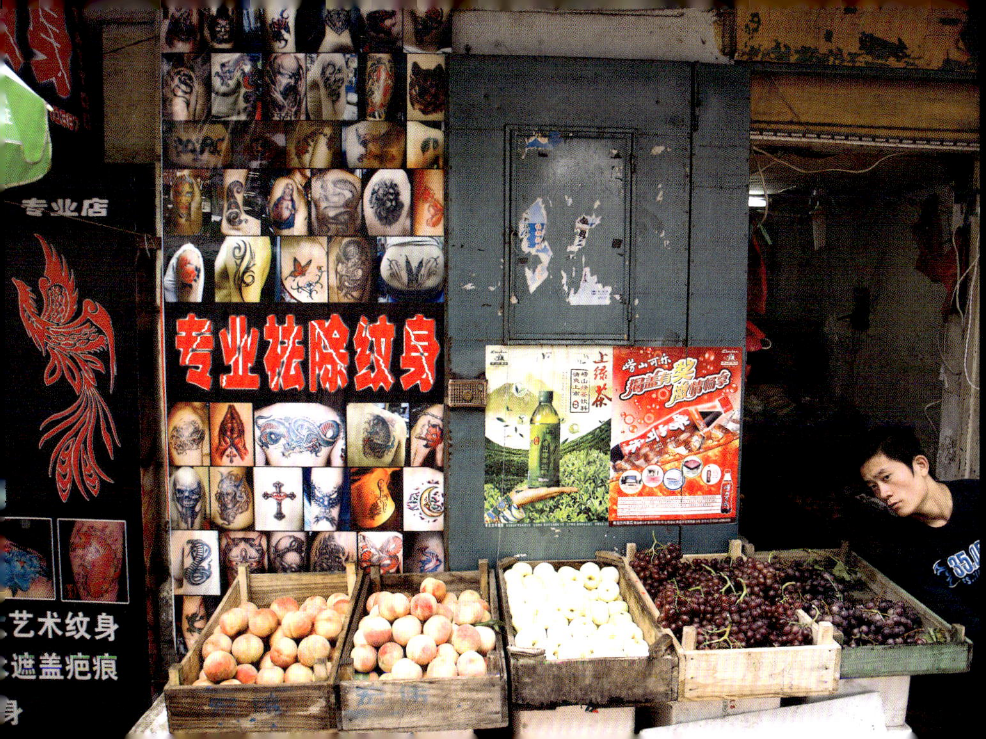
专业店
专业祛除纹身
艺术纹身
遮盖疤痕

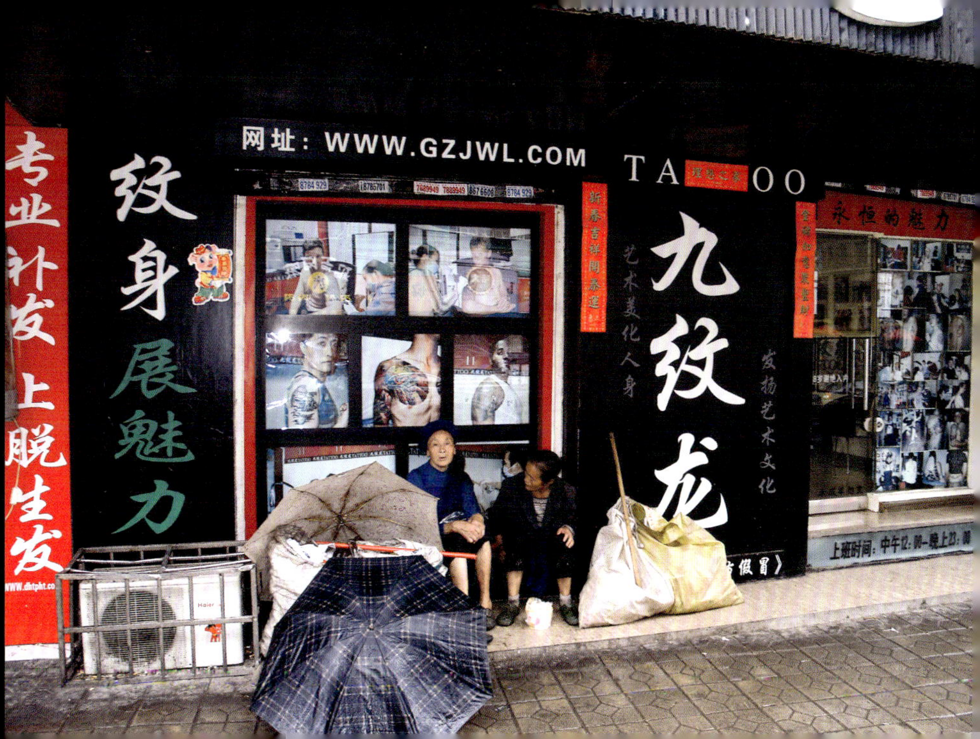
网址：WWW.GZJWL.COM
专业补发
上脱生发
纹身
展魅力
九纹龙
艺术美化人身
发扬艺术文化
永恒的魅力

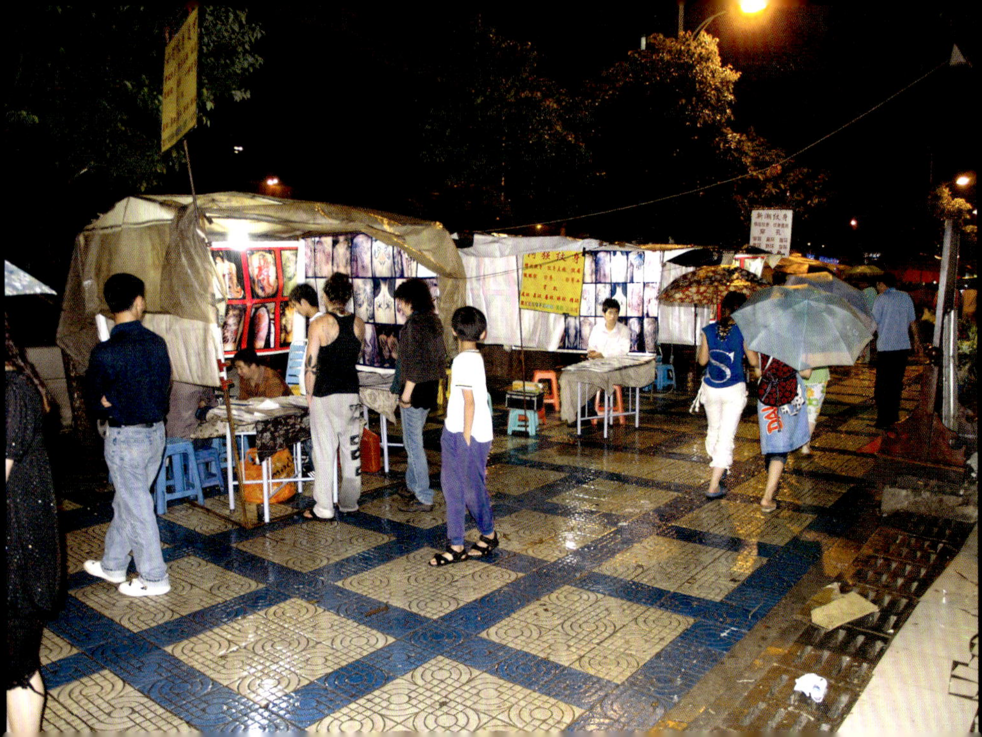

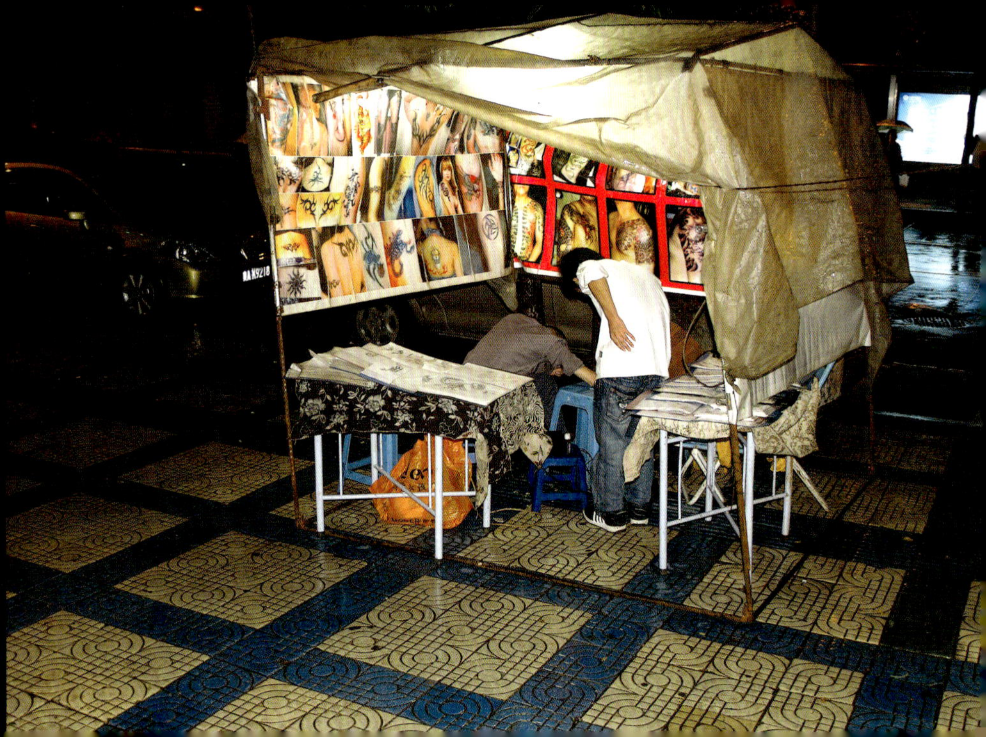

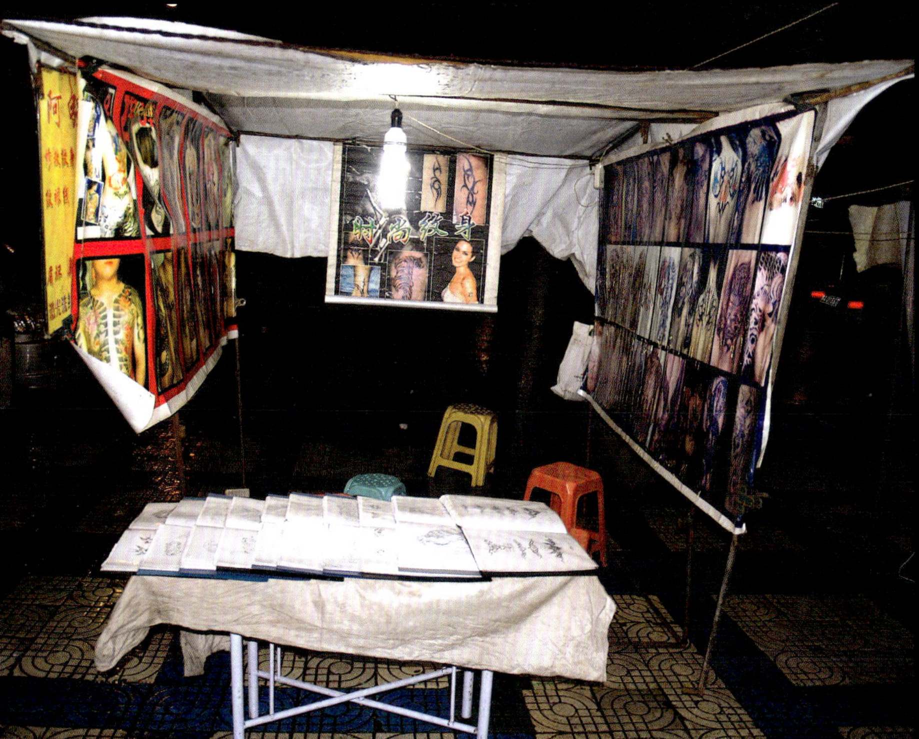
时尚纹身

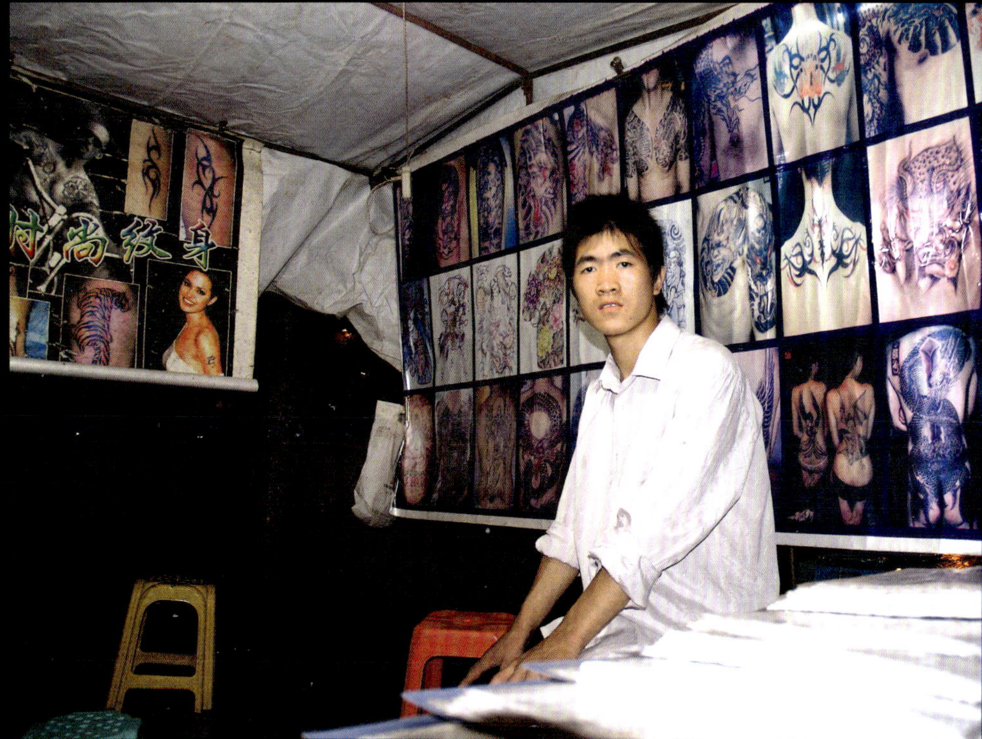
时尚纹身

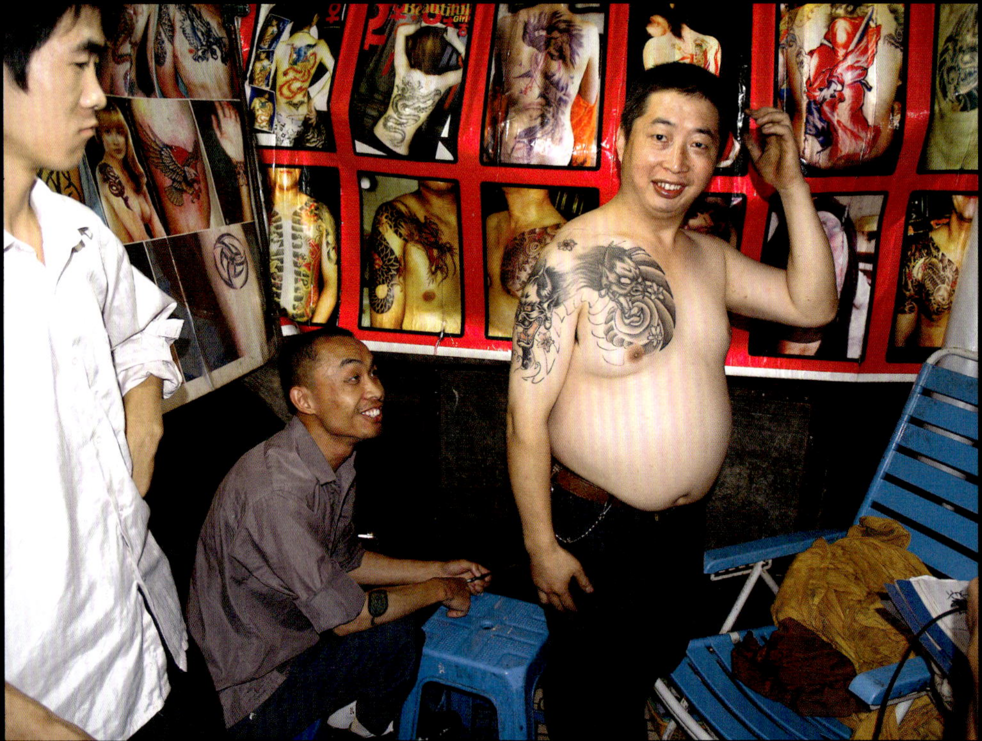

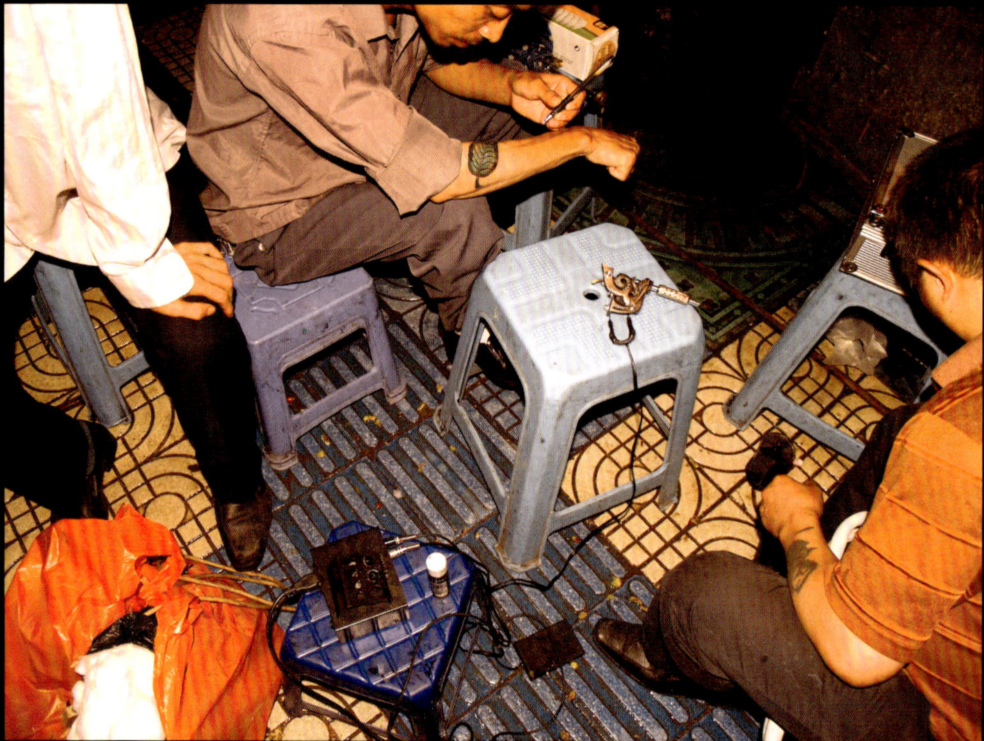

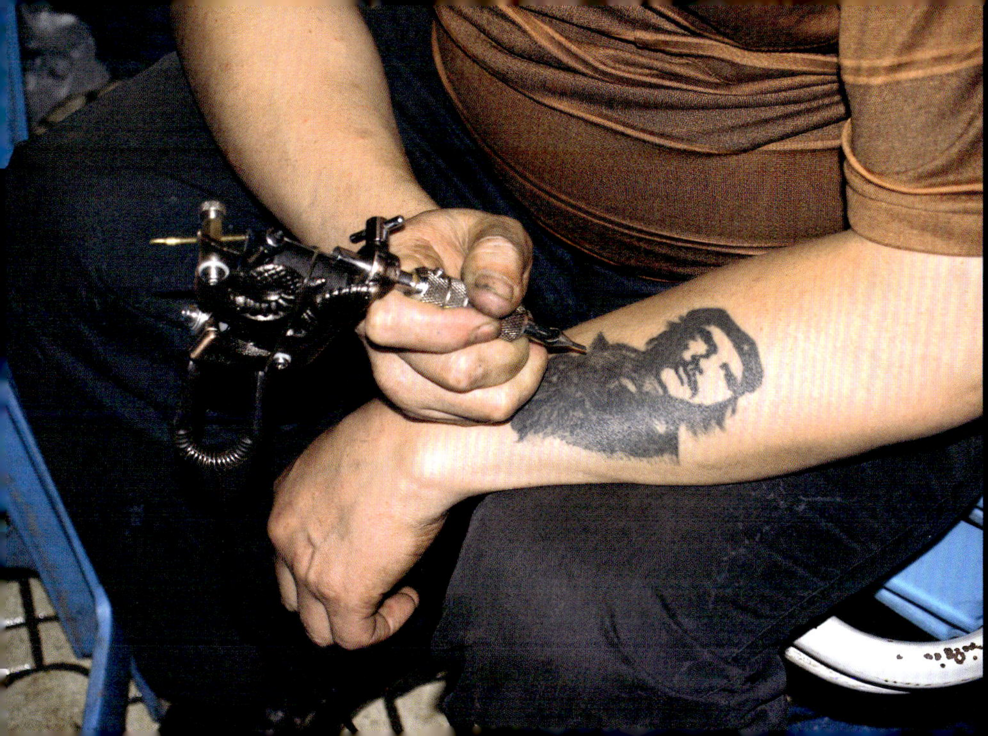

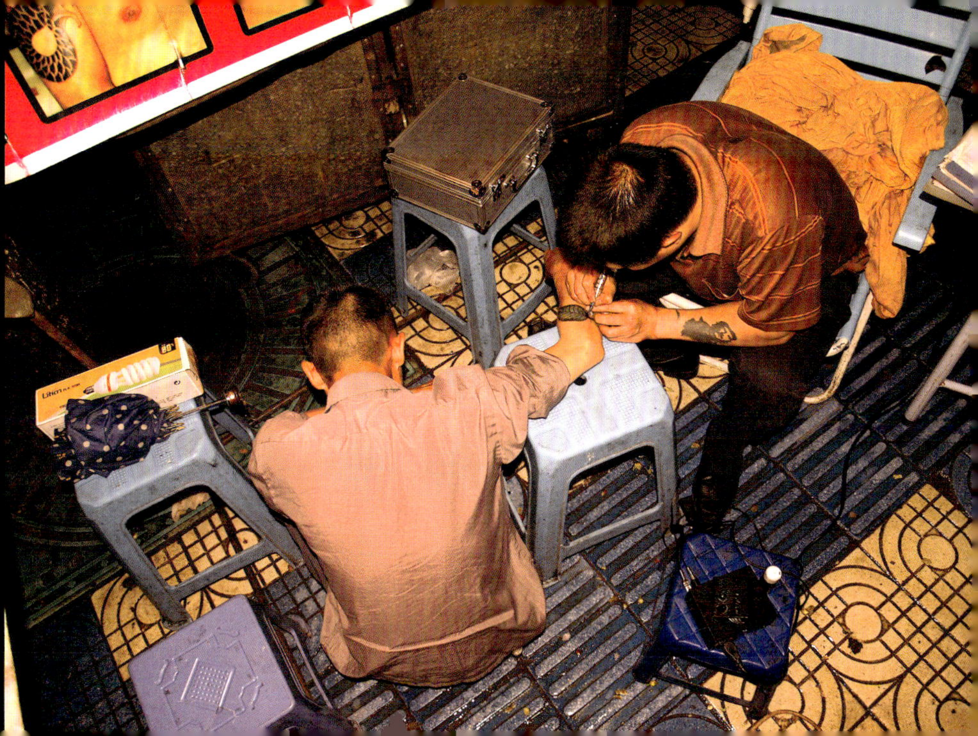

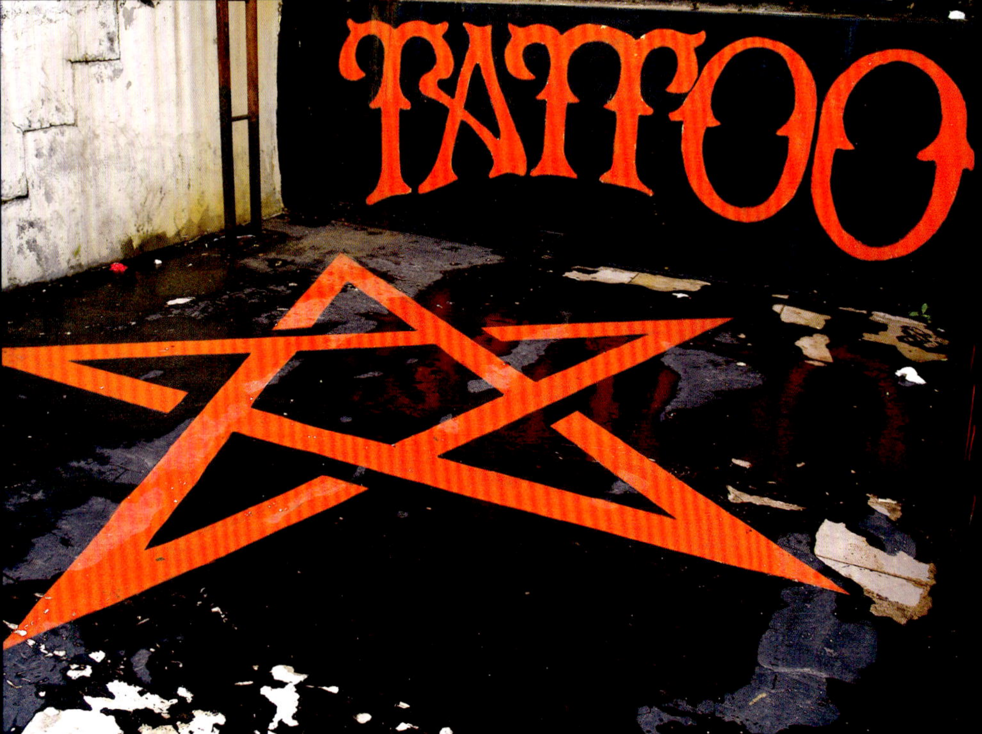
TATTOO

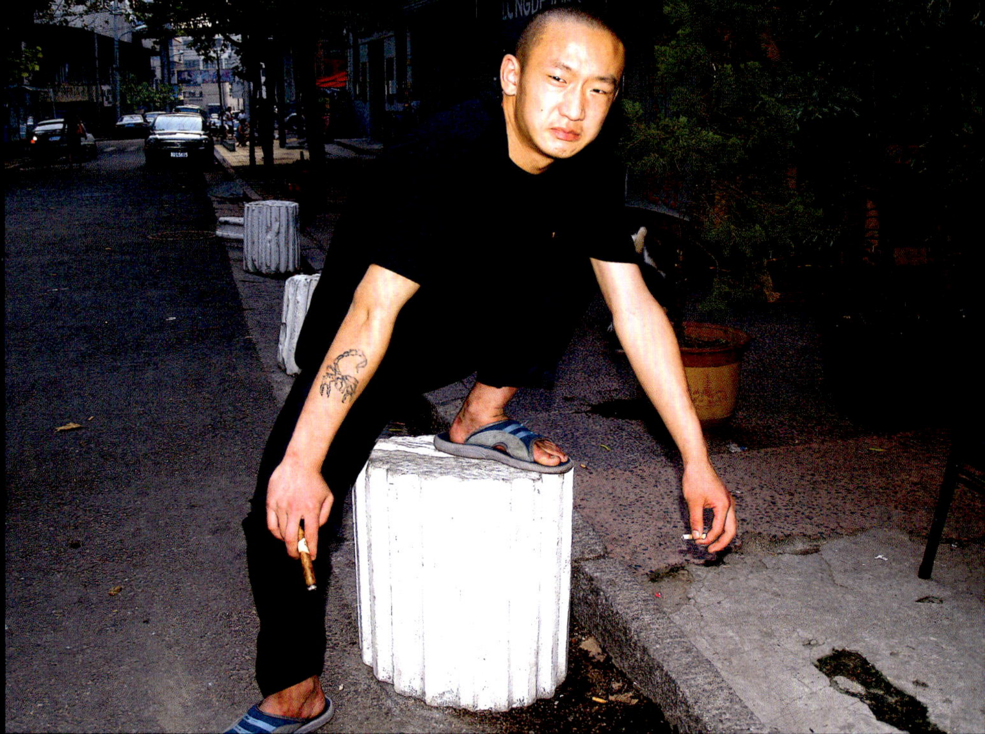

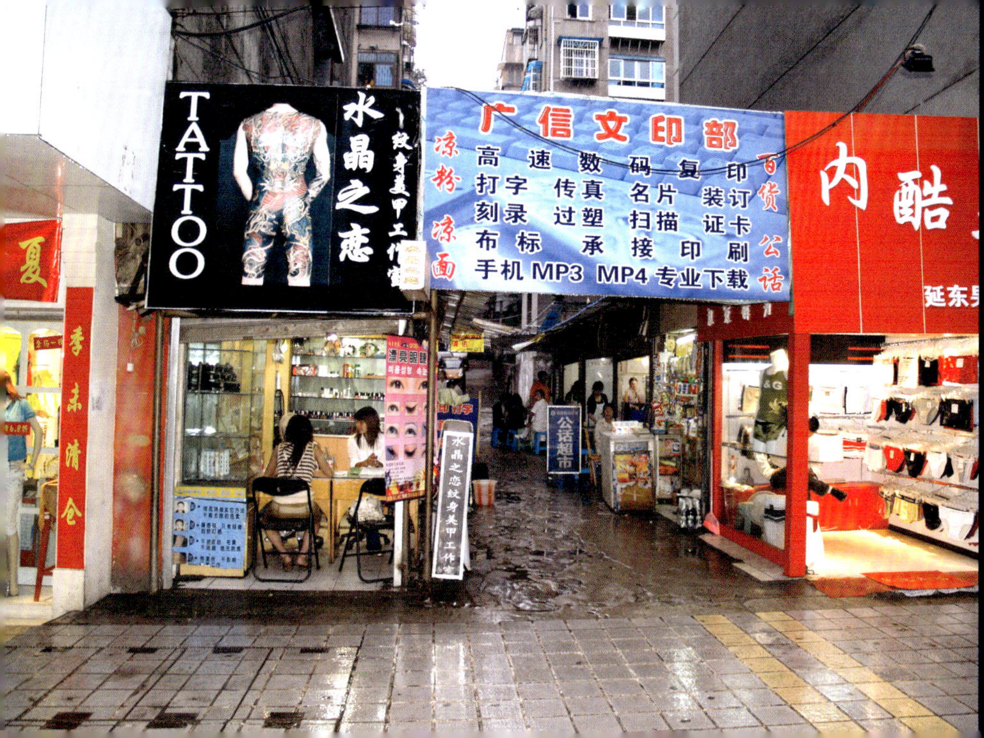
TATTOO
水晶之恋
广信文印部
高速 数码 复印
打字 传真 名片 装订
刻录 过塑 扫描 证卡
布标 承接 印刷
手机 MP3 MP4 专业下载
凉粉 凉面
百货 公话
内 酷
延东
夏
季末清仓
公话超市
水晶之恋 纹身美甲工作室
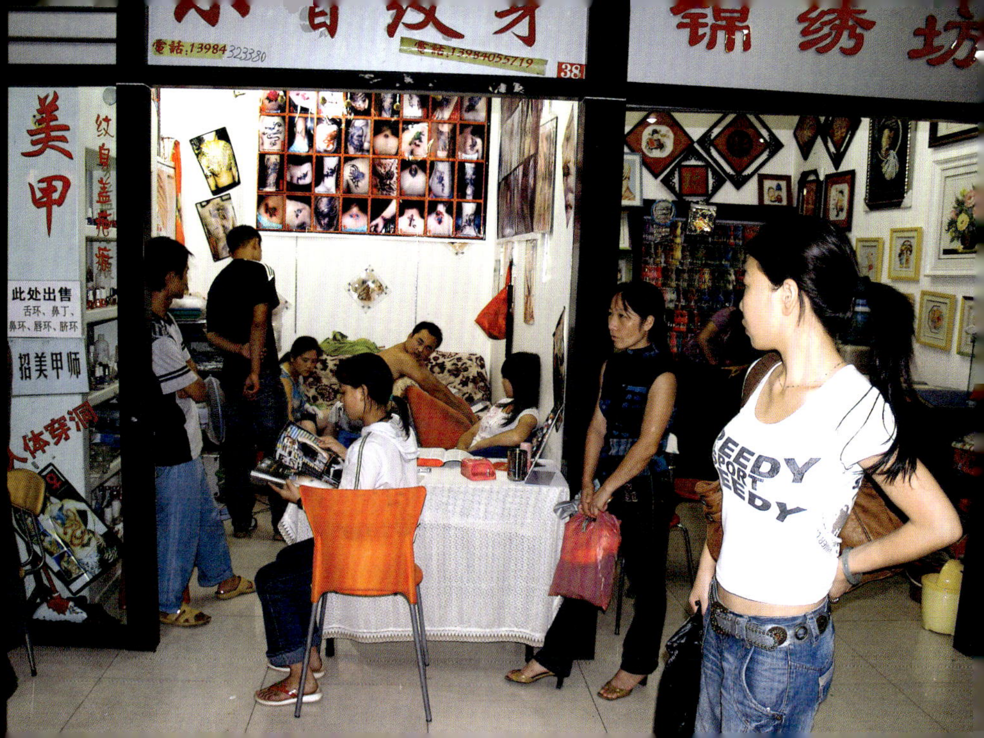
纹身
锦绣坊
38
美甲
此处出售
舌环、鼻丁、
鼻环、唇环、脐环
招美甲师
人体穿洞

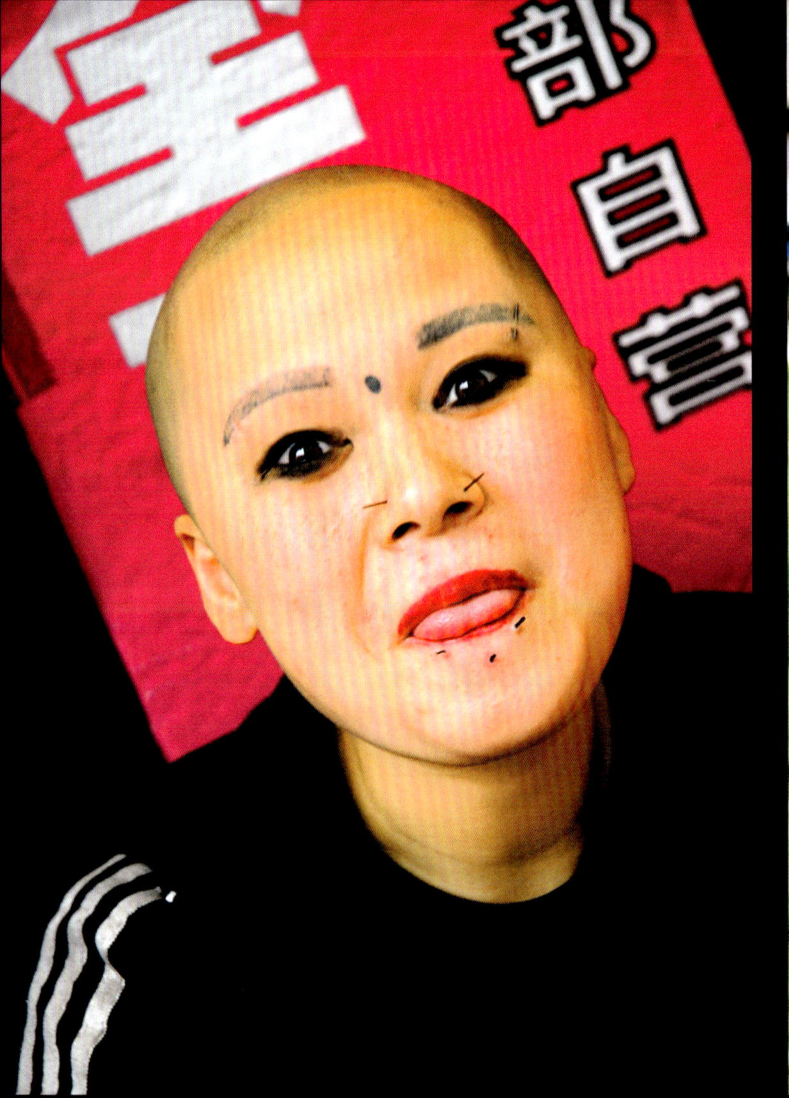
部自営

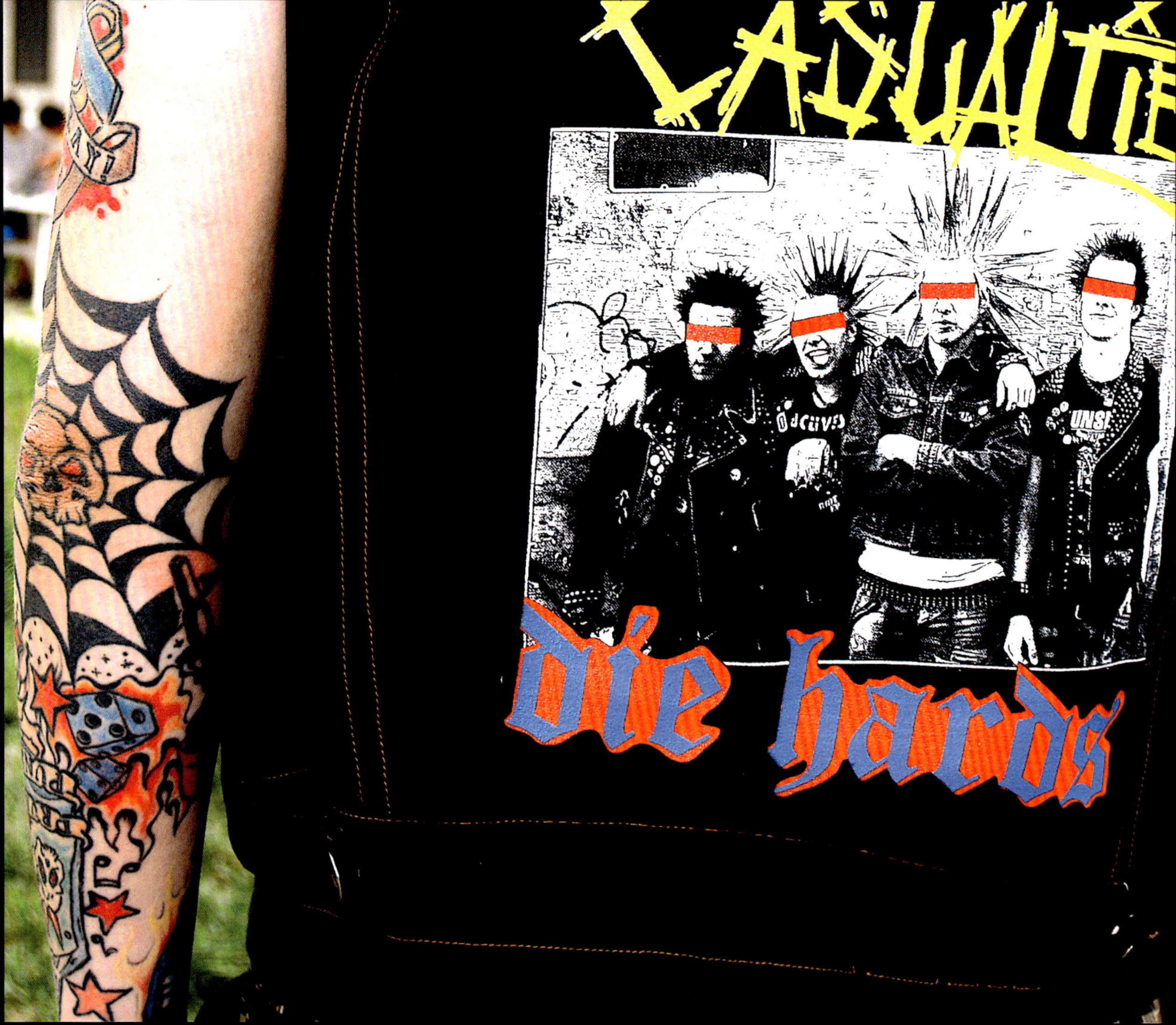
die hards

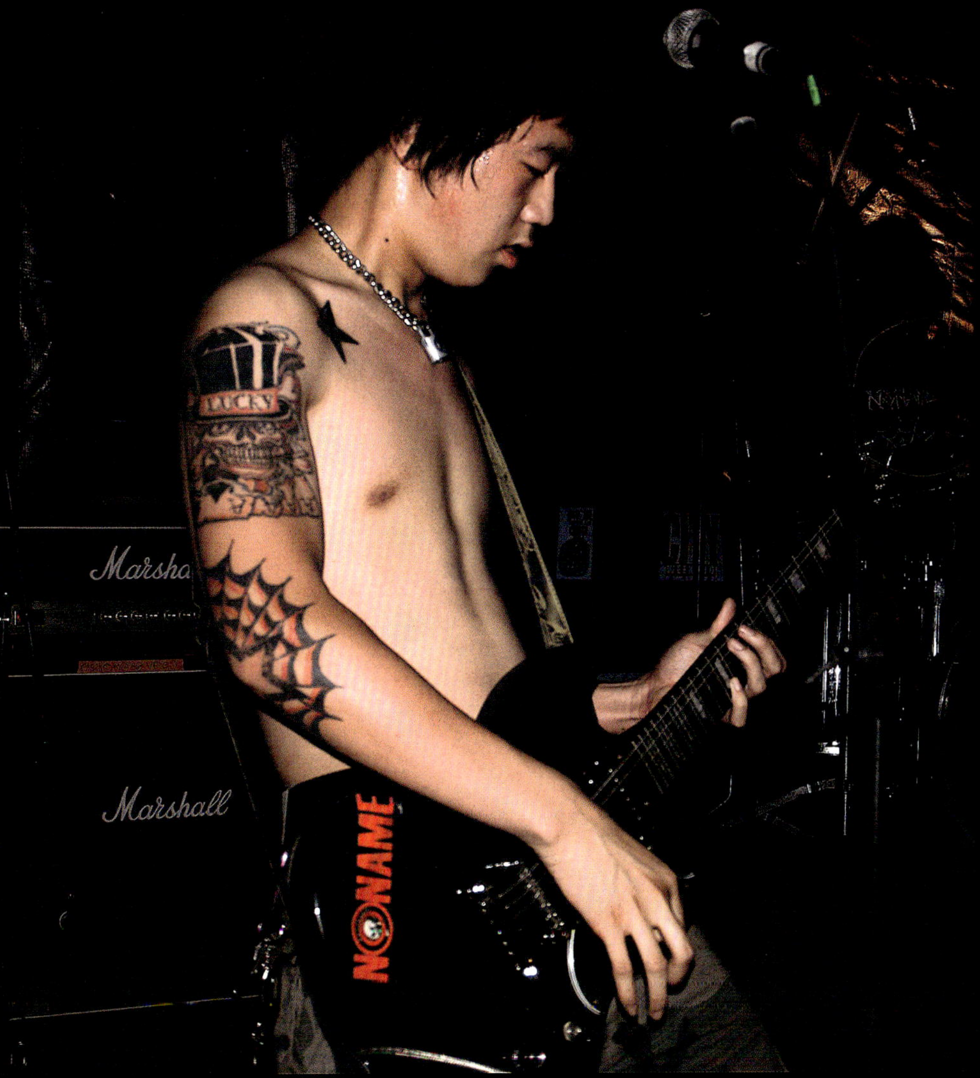
Marshall
NONAME

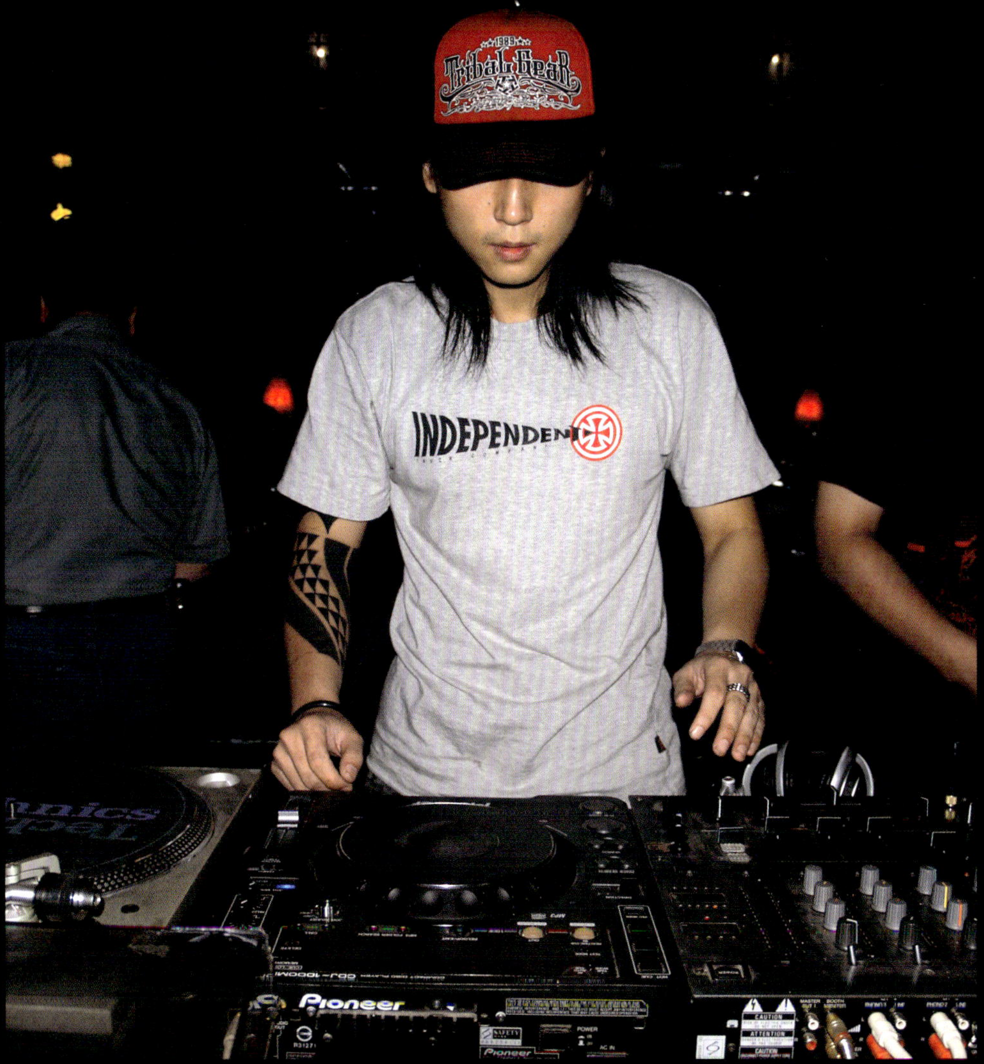
Tribal Gear
Pioneer

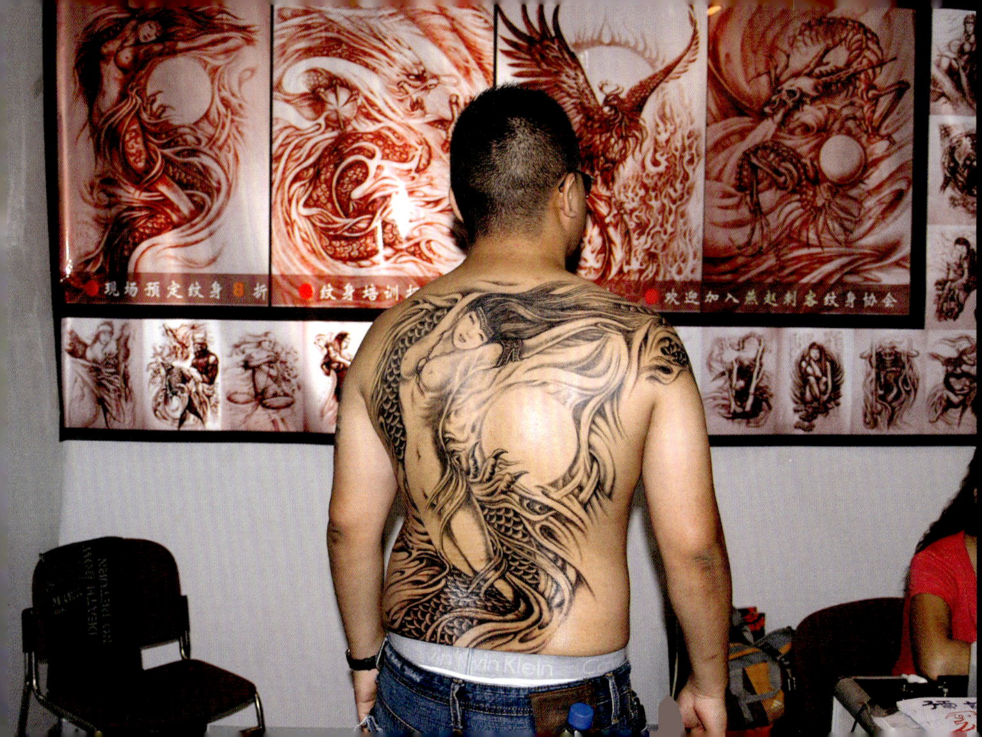
现场预定纹身8折
纹身培训
欢迎加入燕赵刺客纹身协会

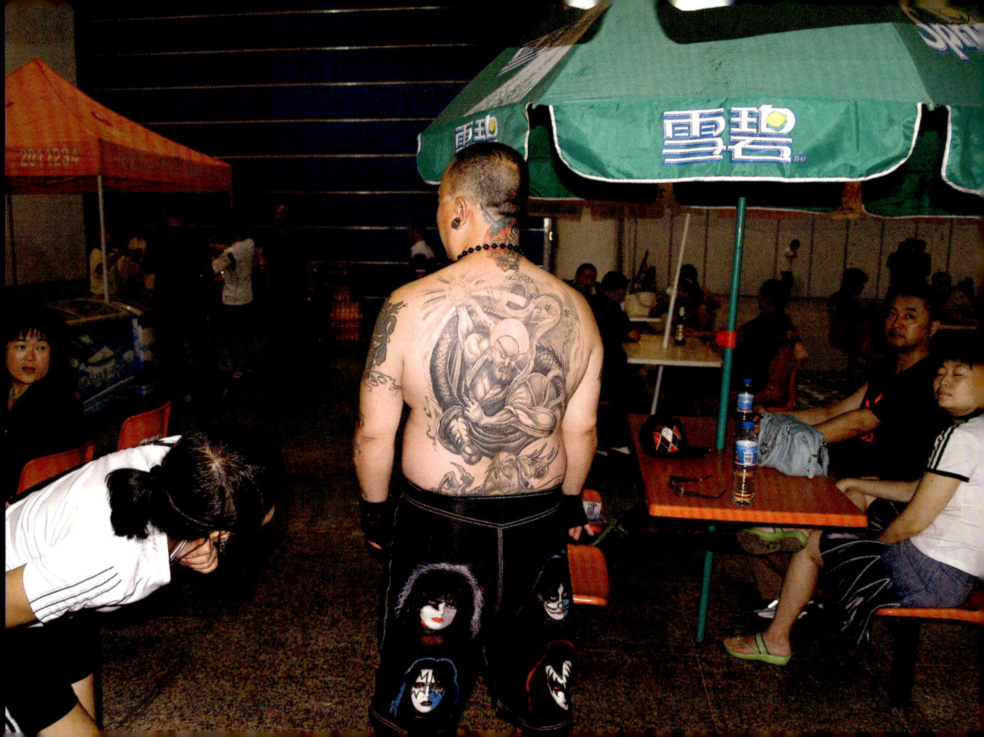
雪碧

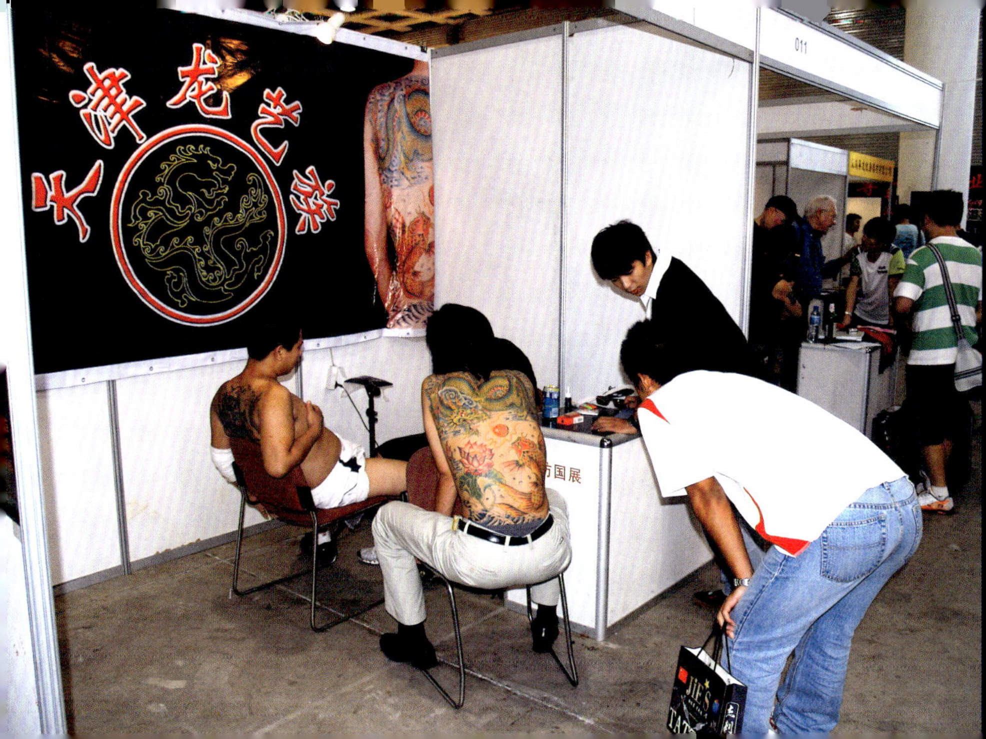
天津龙艺族
011

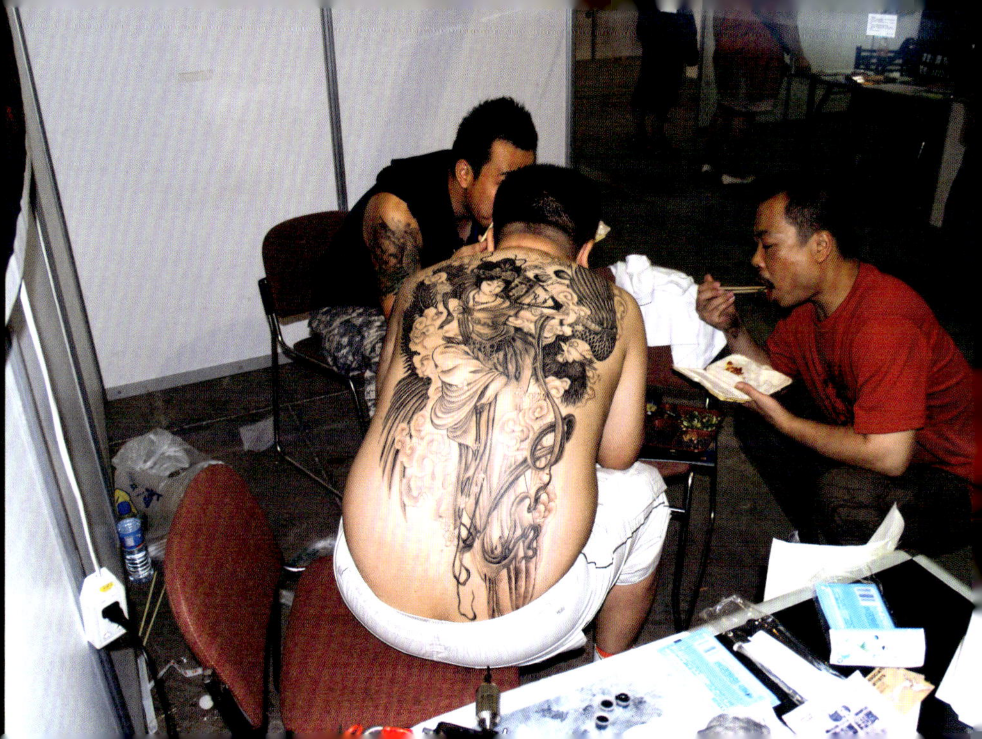

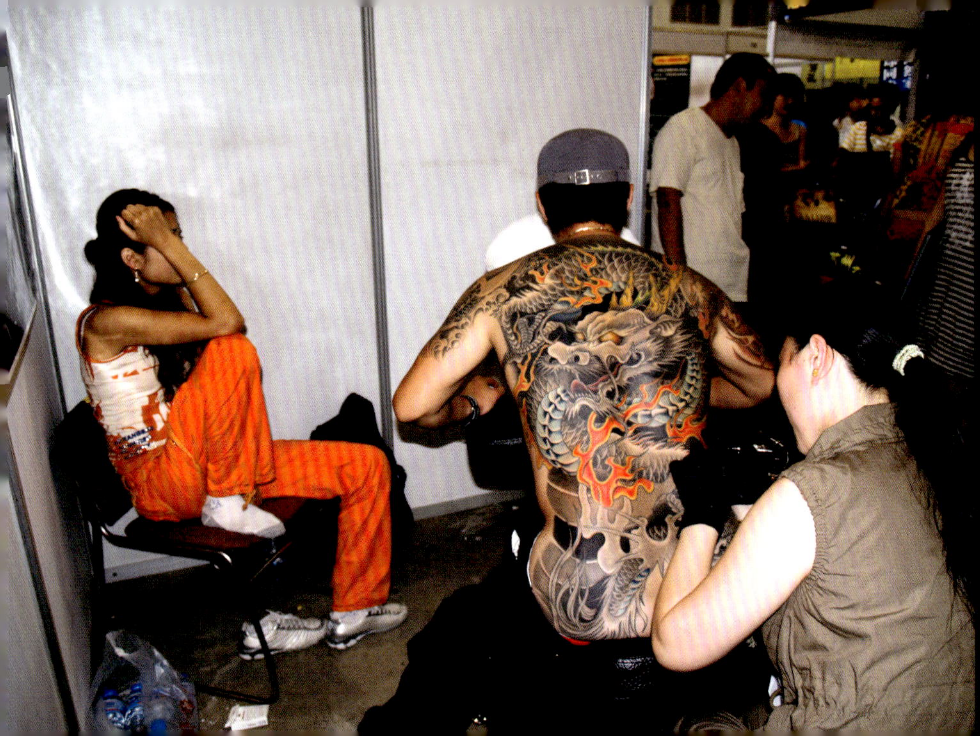

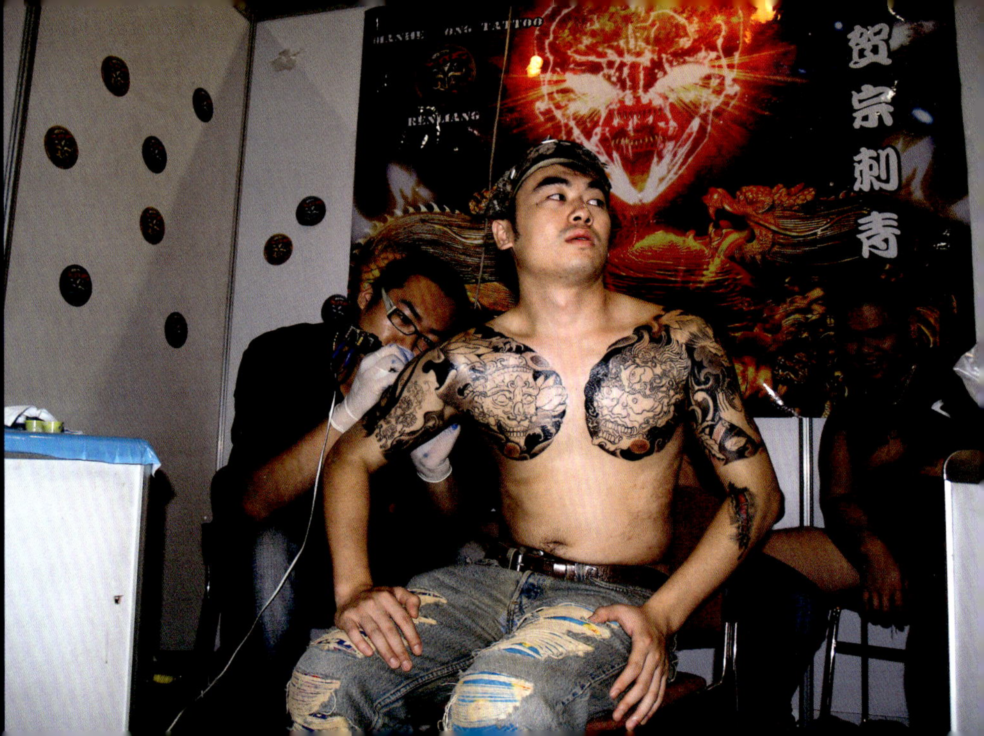
贺宗刺青
RENLIANG

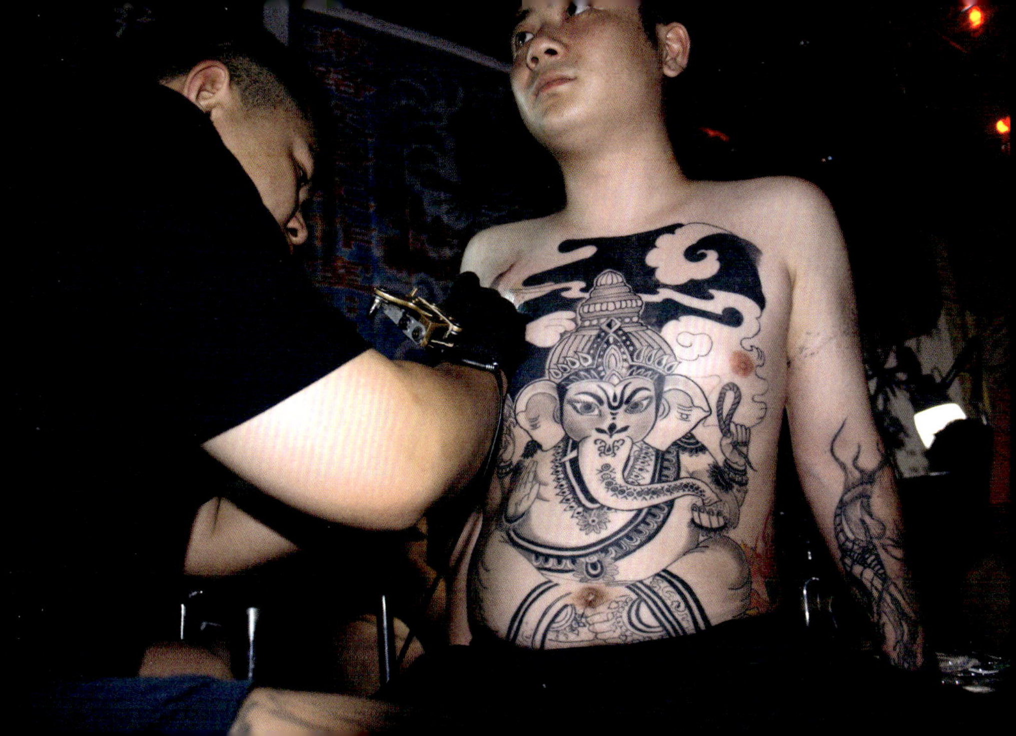

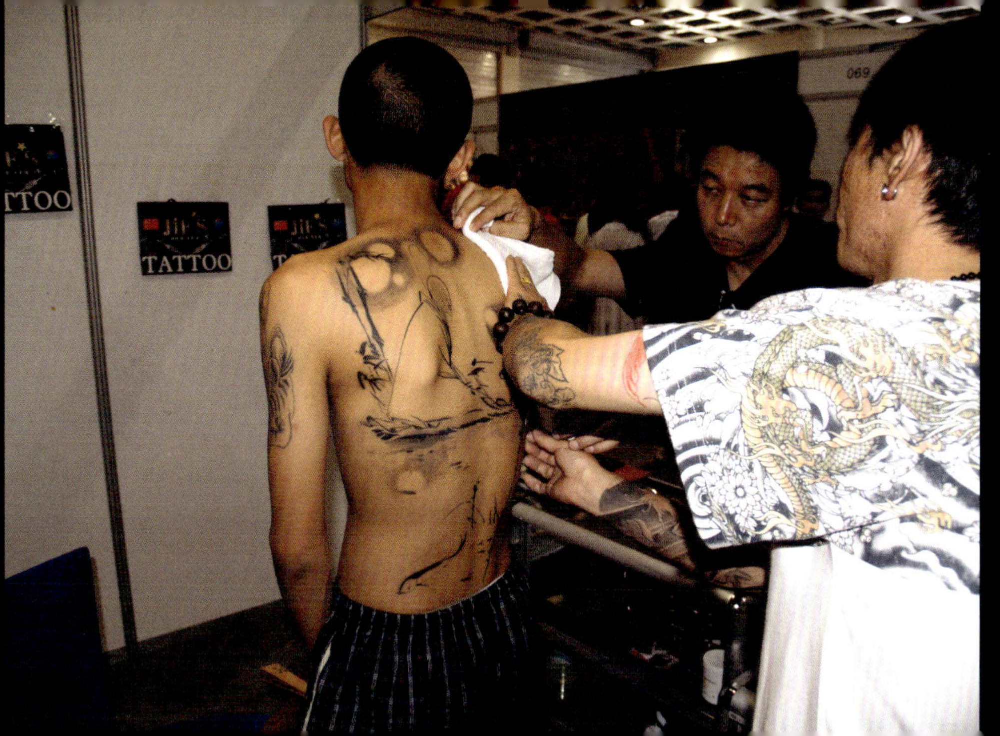

TATTOO
TATTOO
069

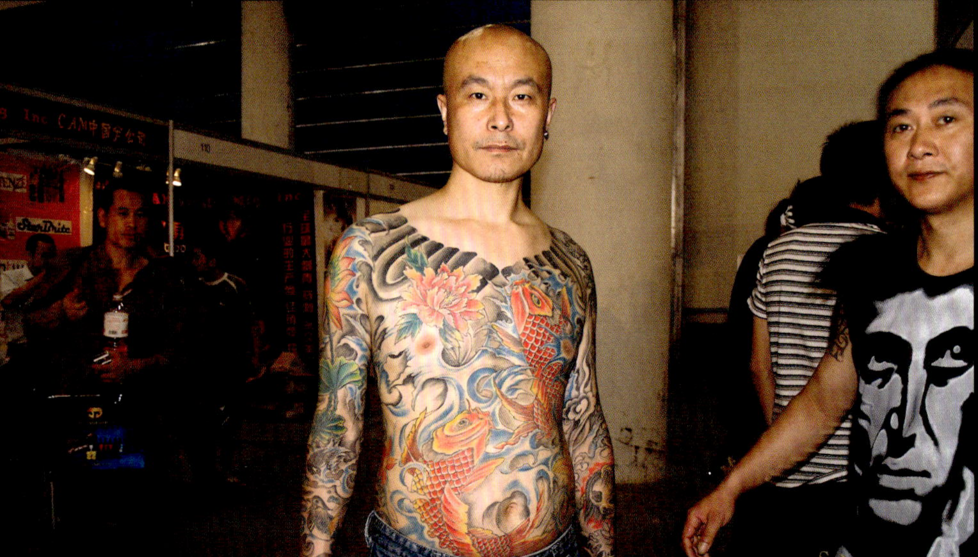

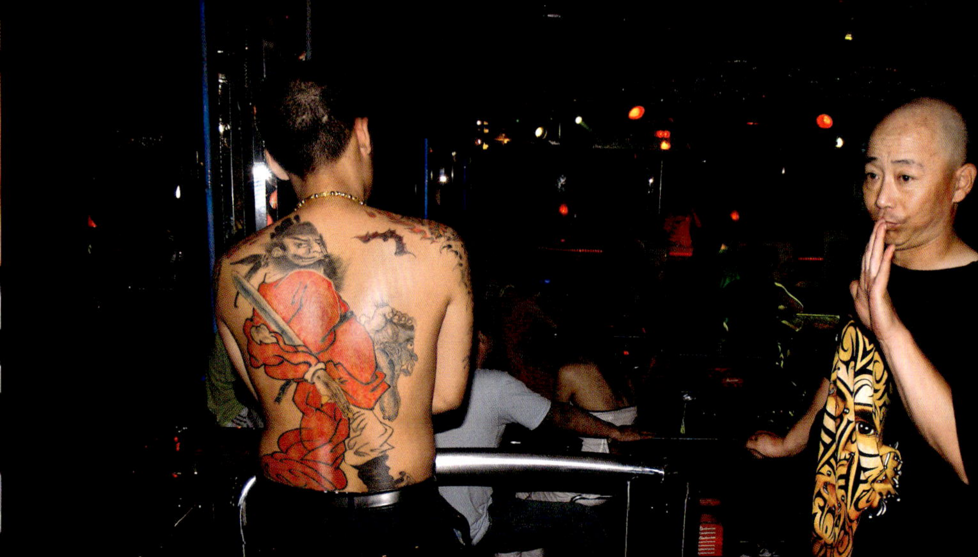

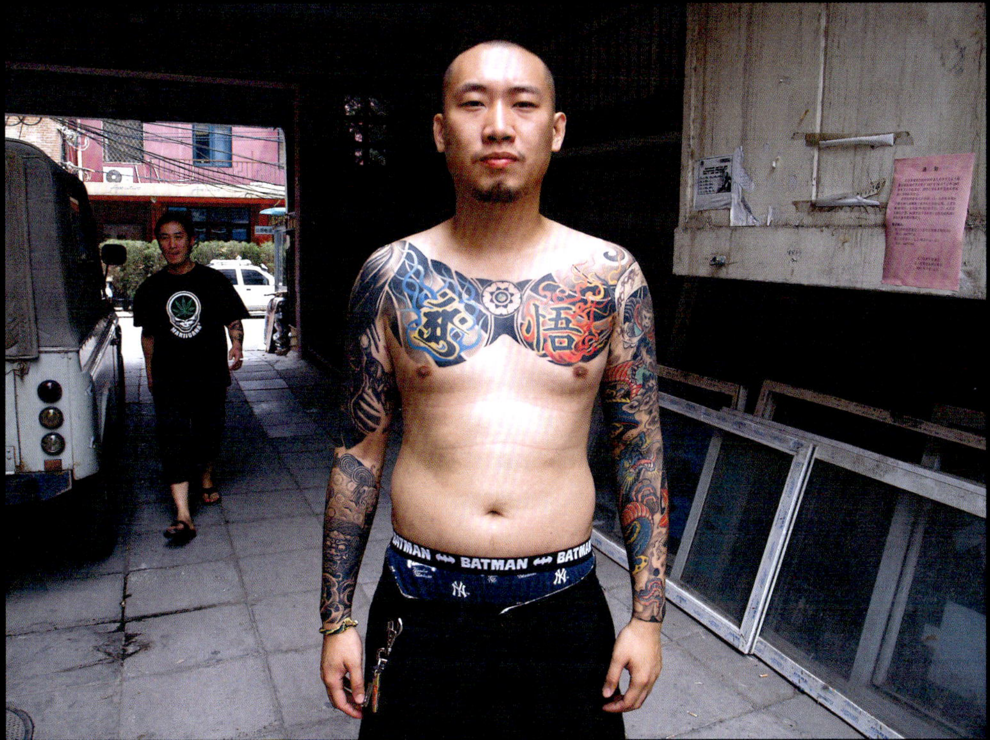
BATMAN

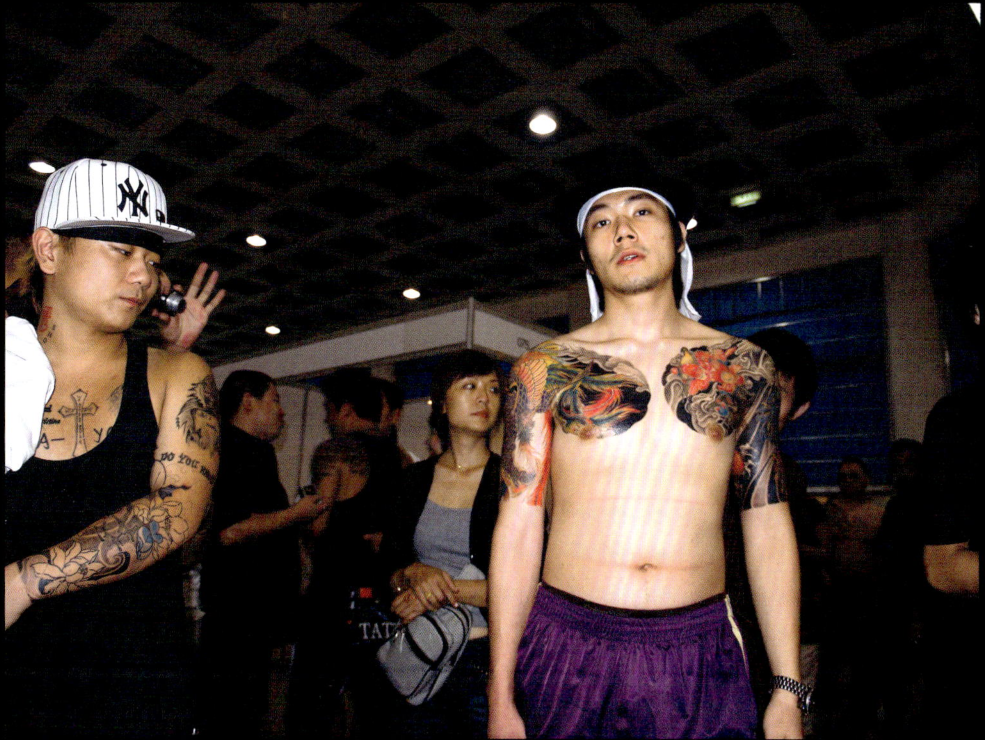

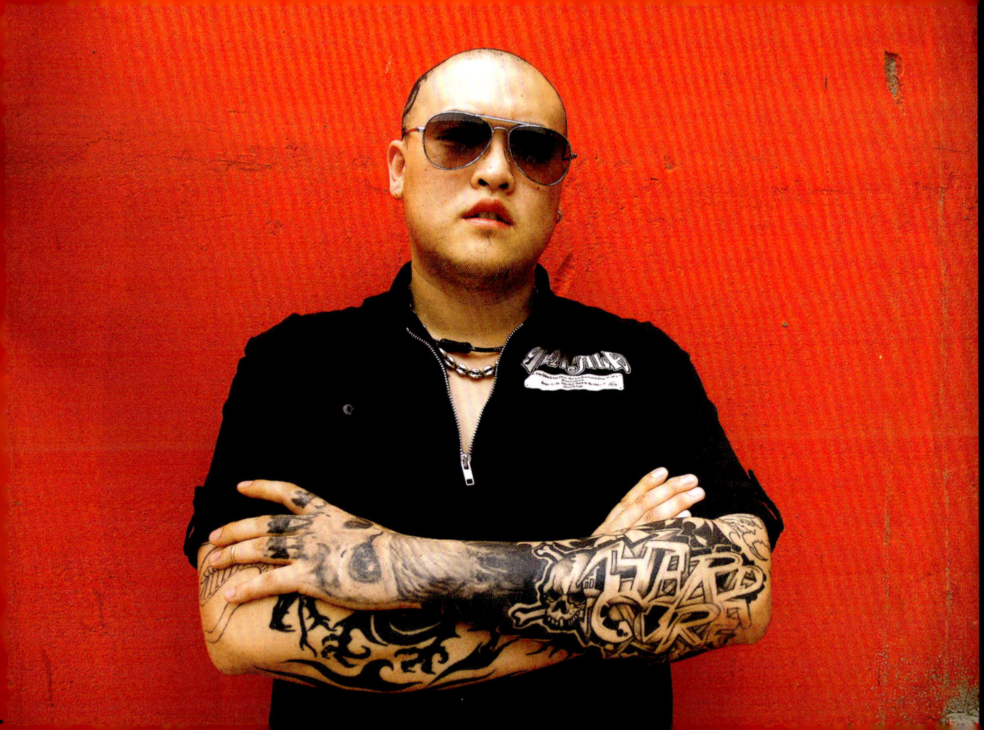

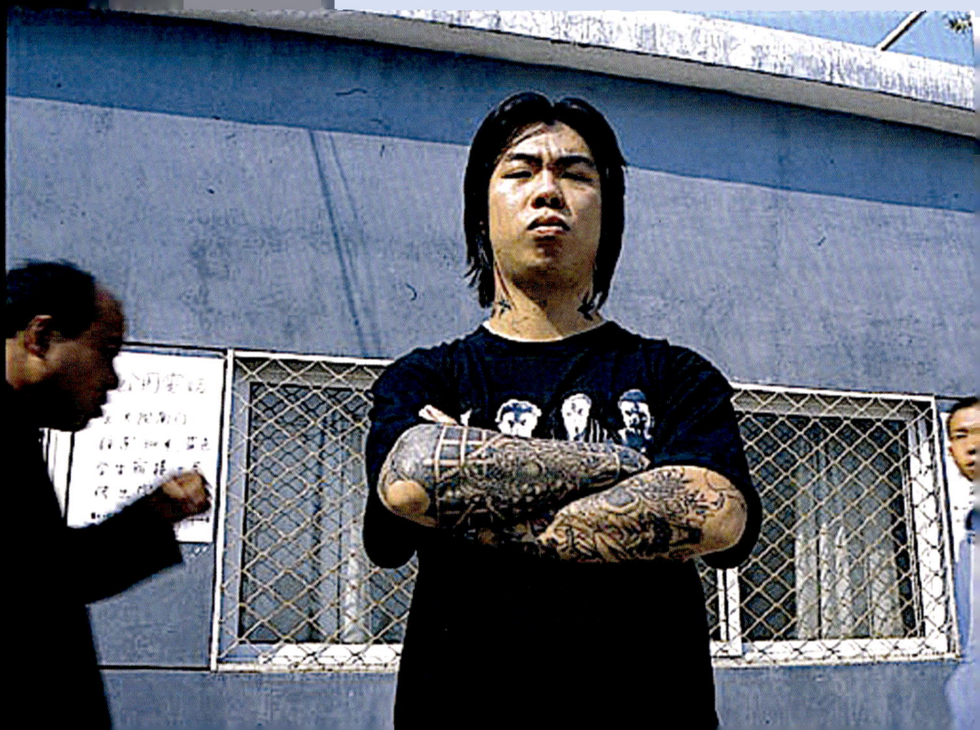

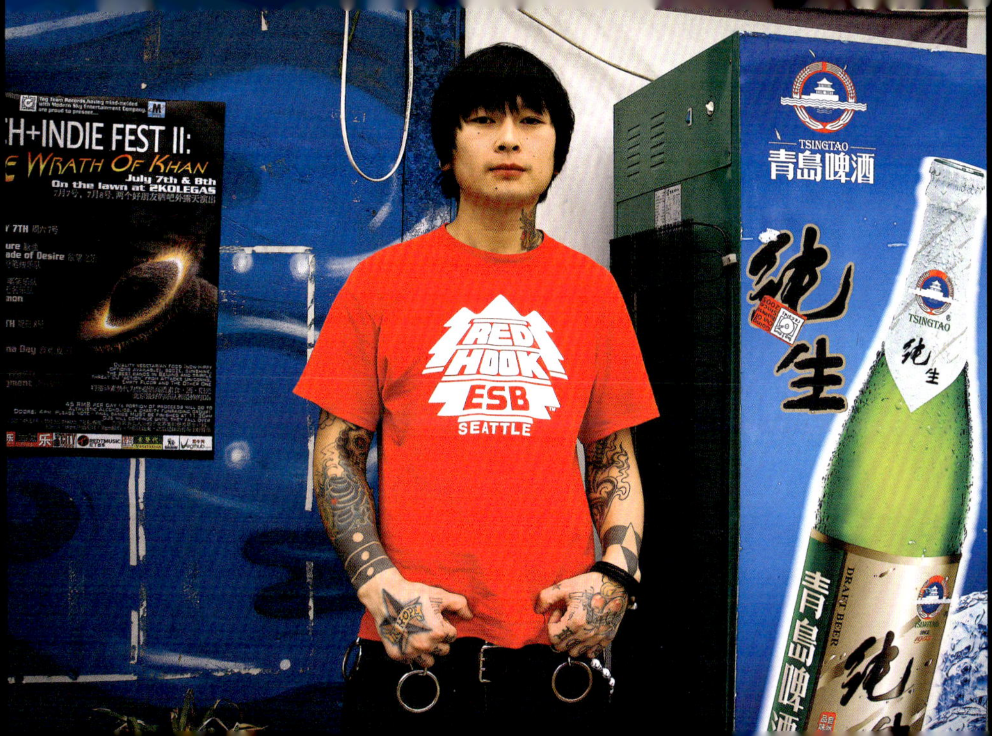
TH+INDIE FEST II:
WRATH OF KHAN
July 7th & 8th
On the lawn at 2KOLEGAS
RED HOOK
ESB
SEATTLE
TSINGTAO
青島啤酒
纯生
DRAFT BEER

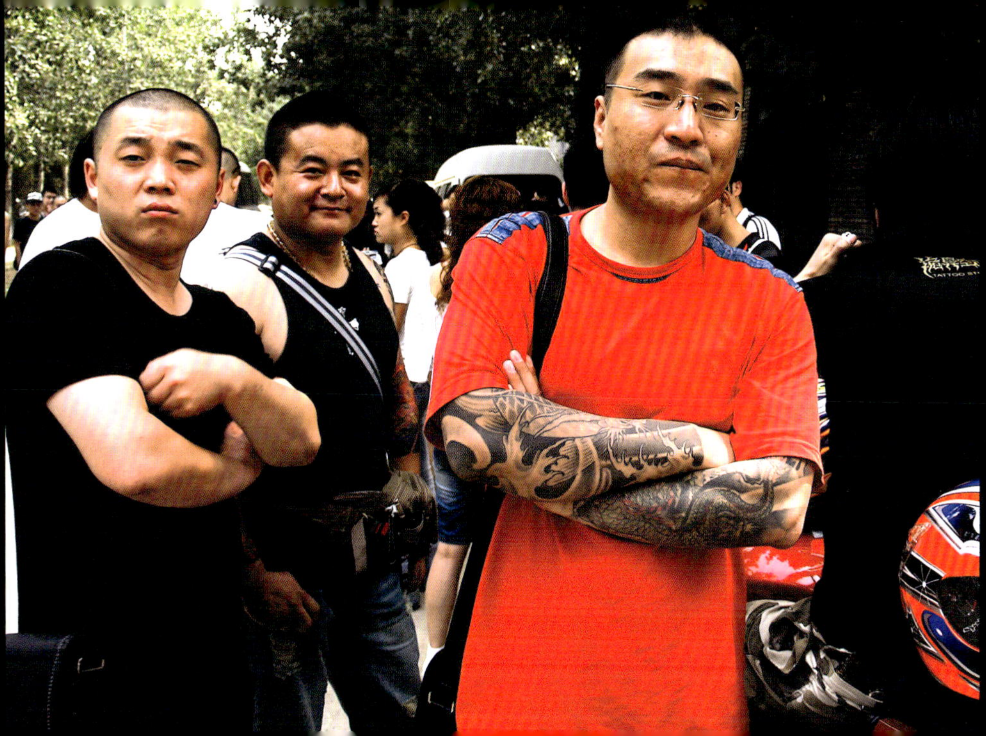

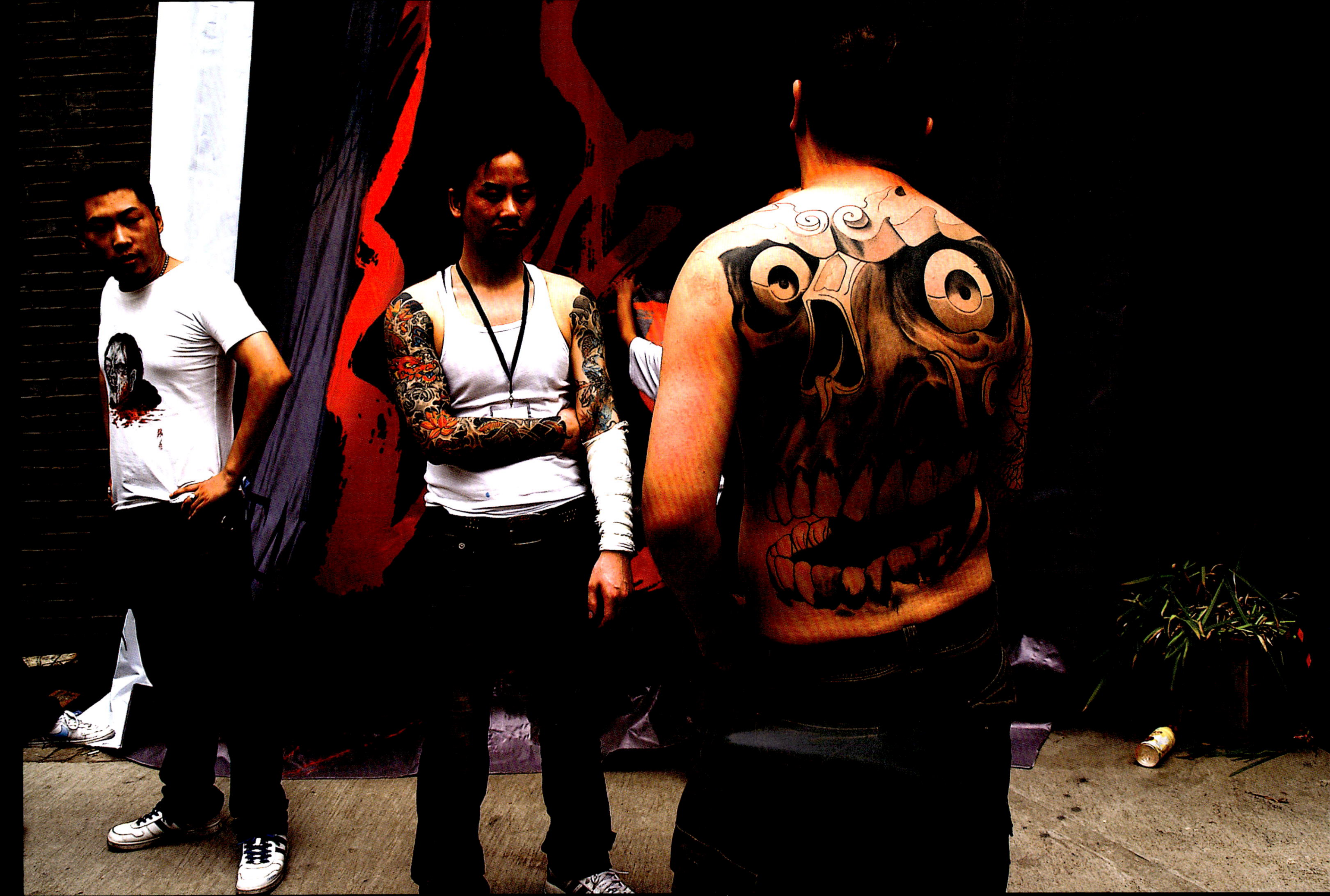

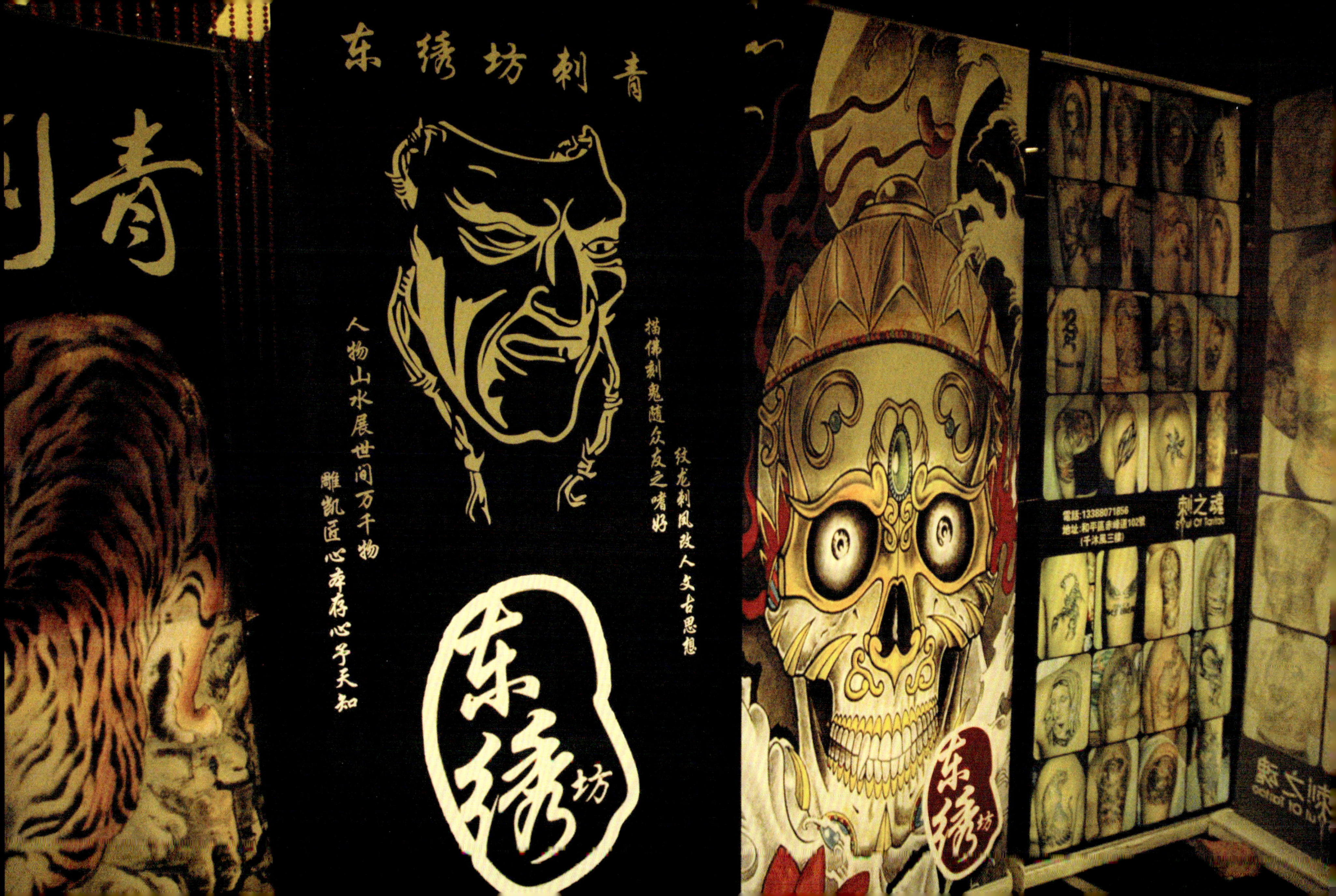
刺青
东绣坊刺青
人物山水展世间万千物
雕凯匠心本存心予天知
描佛刺鬼随众友之嗜好
纹龙刺凤改人文古思想
东绣坊
东绣坊
刺之魂

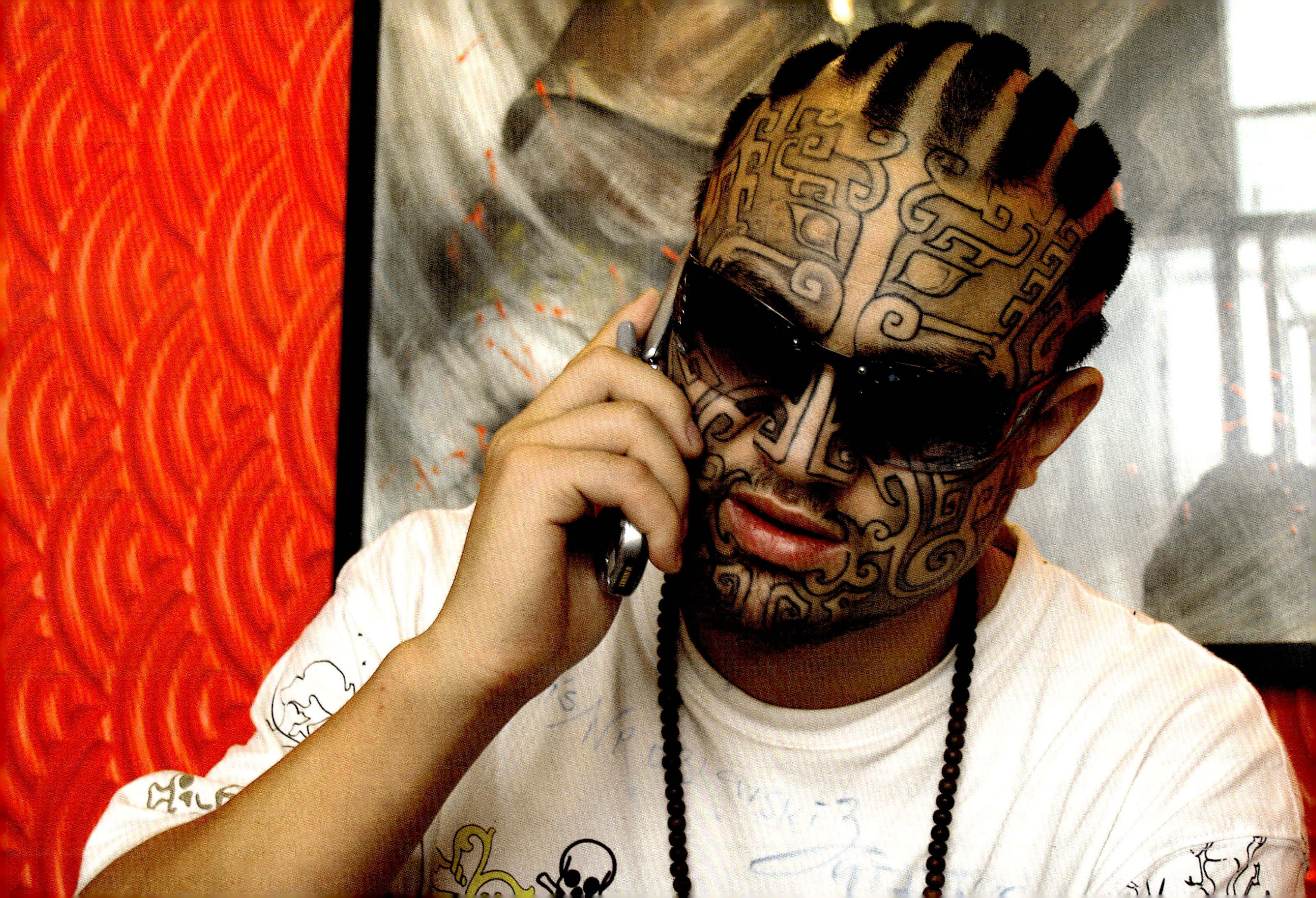

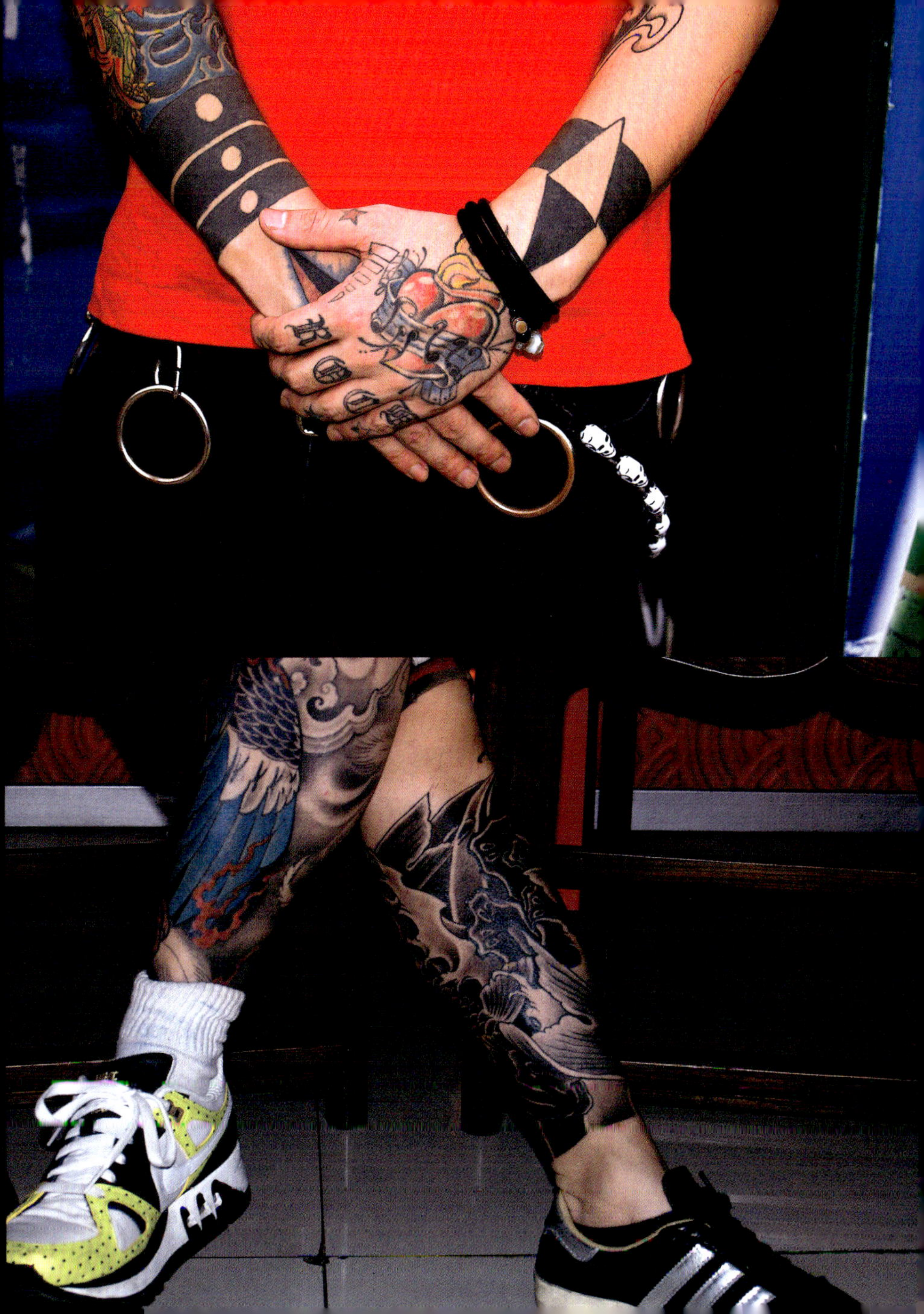

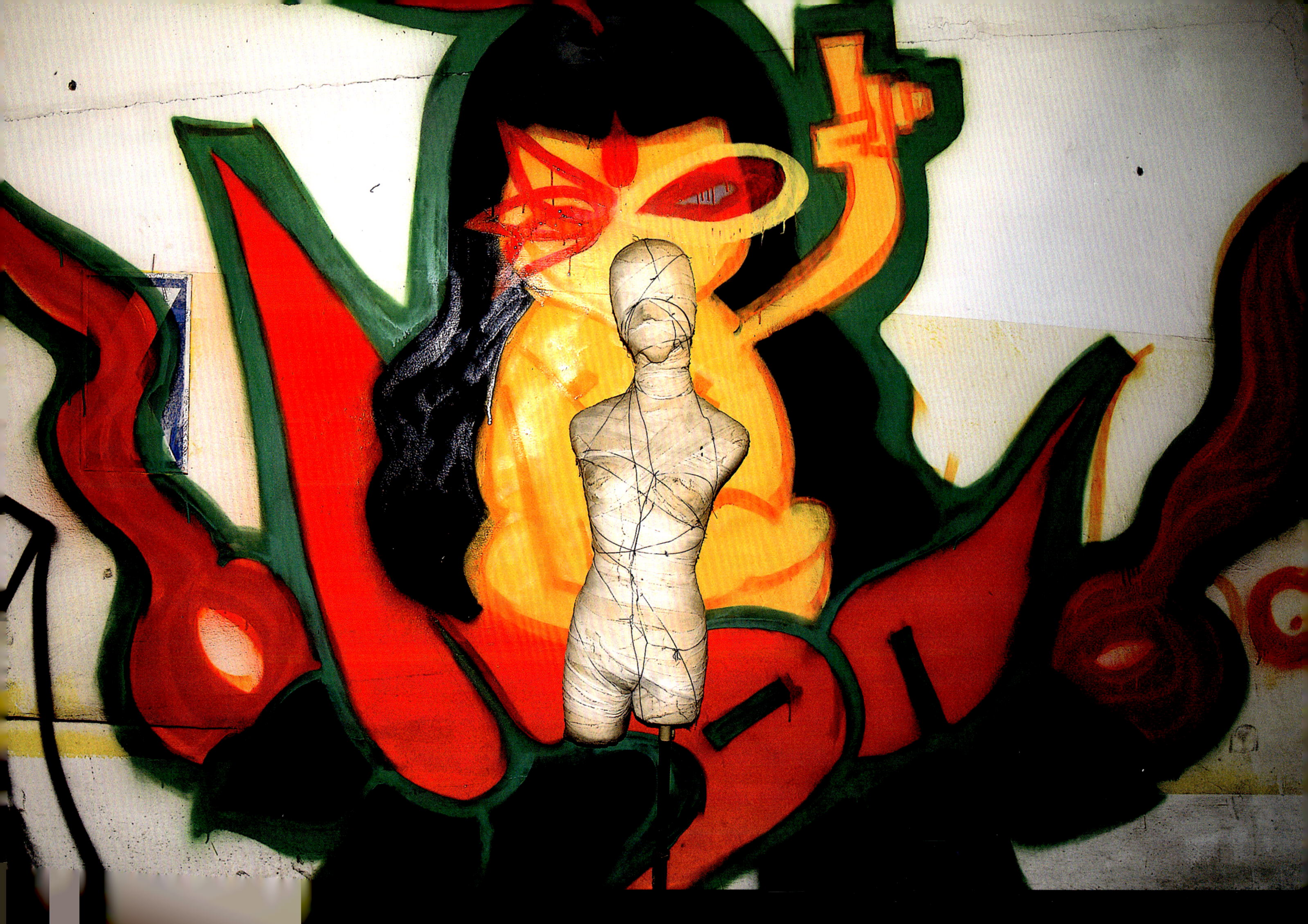

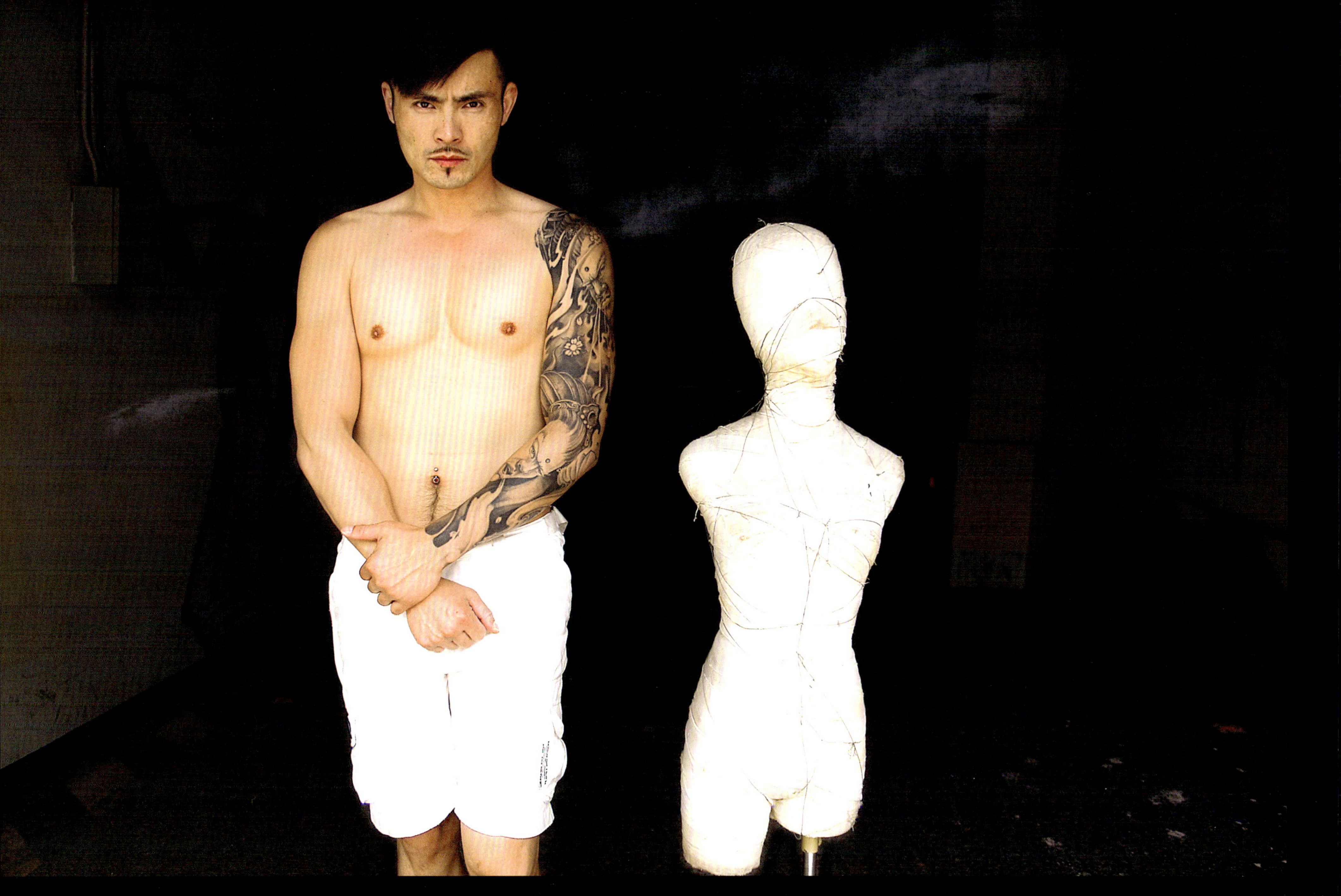

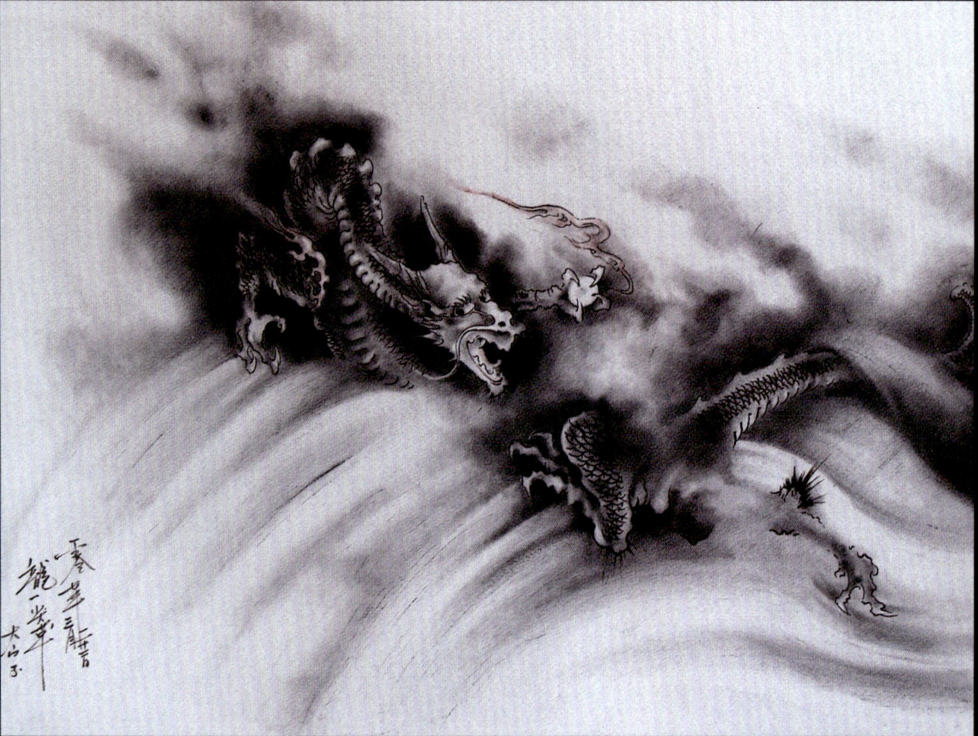

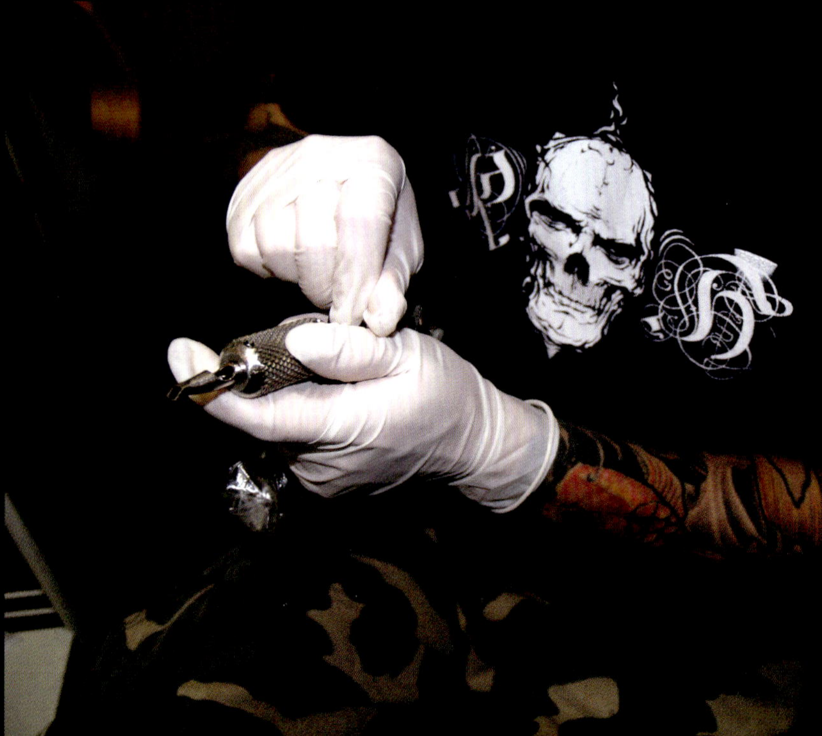

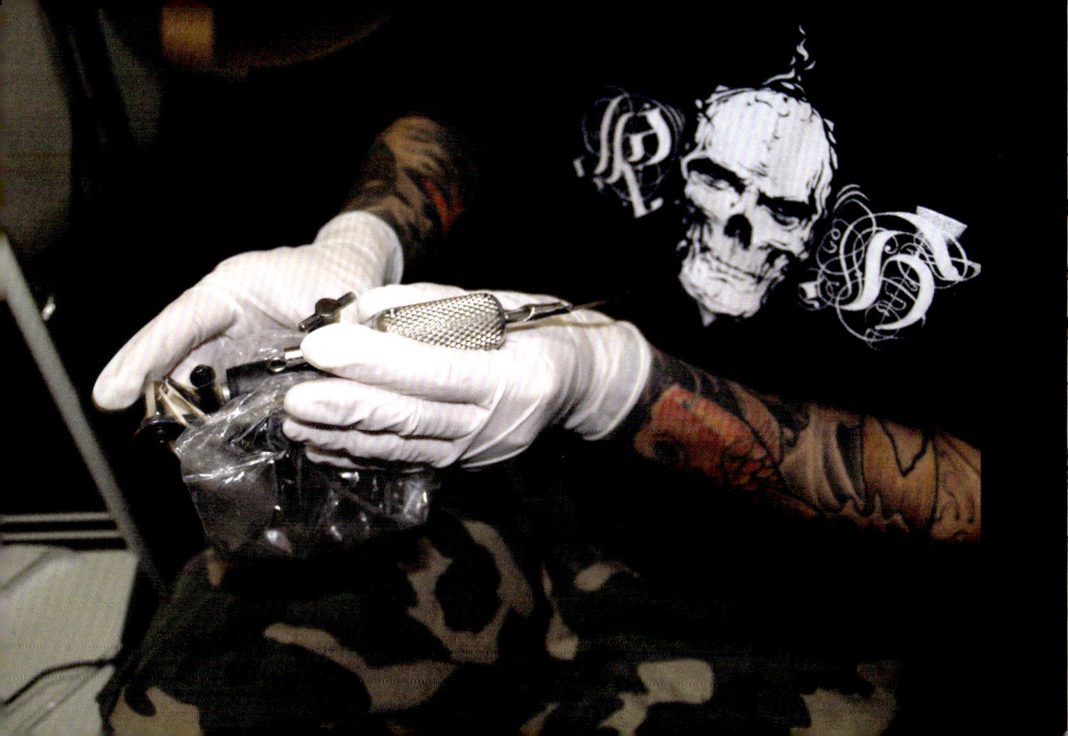

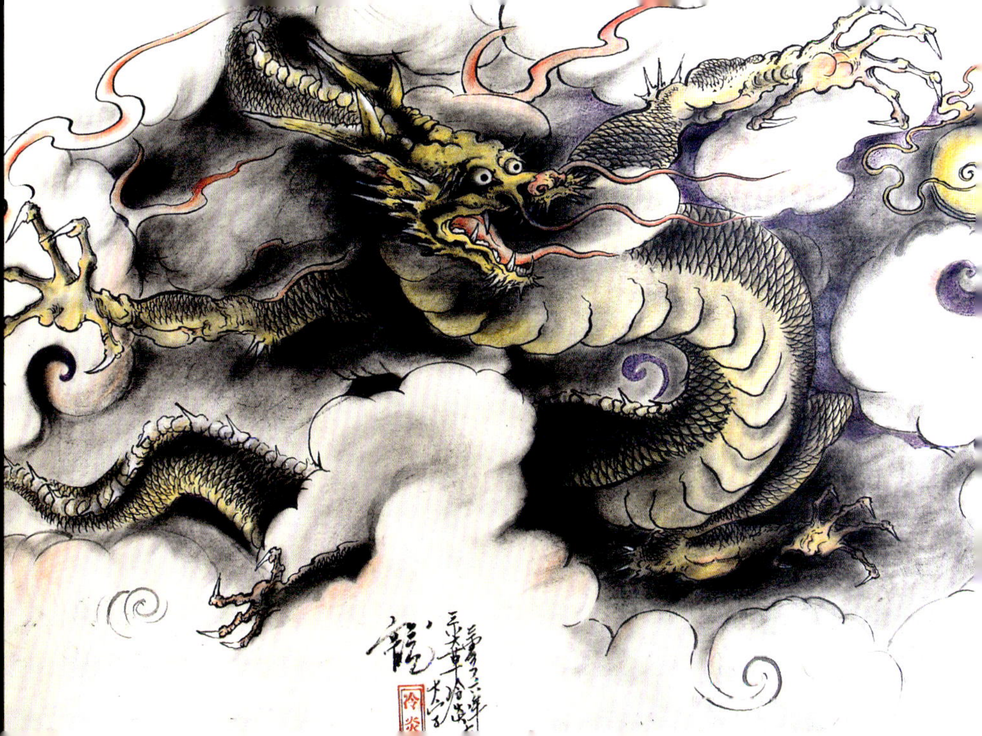

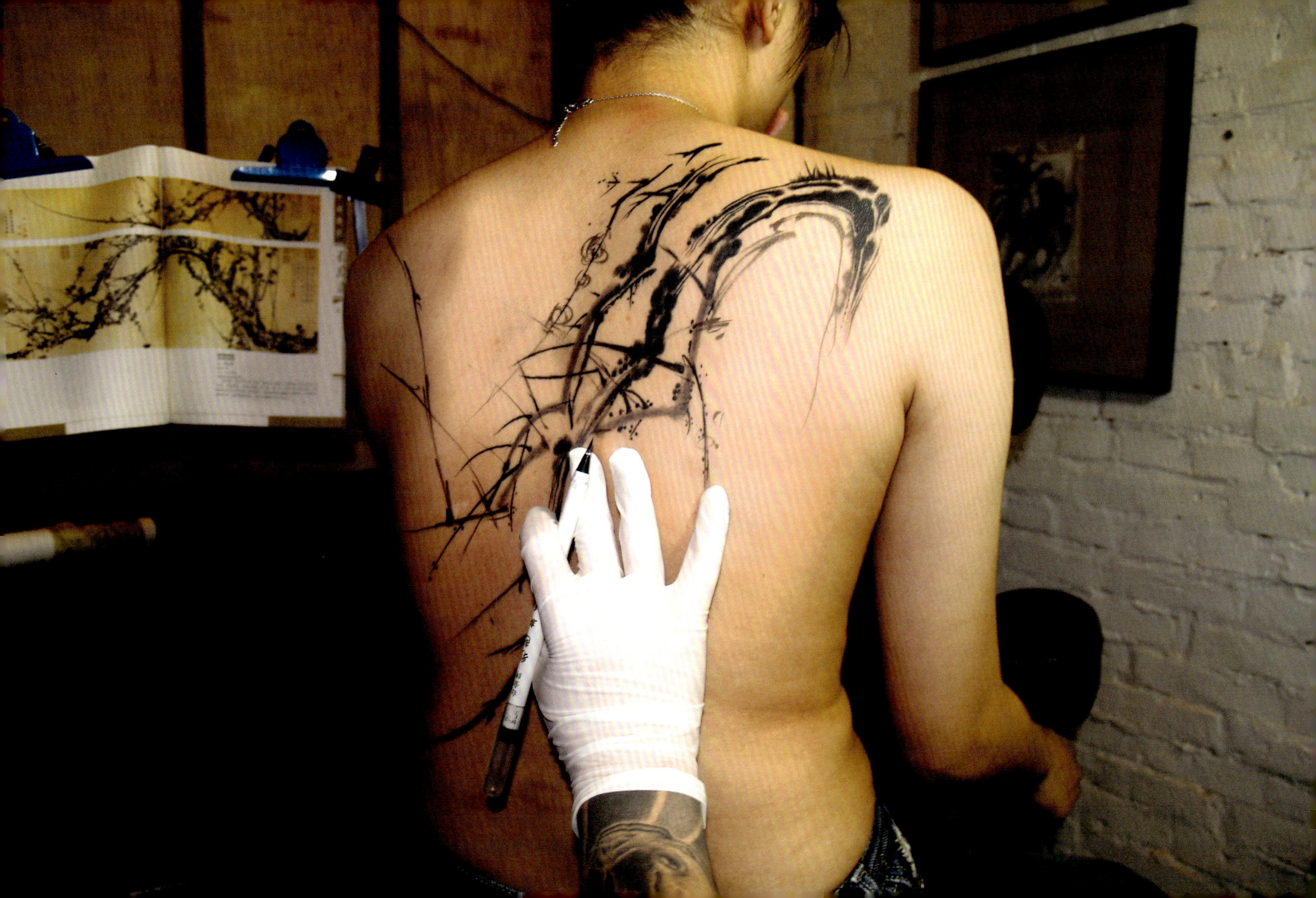

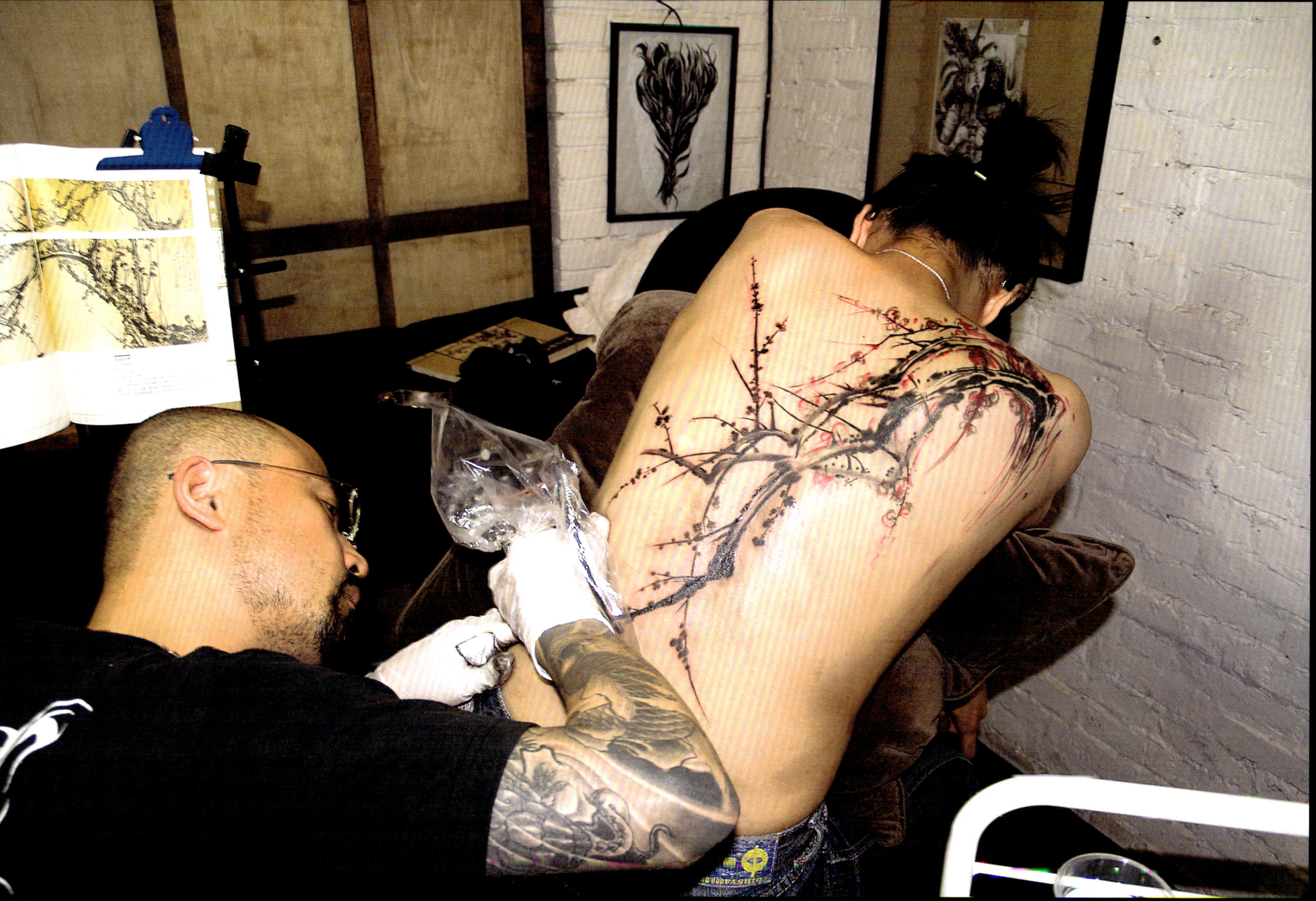

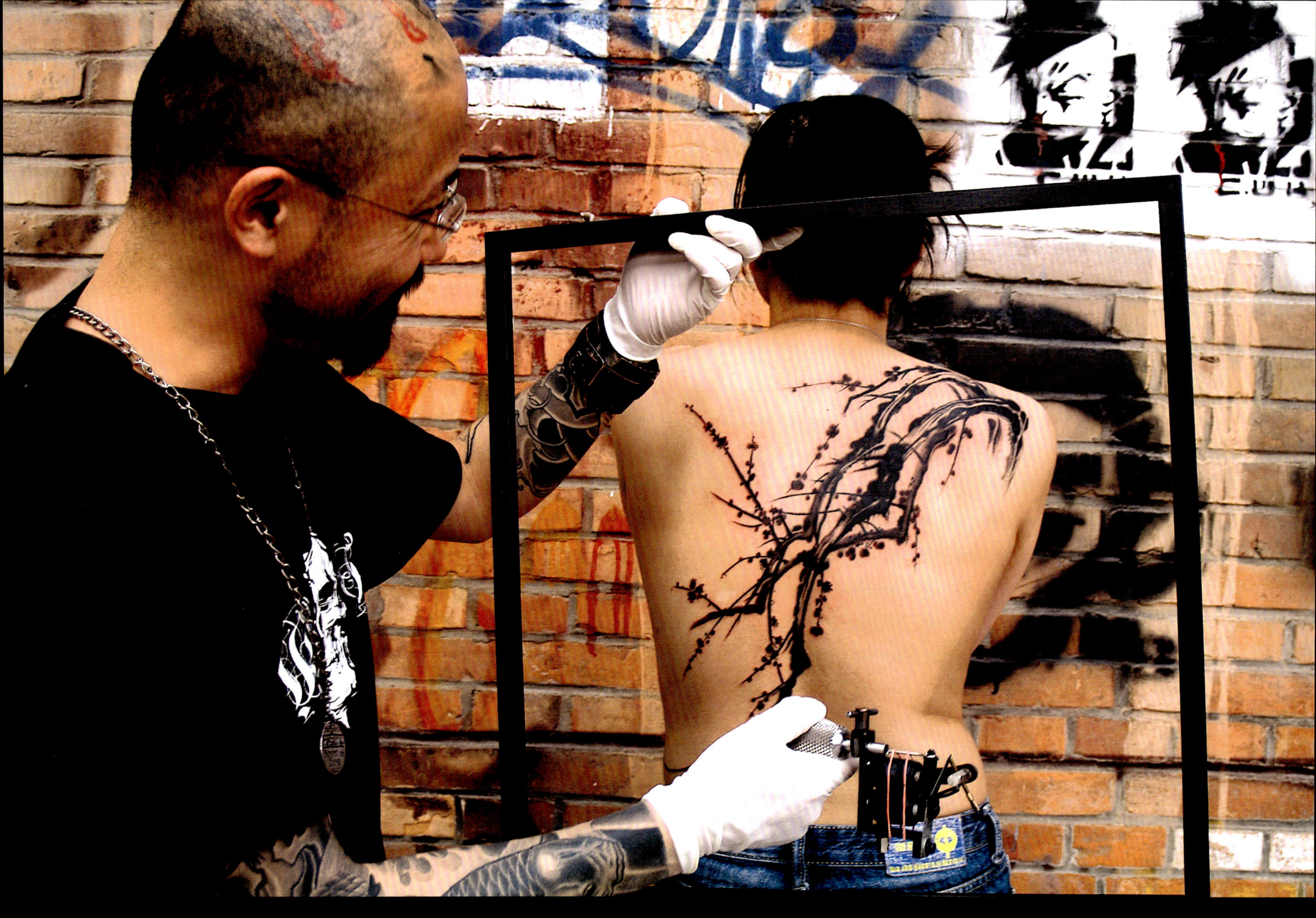

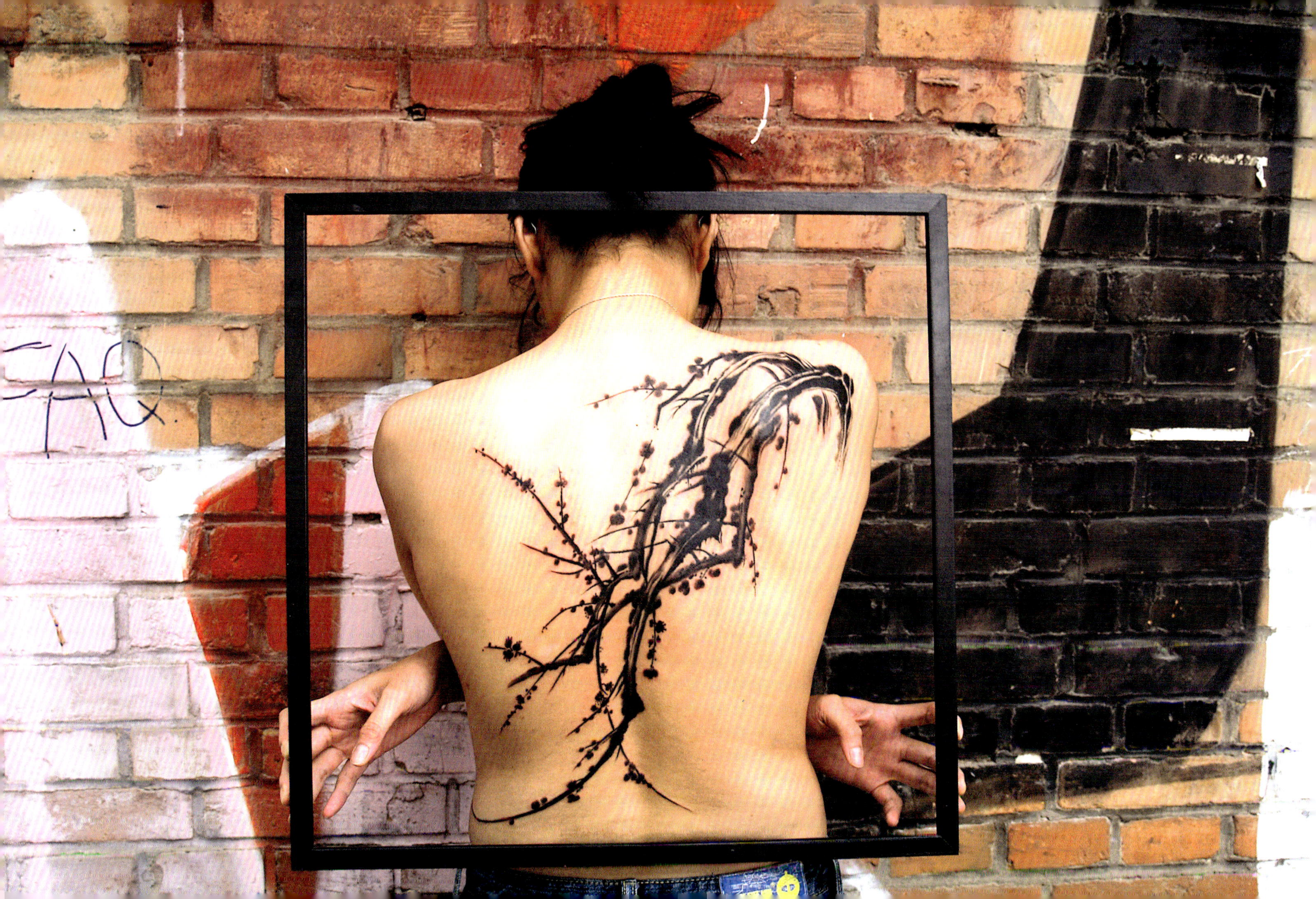

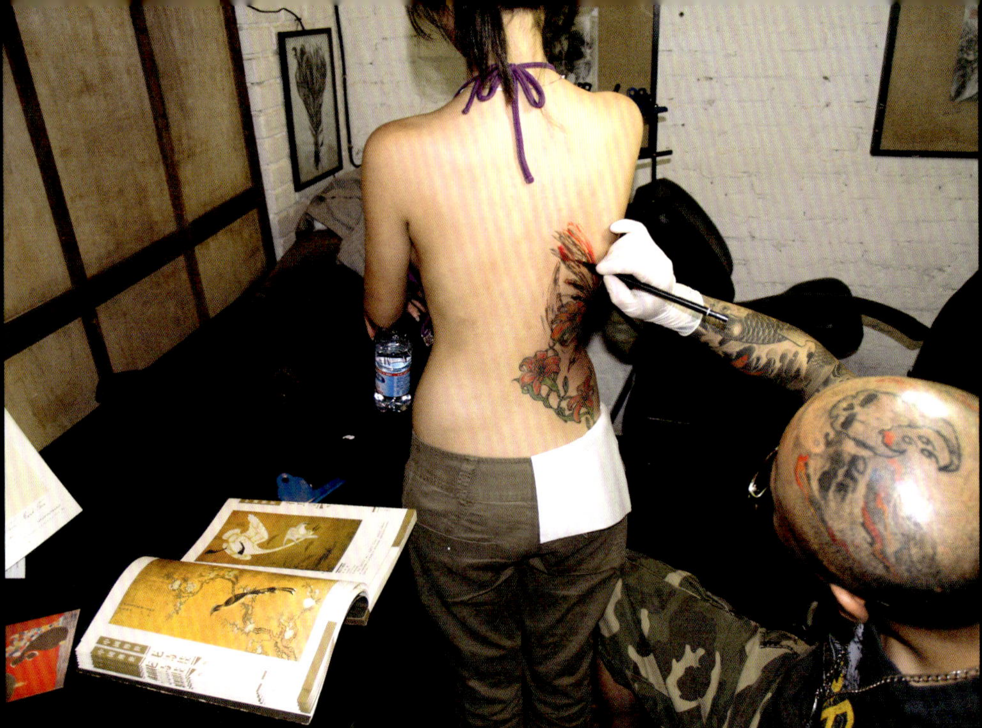

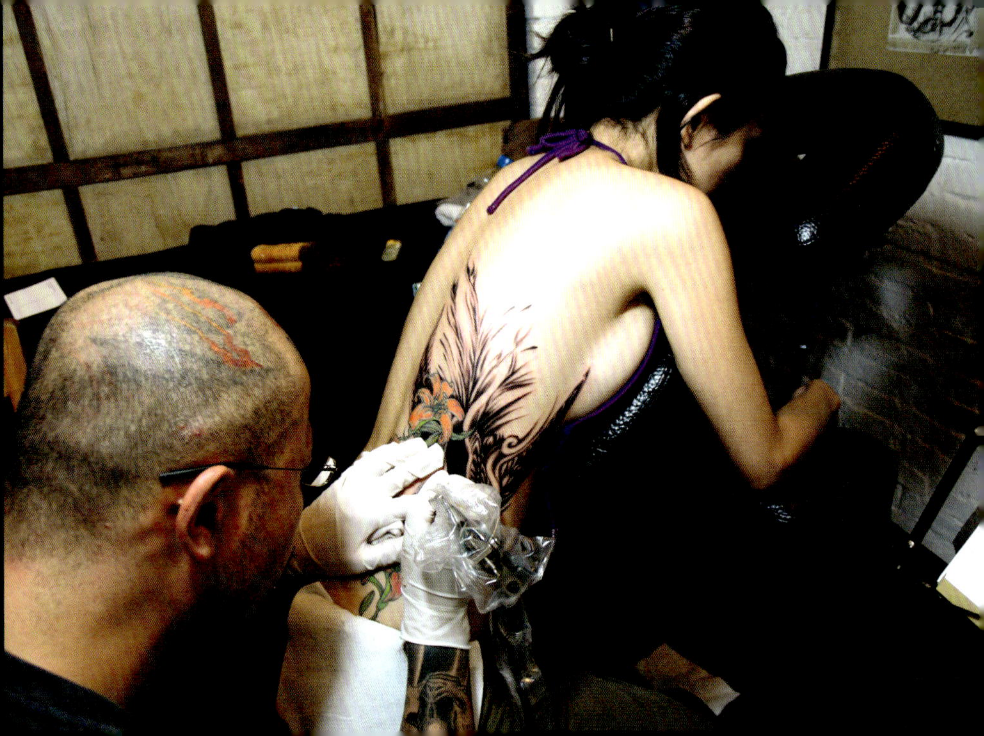

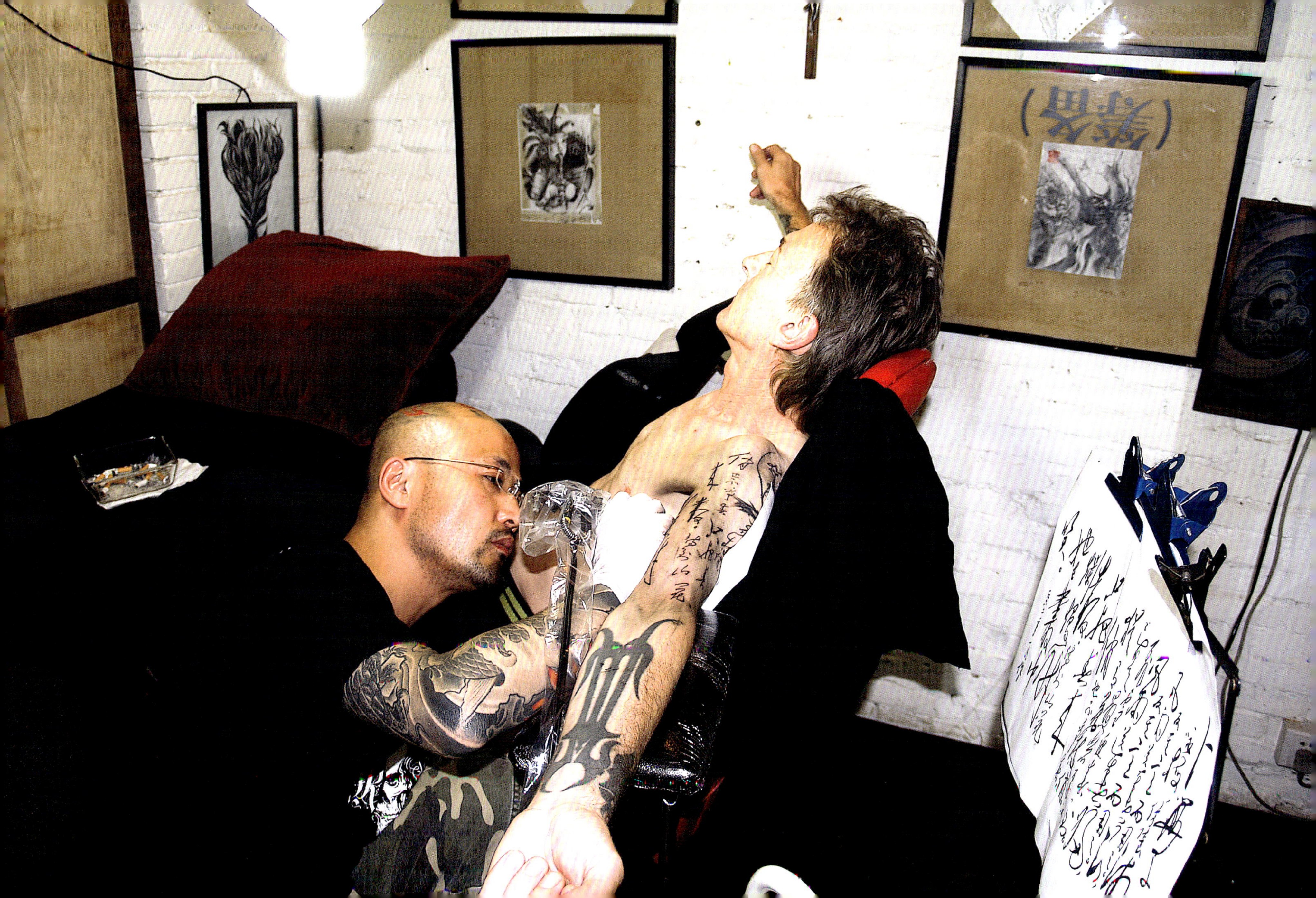

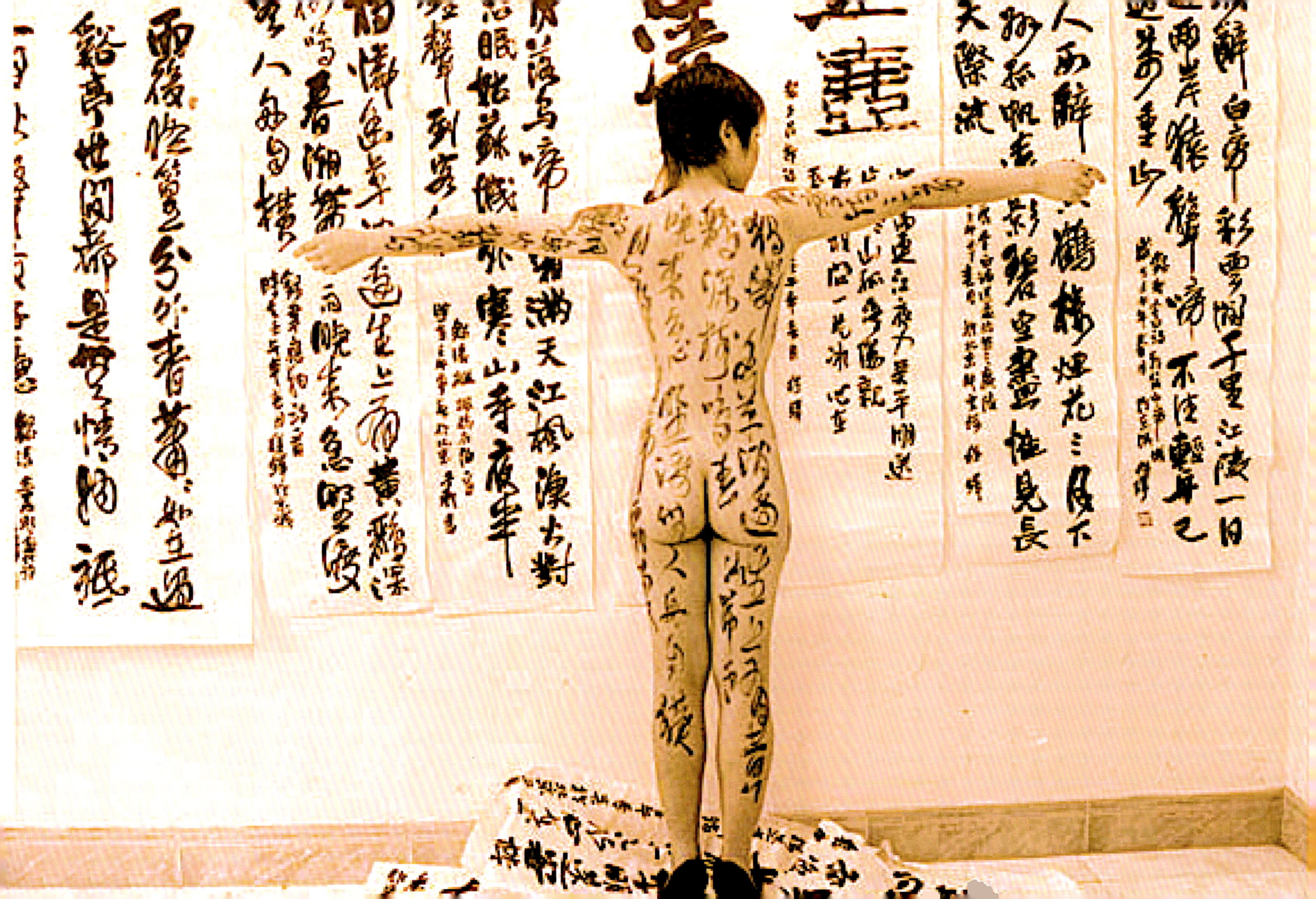

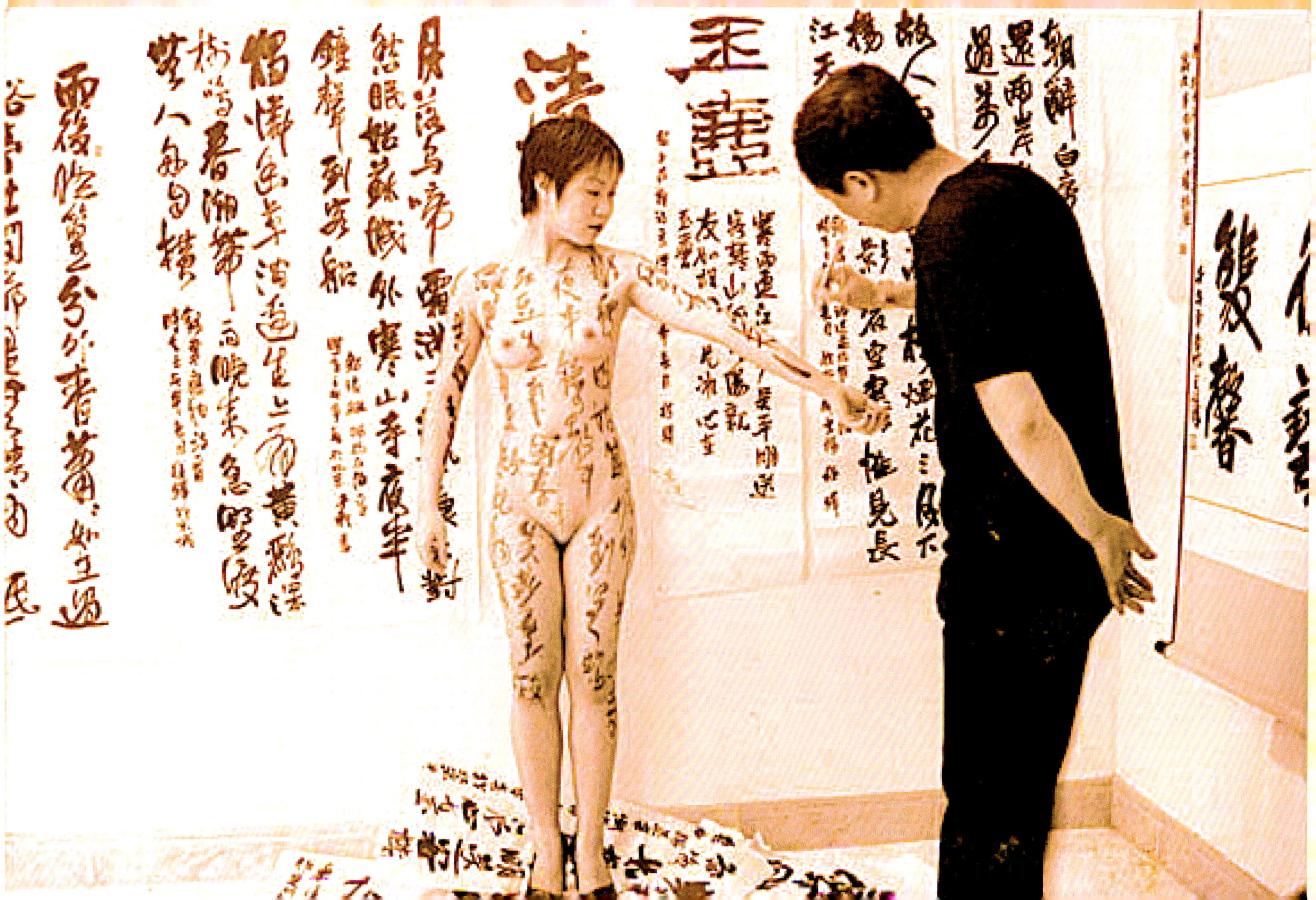

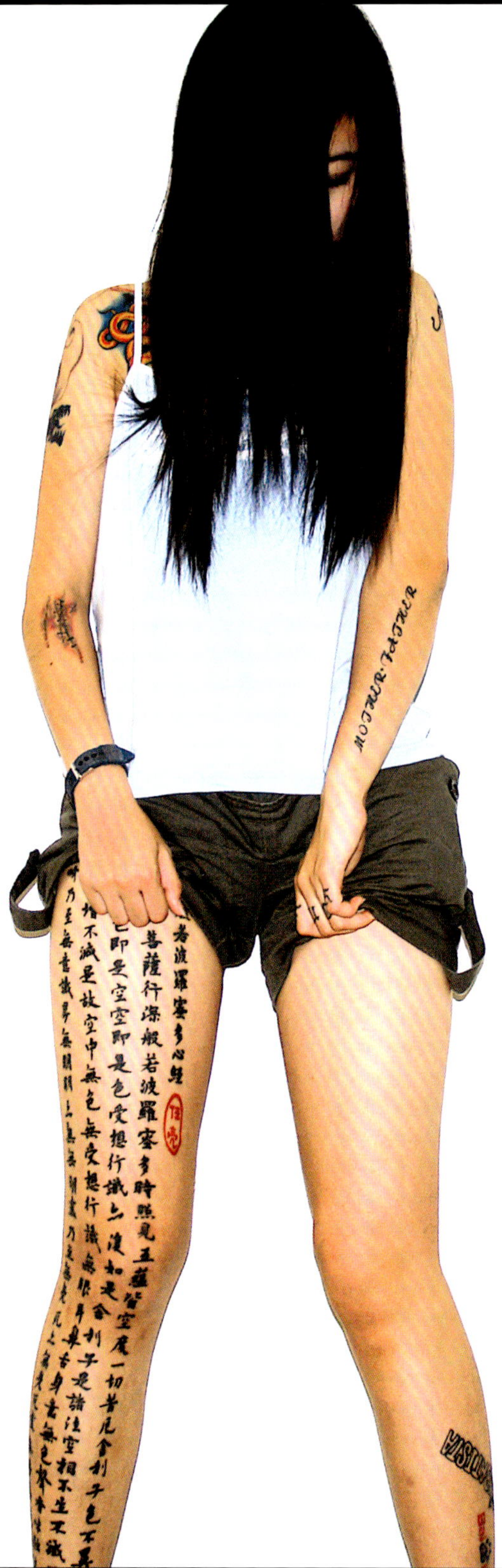

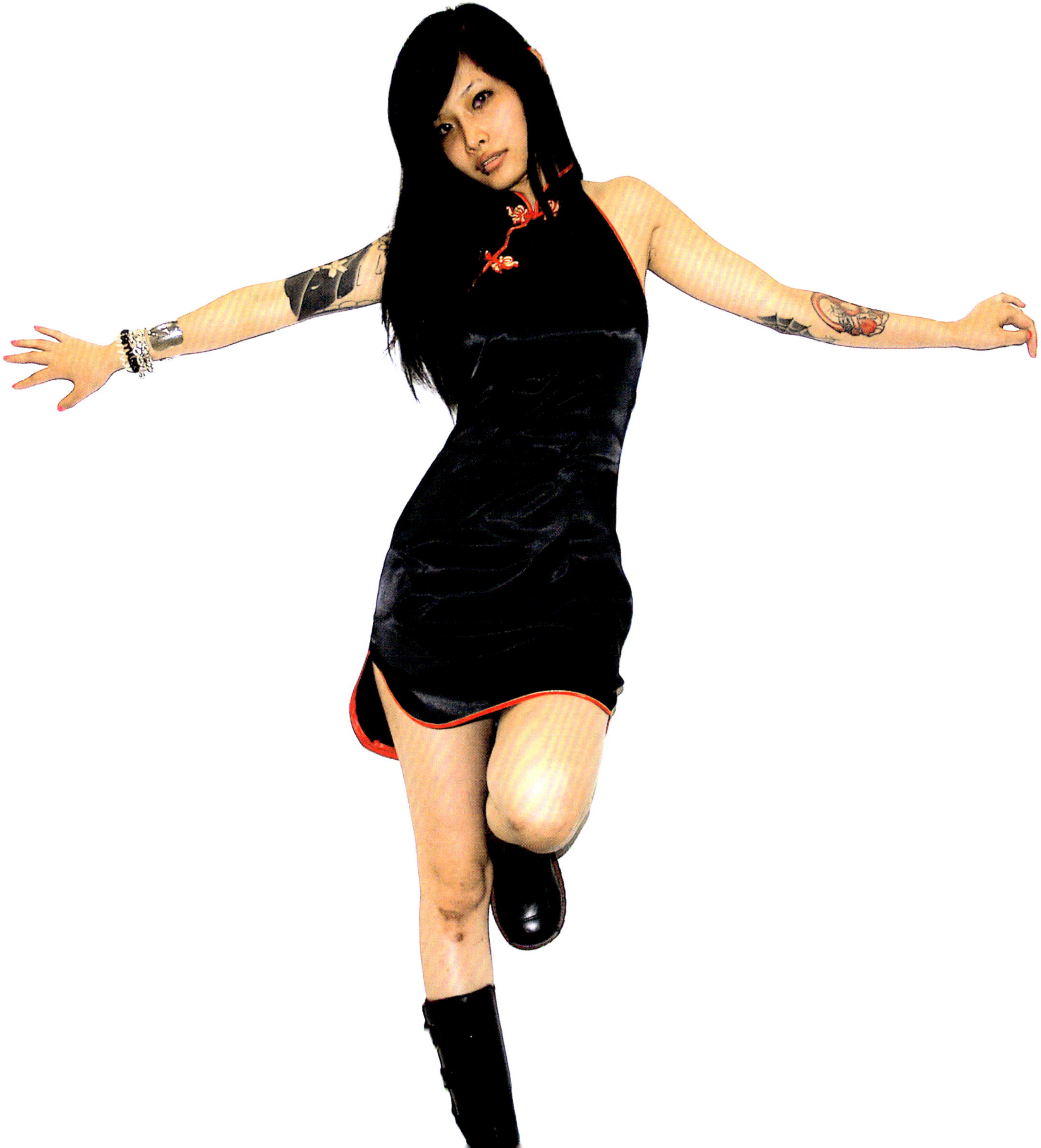

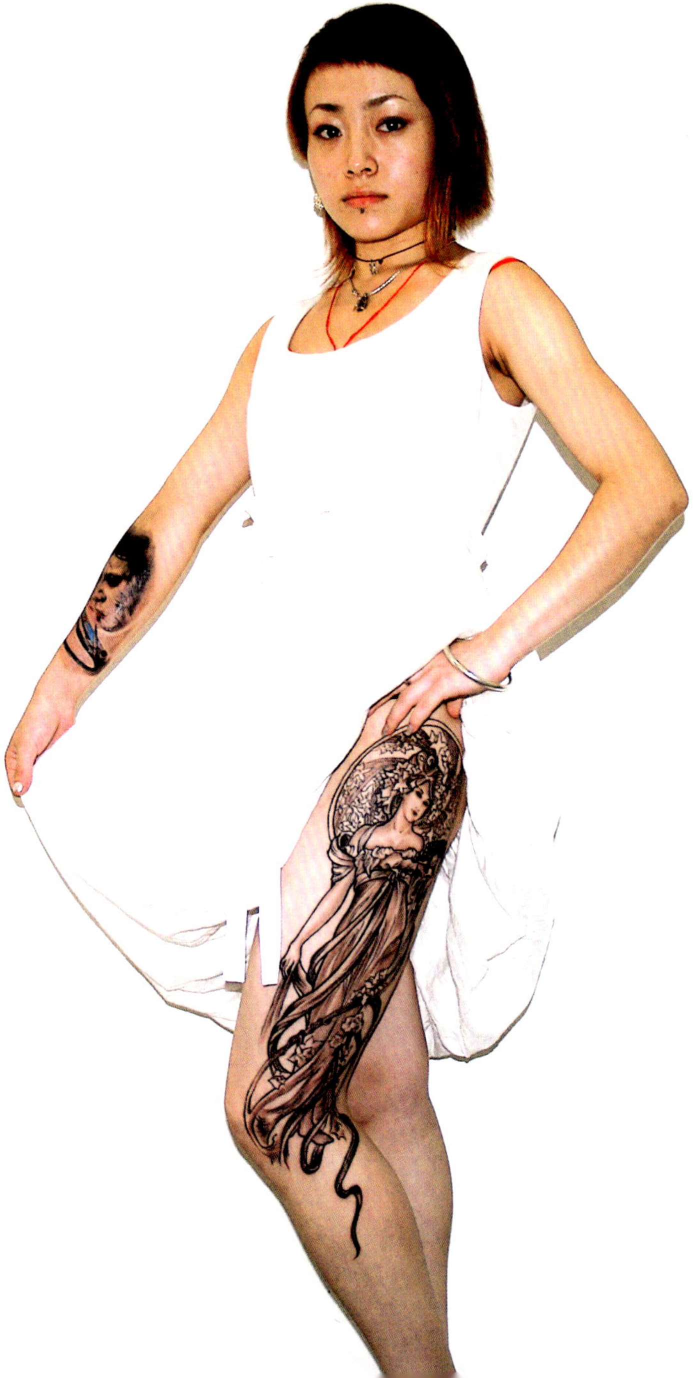

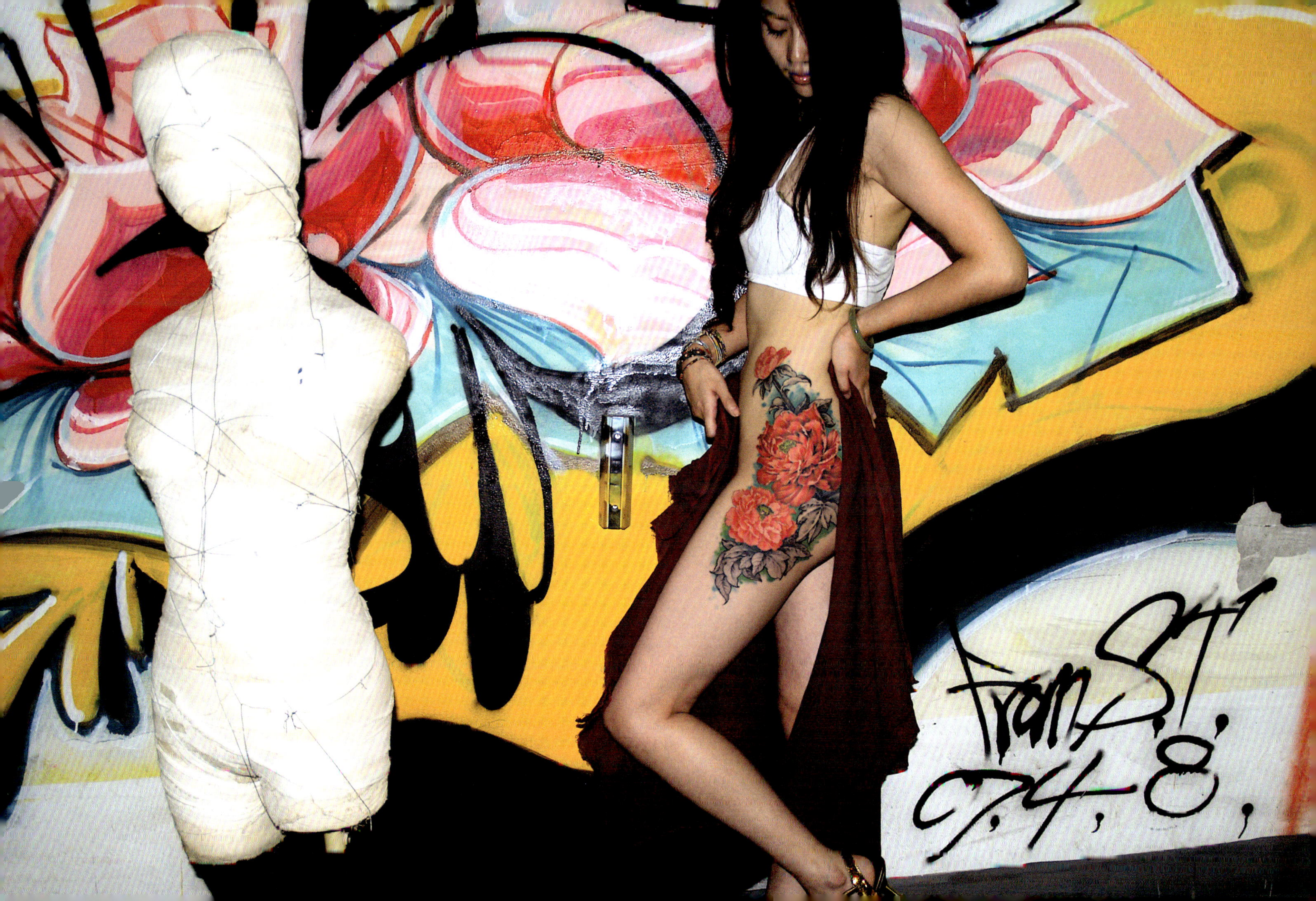

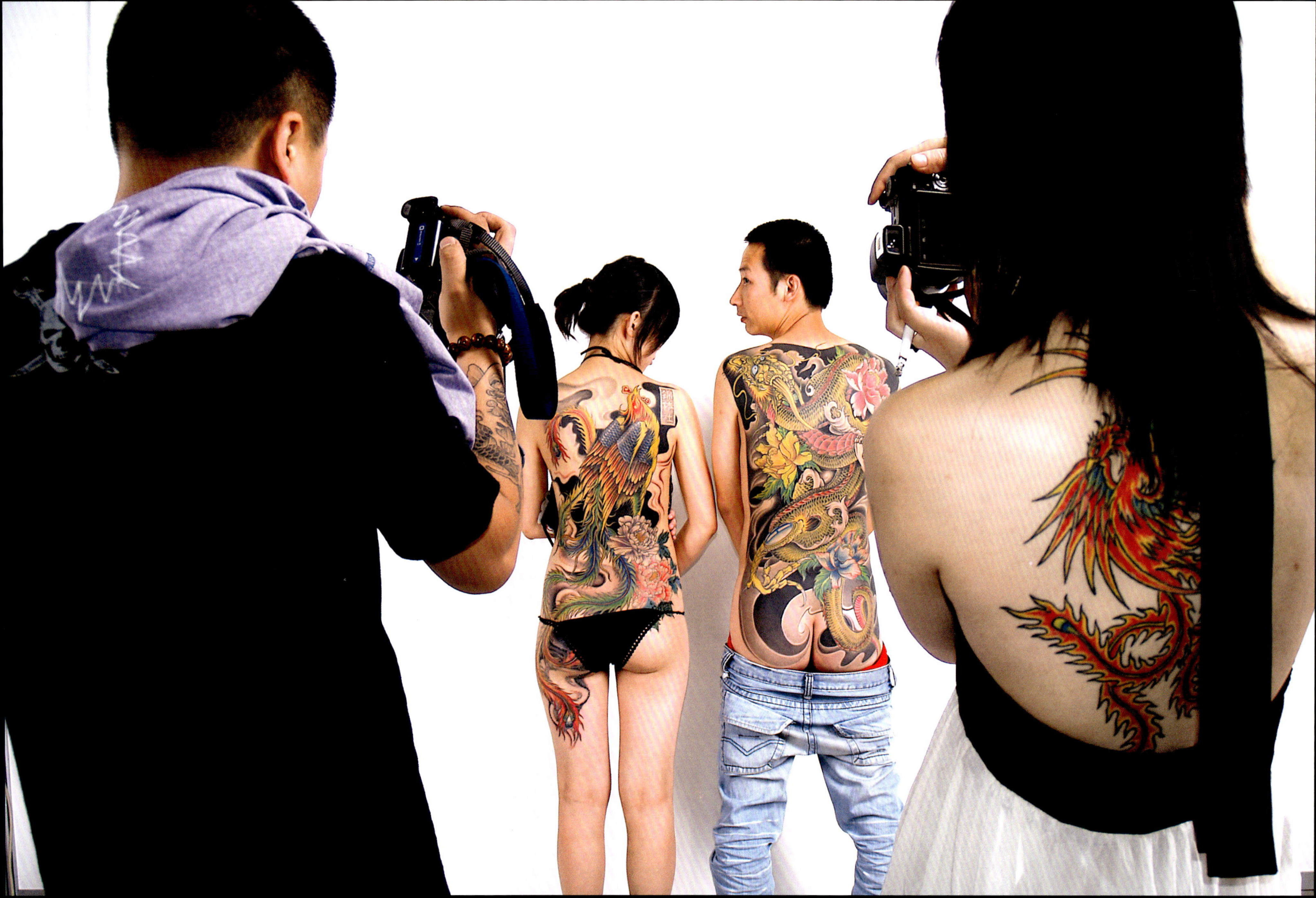

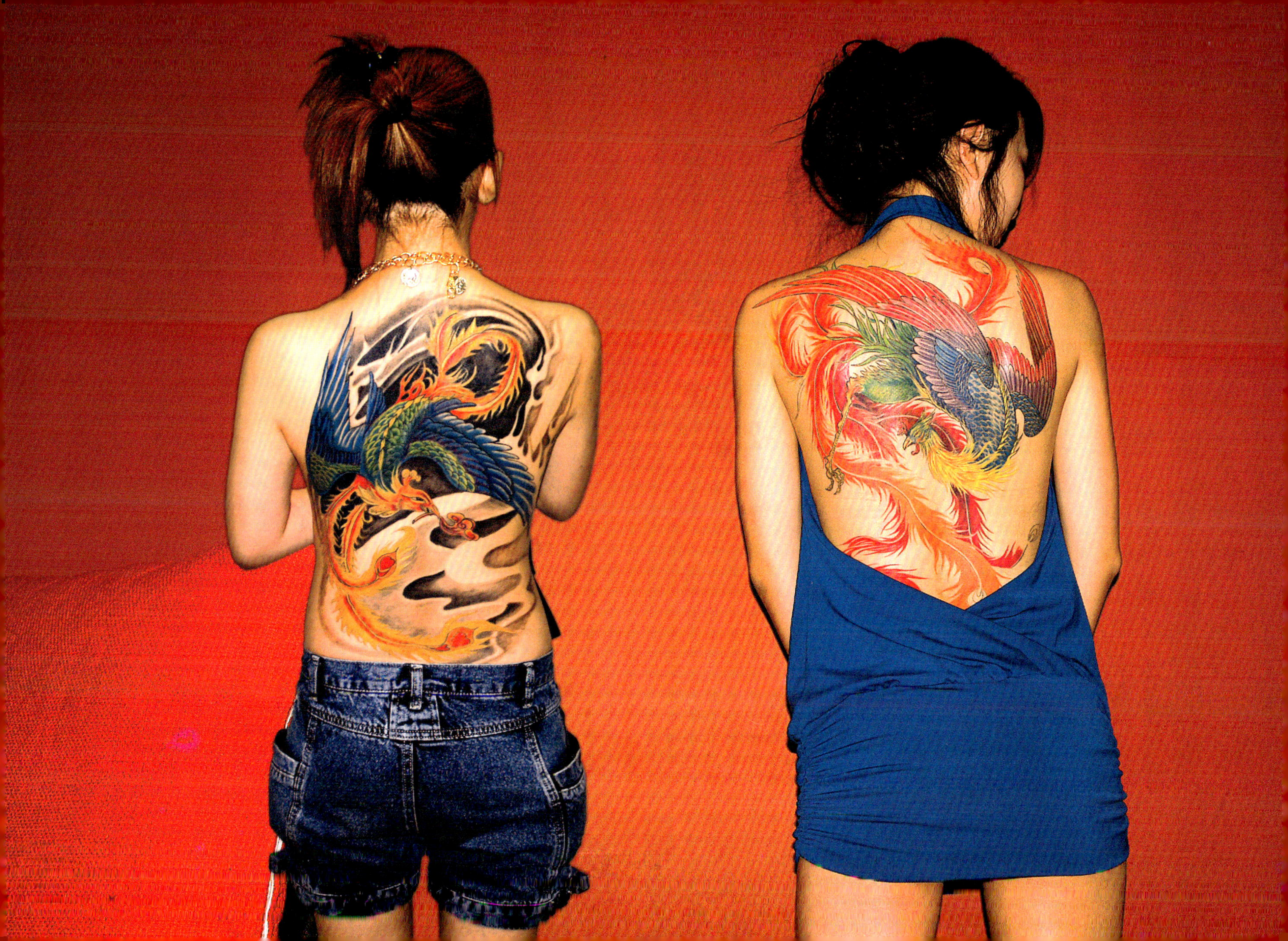

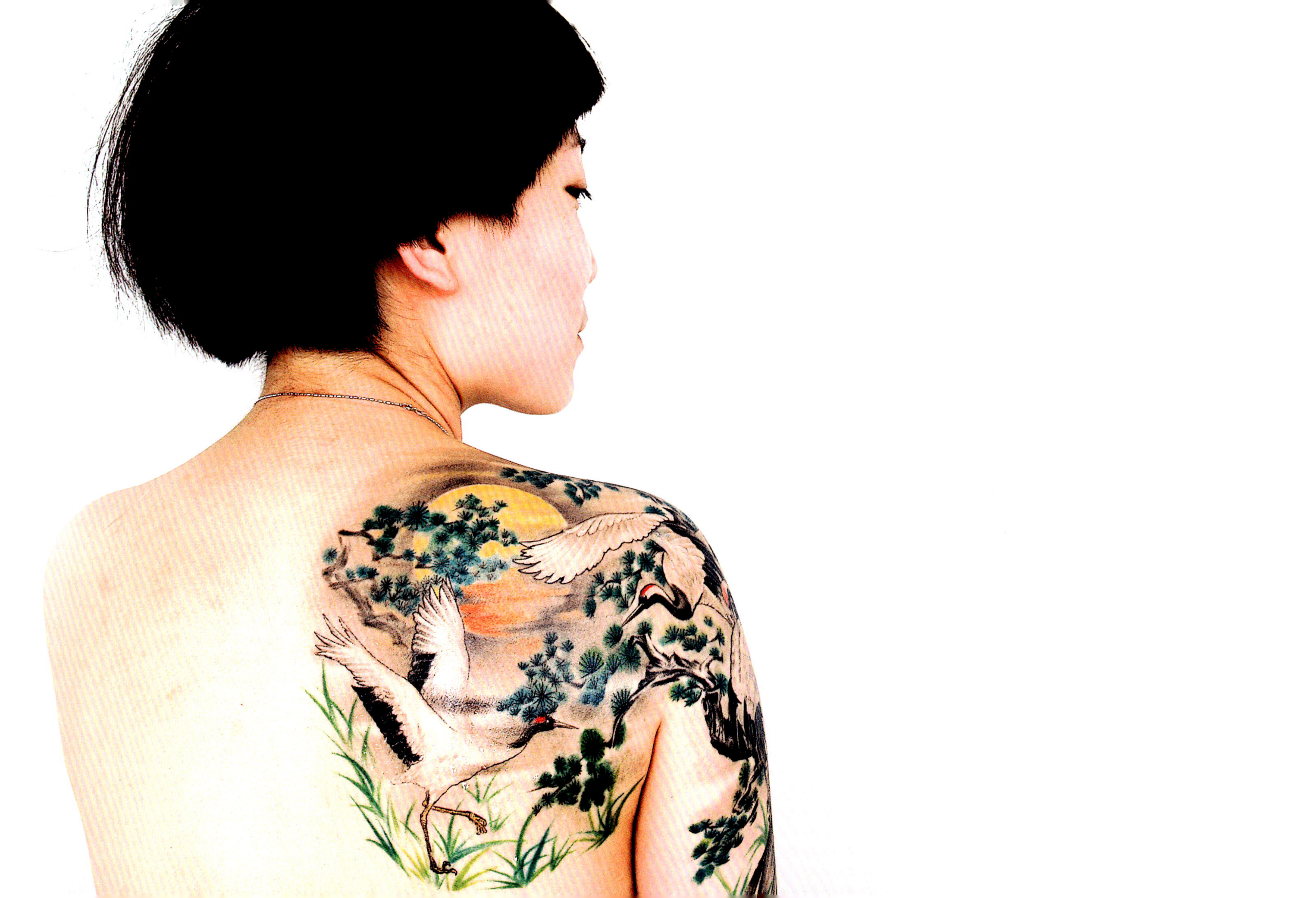

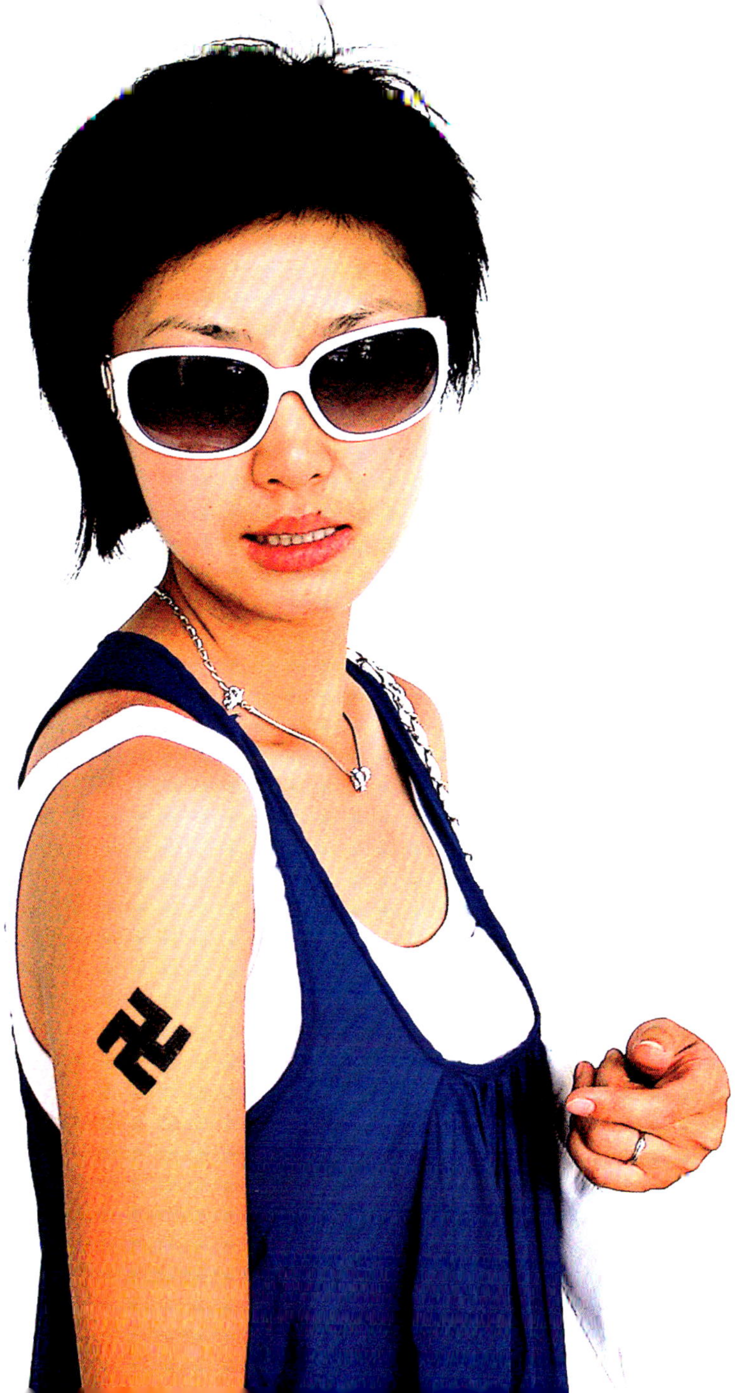

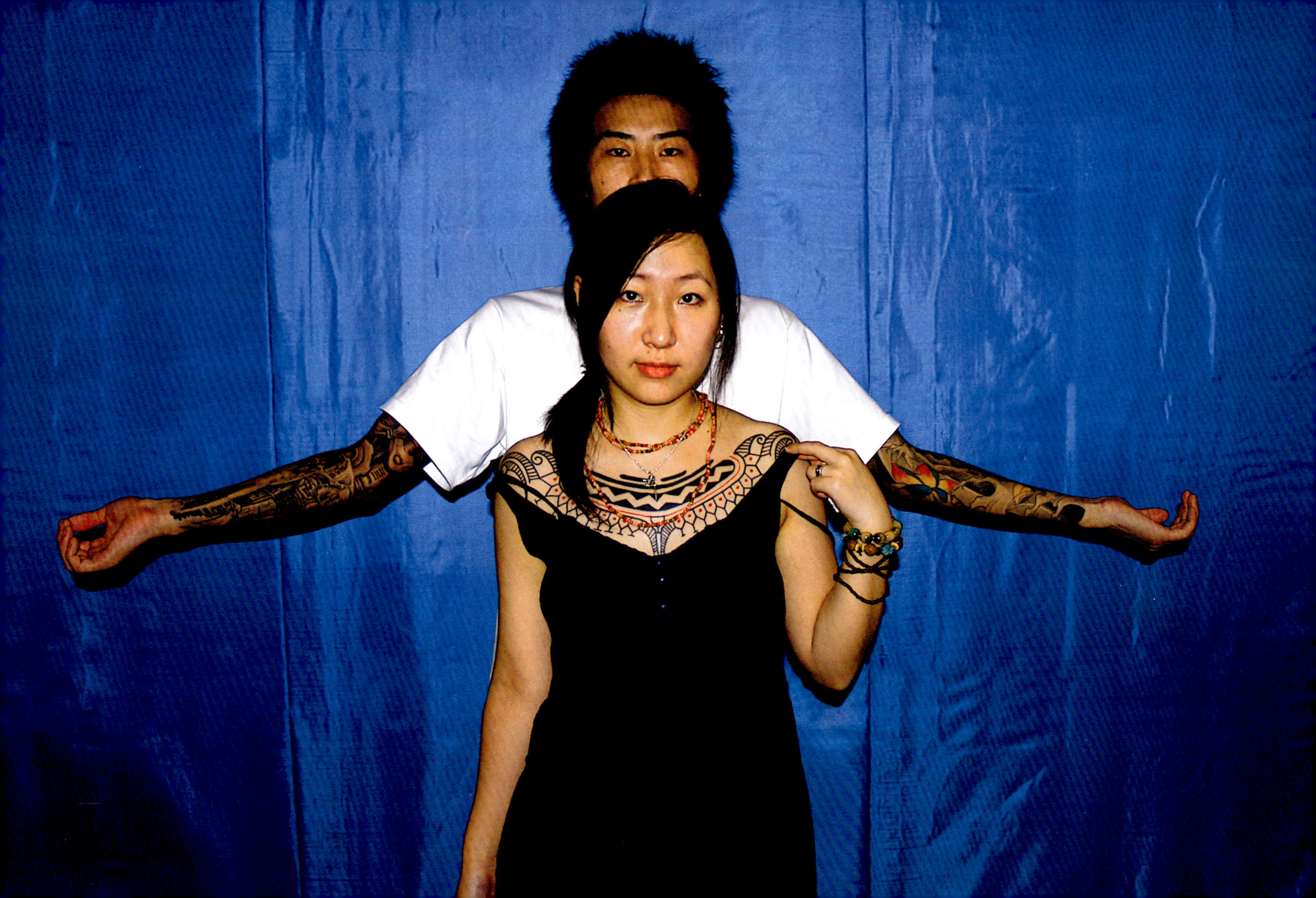

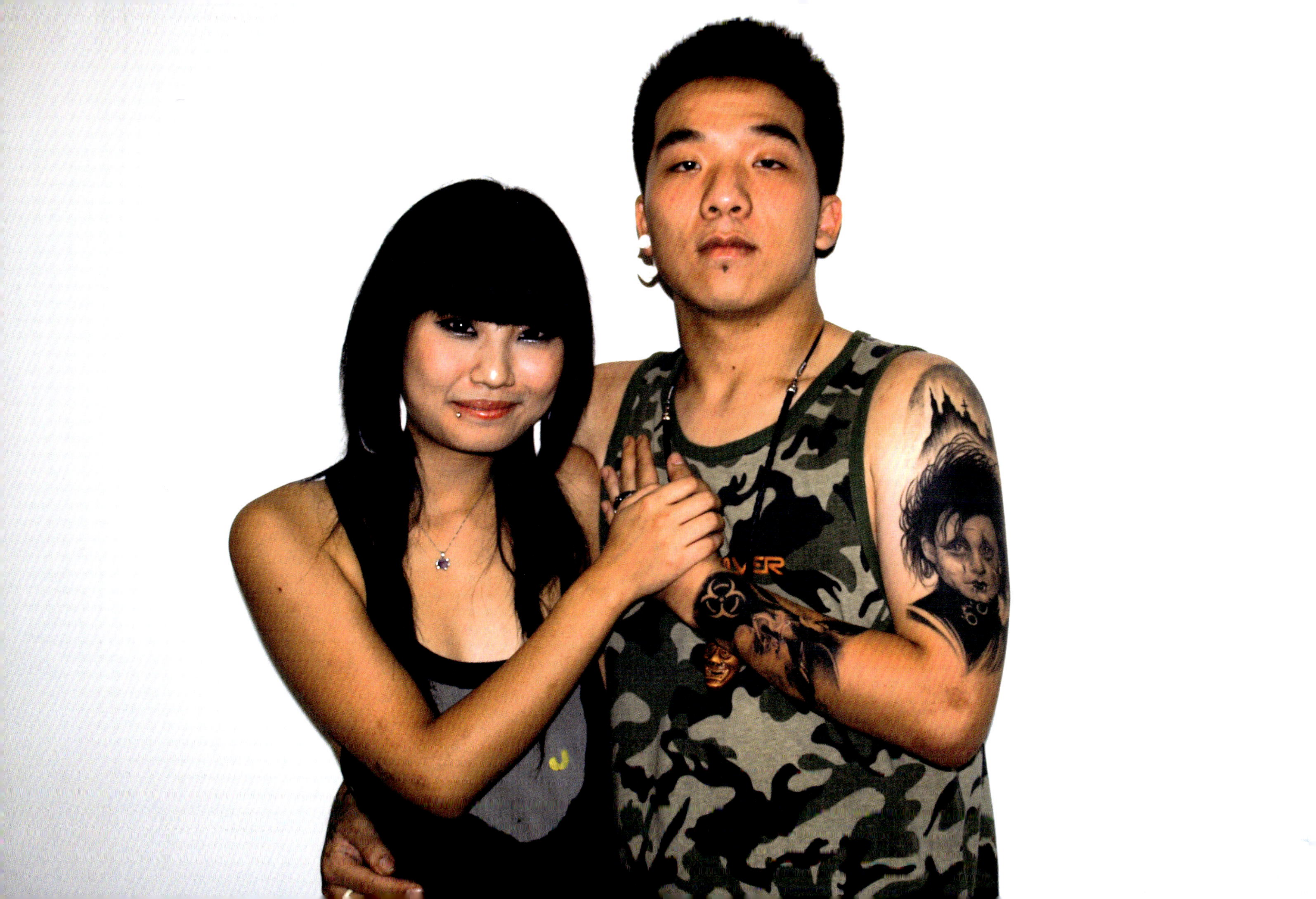

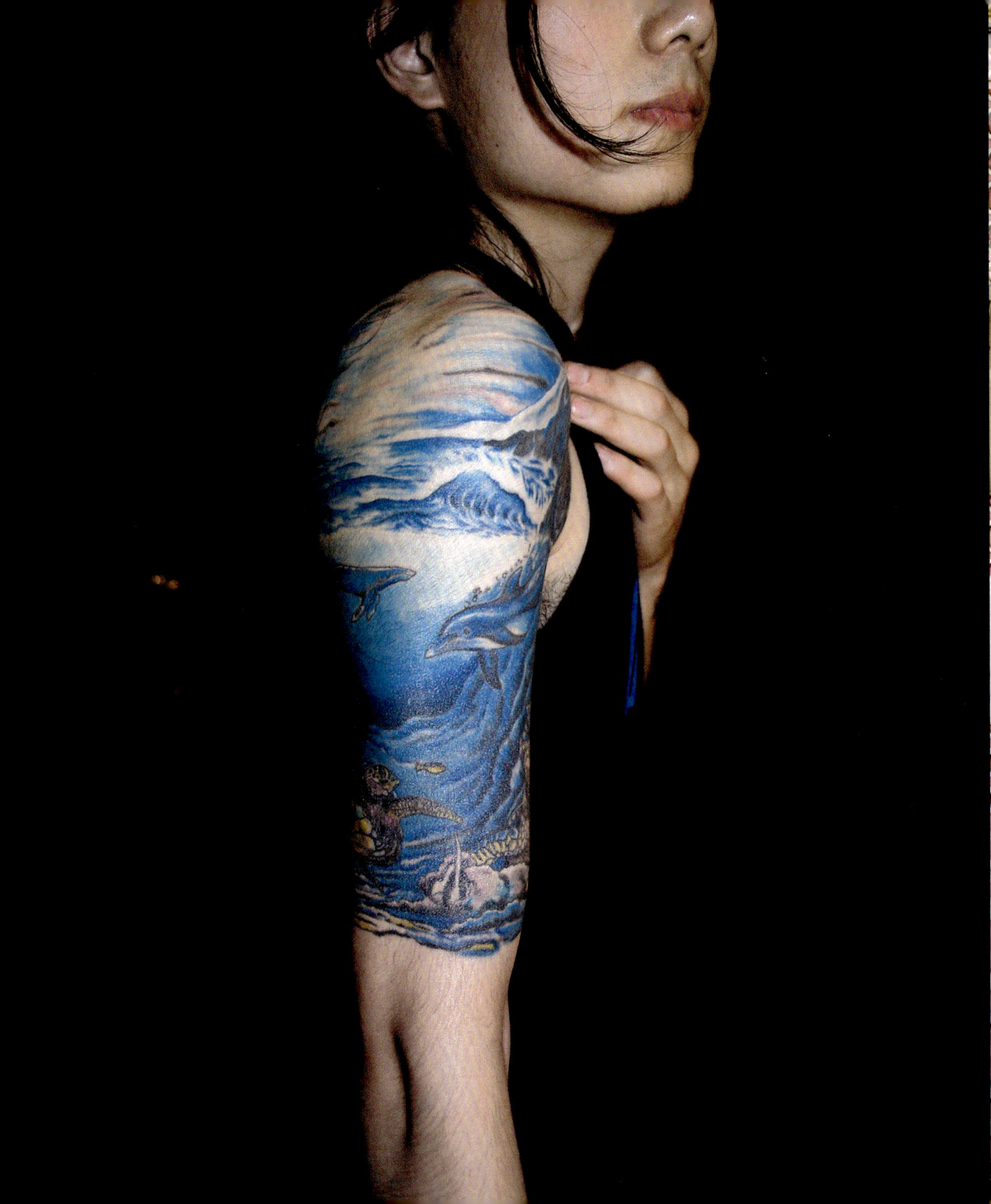
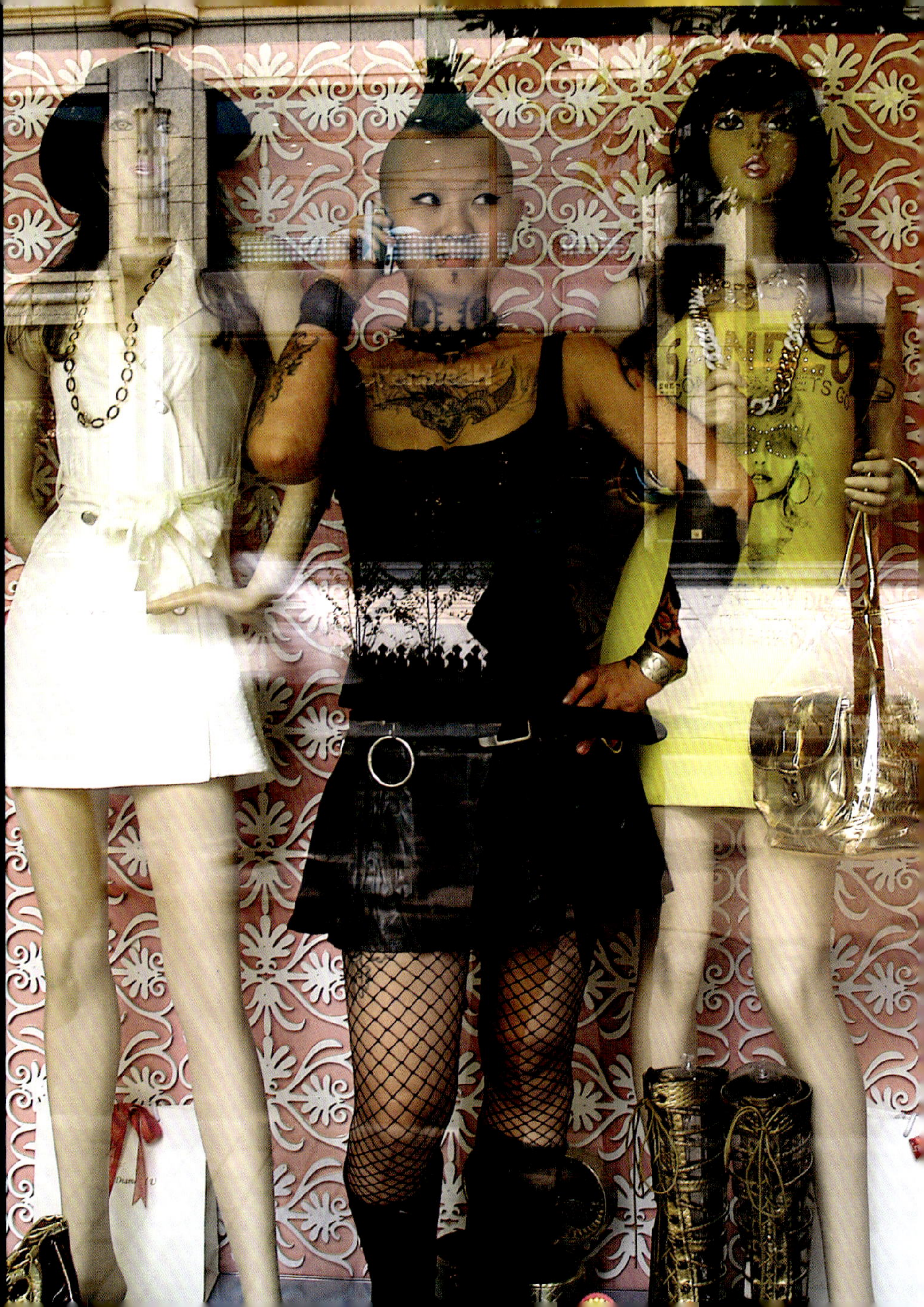

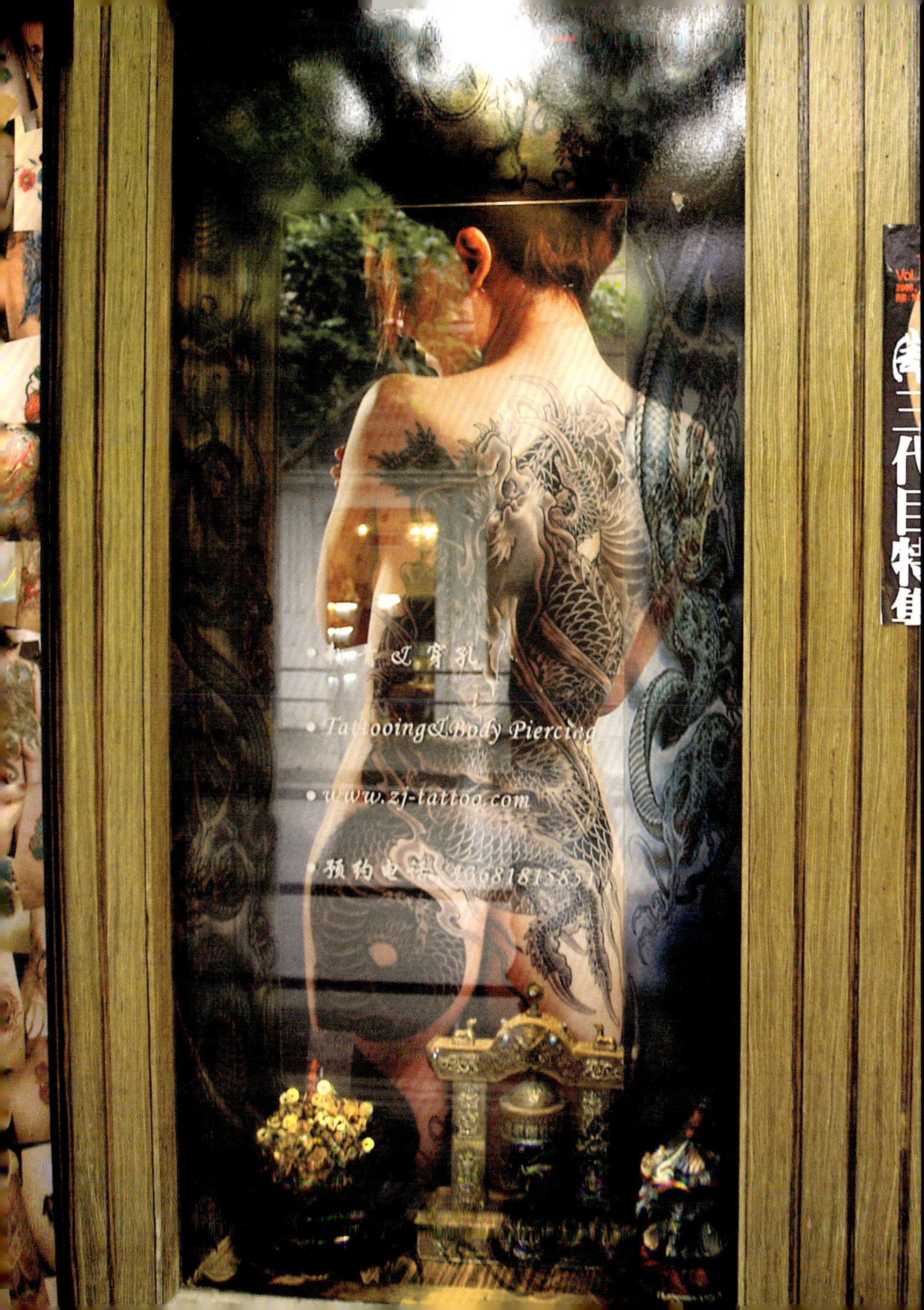
www.zj-tattoo.com
预约电话

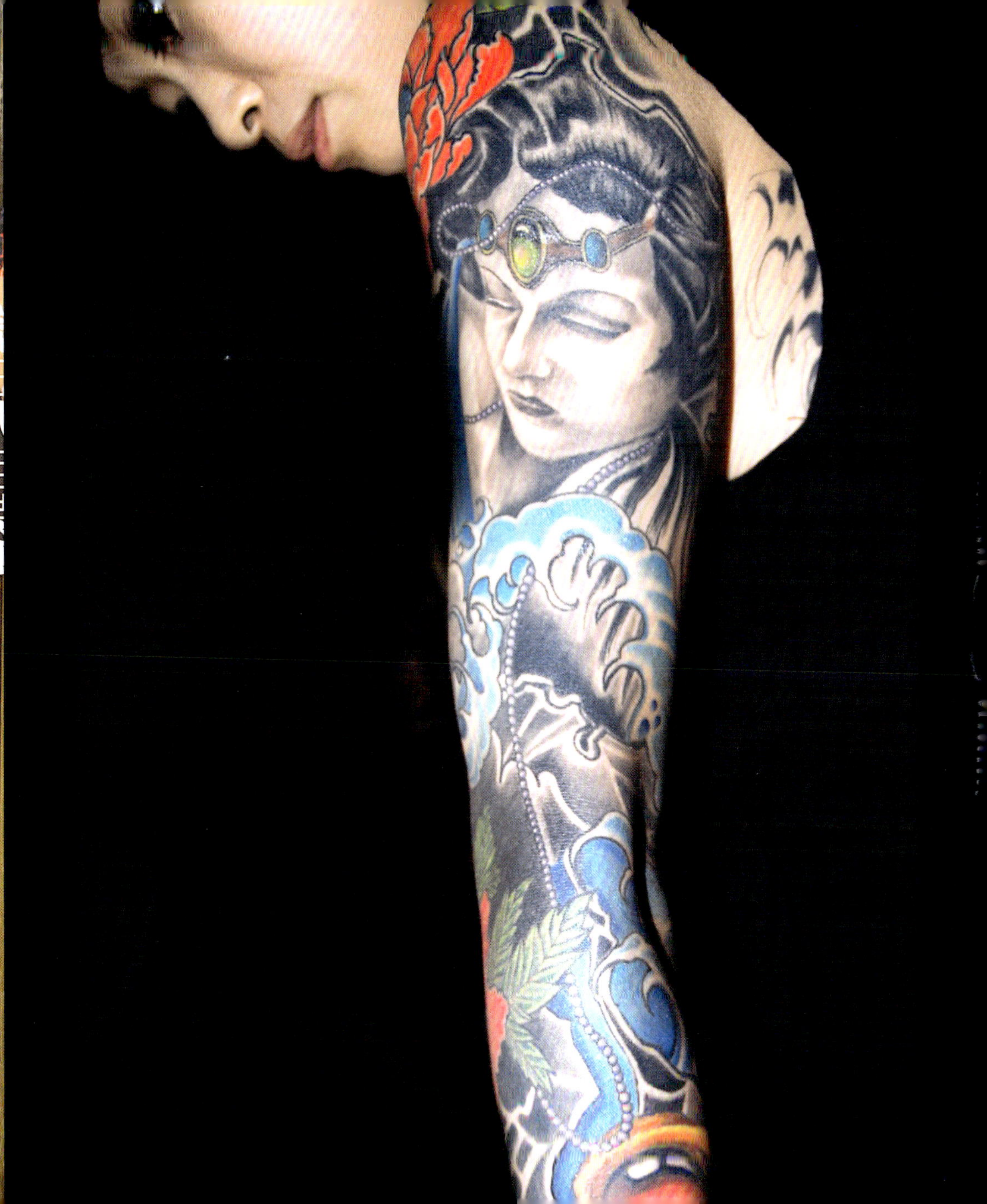

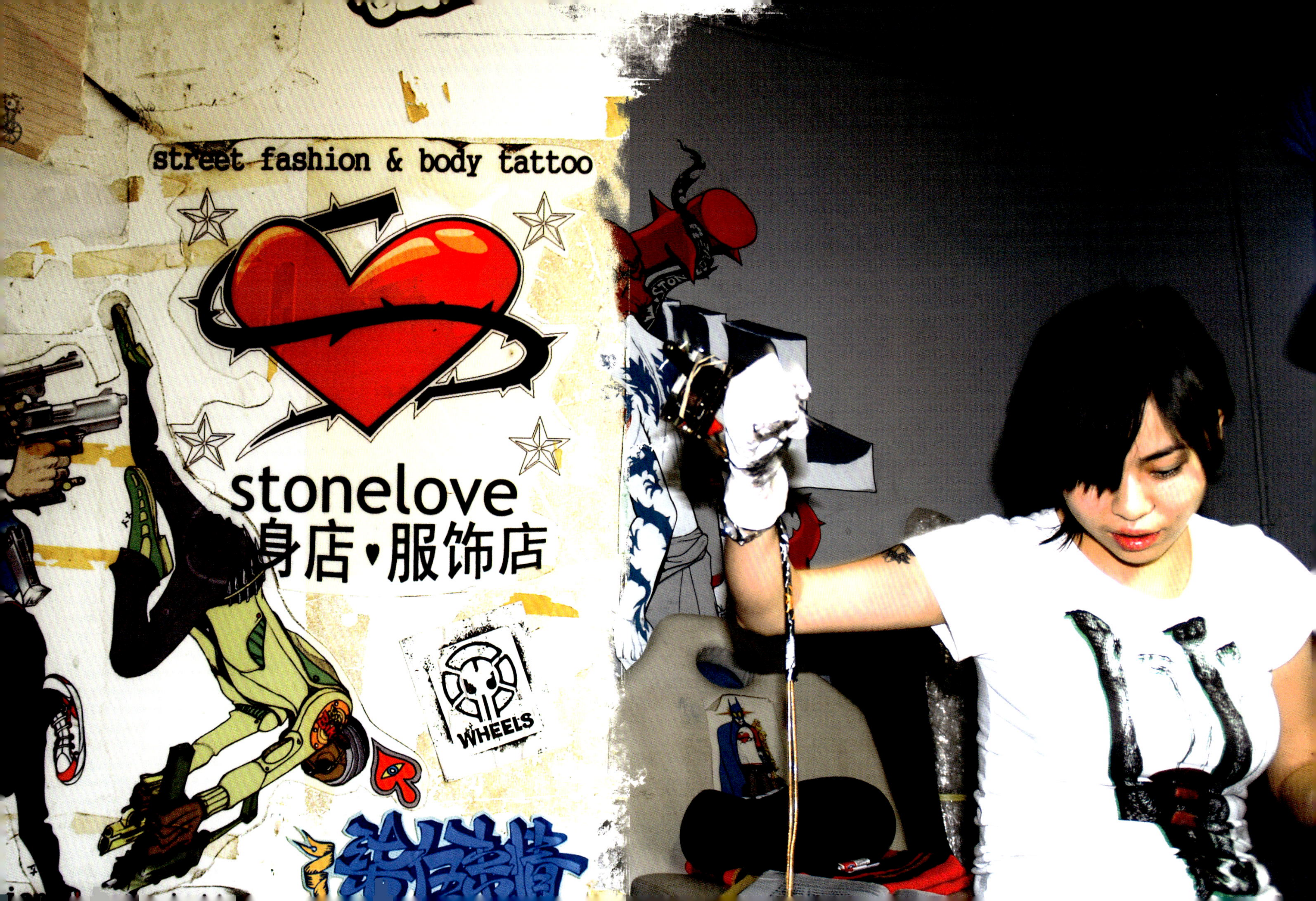
street fashion & body tattoo
stonelove
身店•服饰店
WHEELS

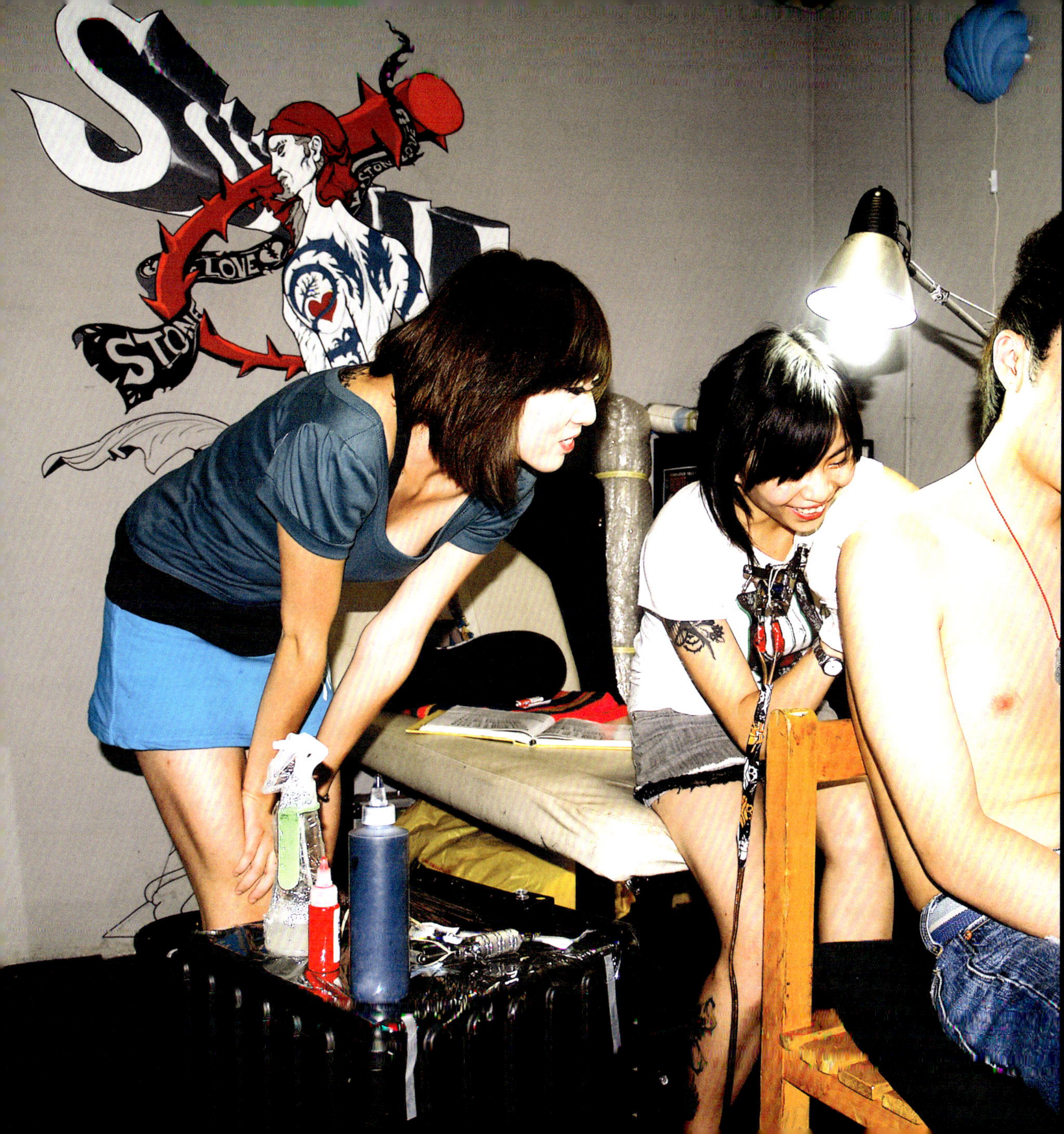
LOVE
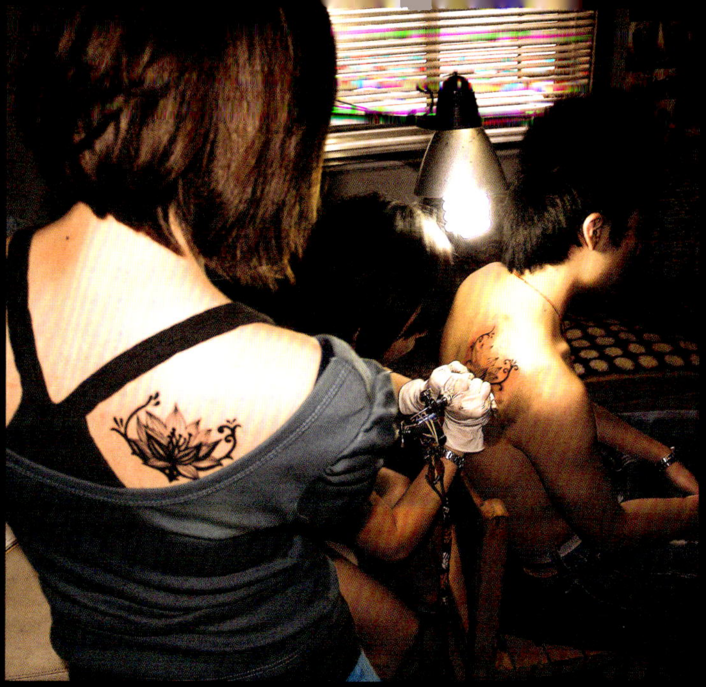
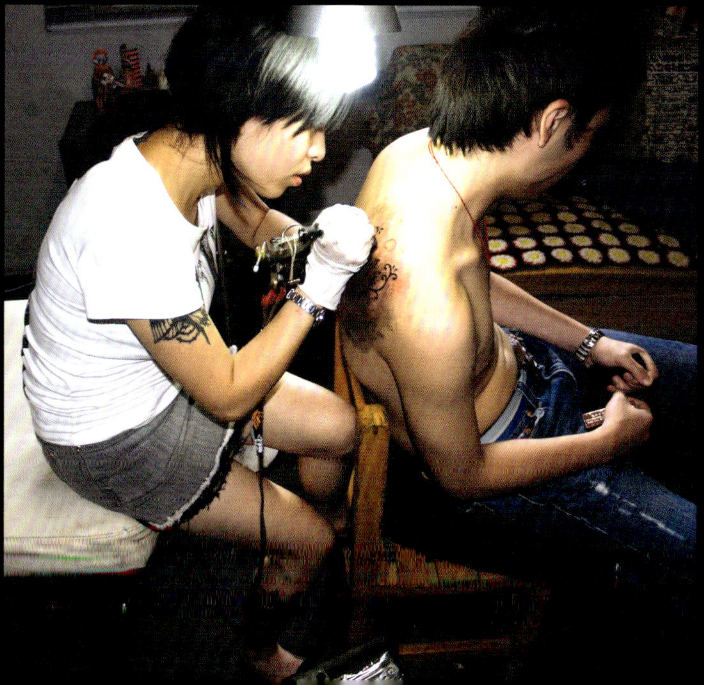

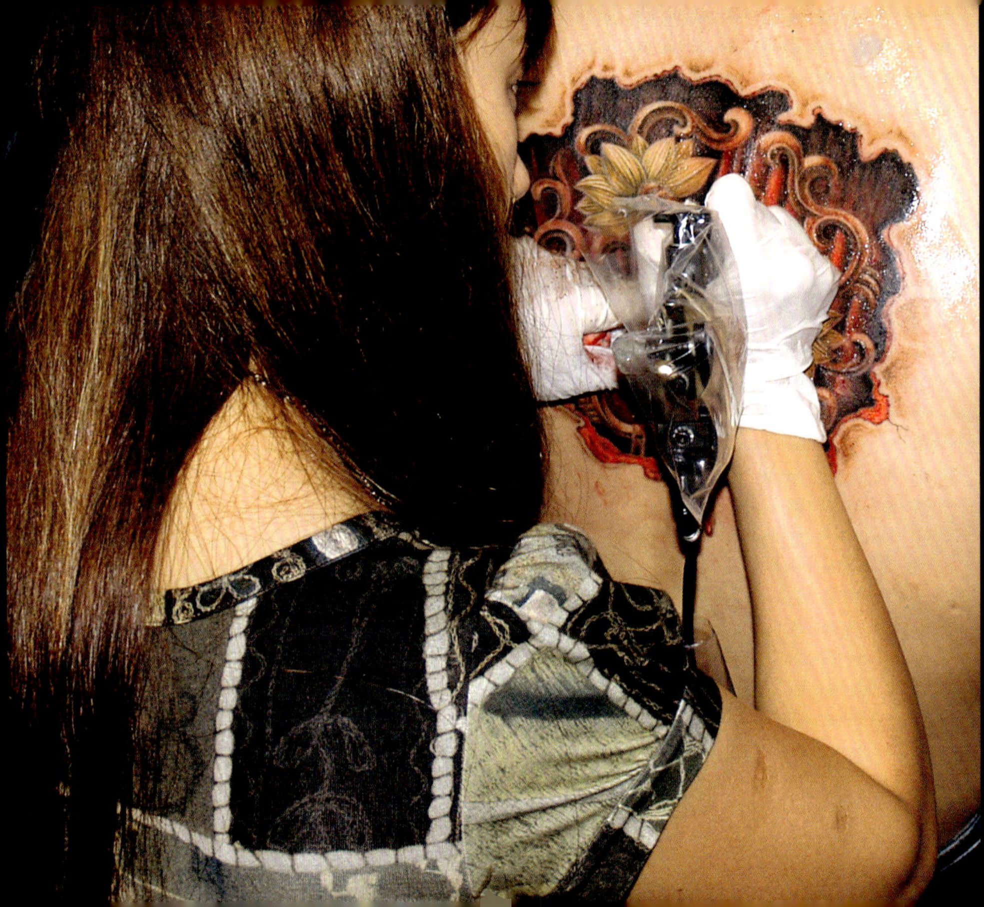

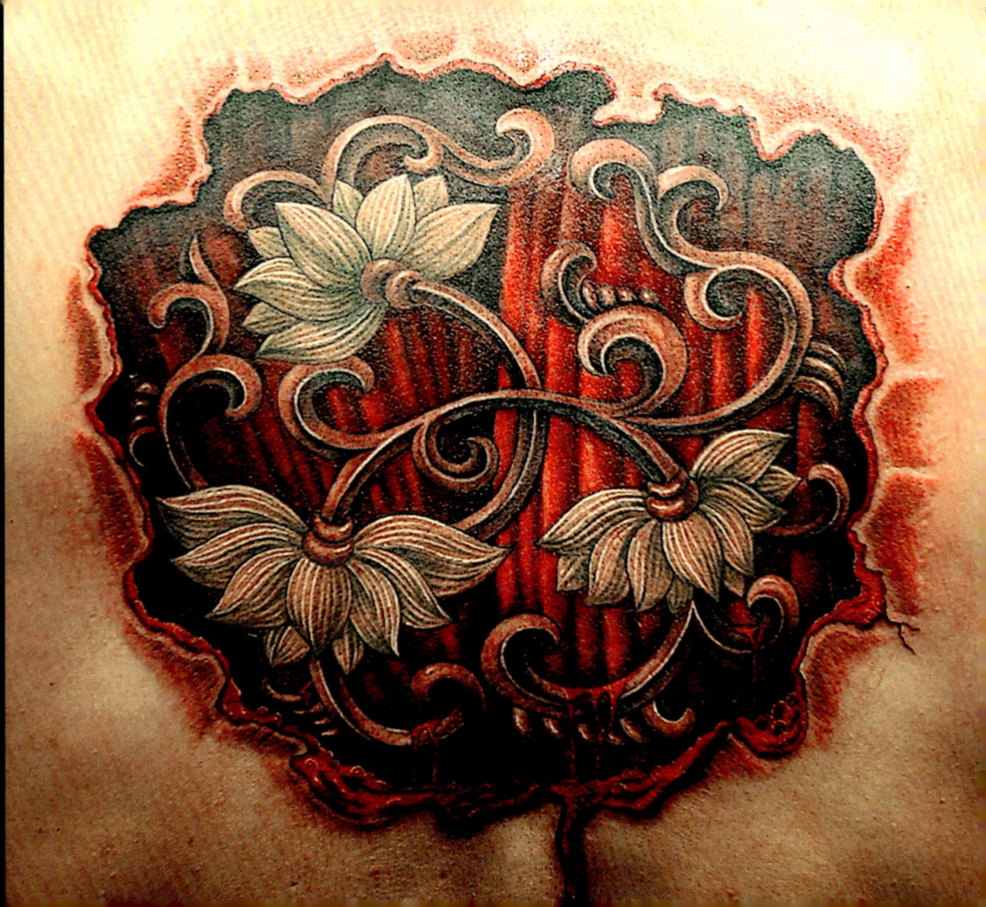

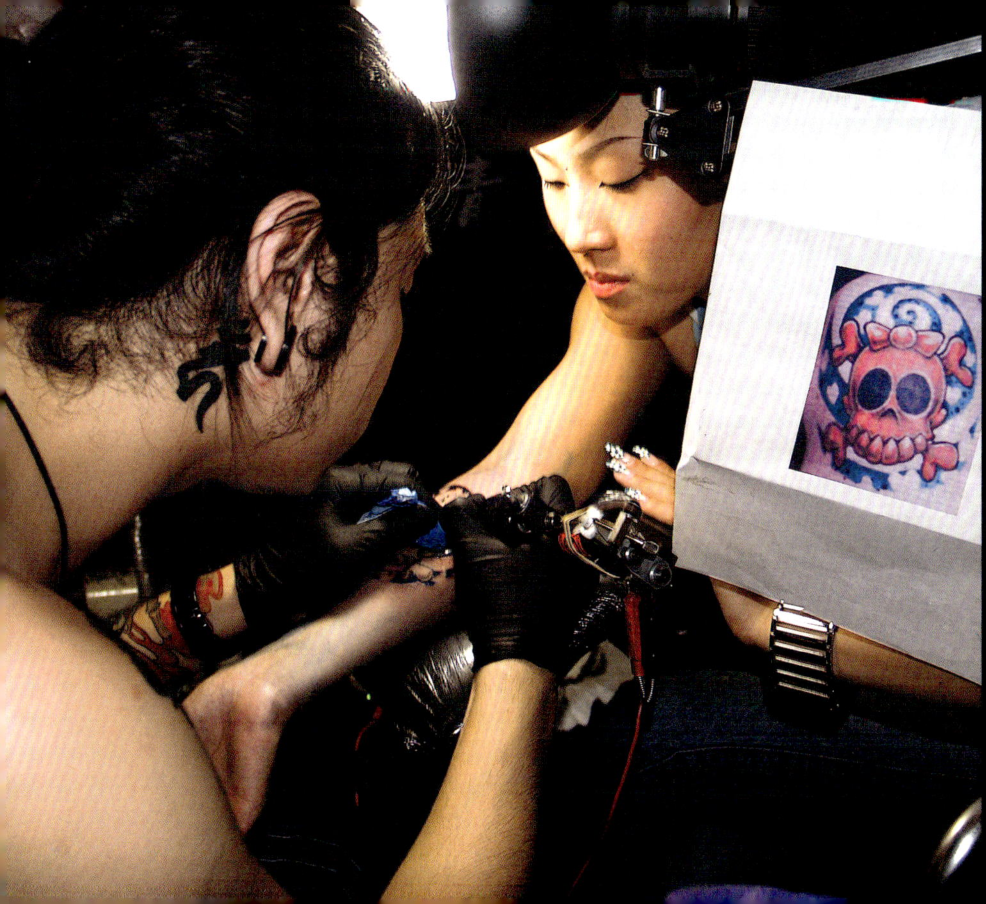

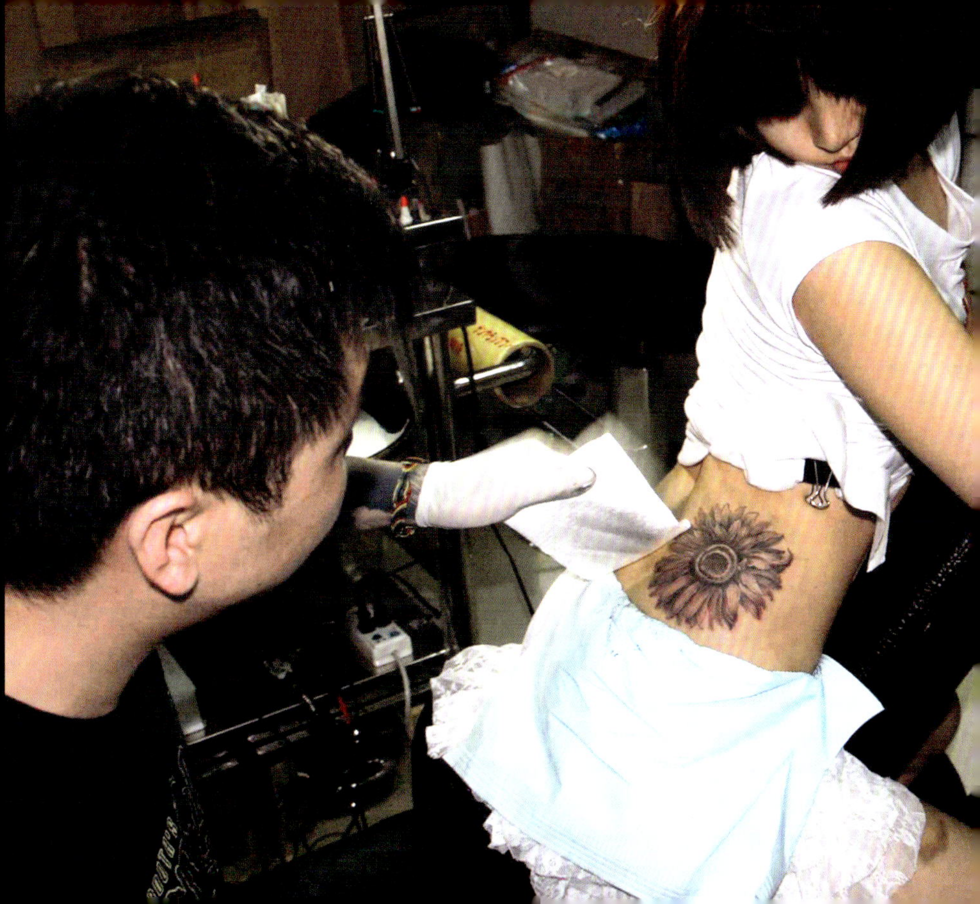

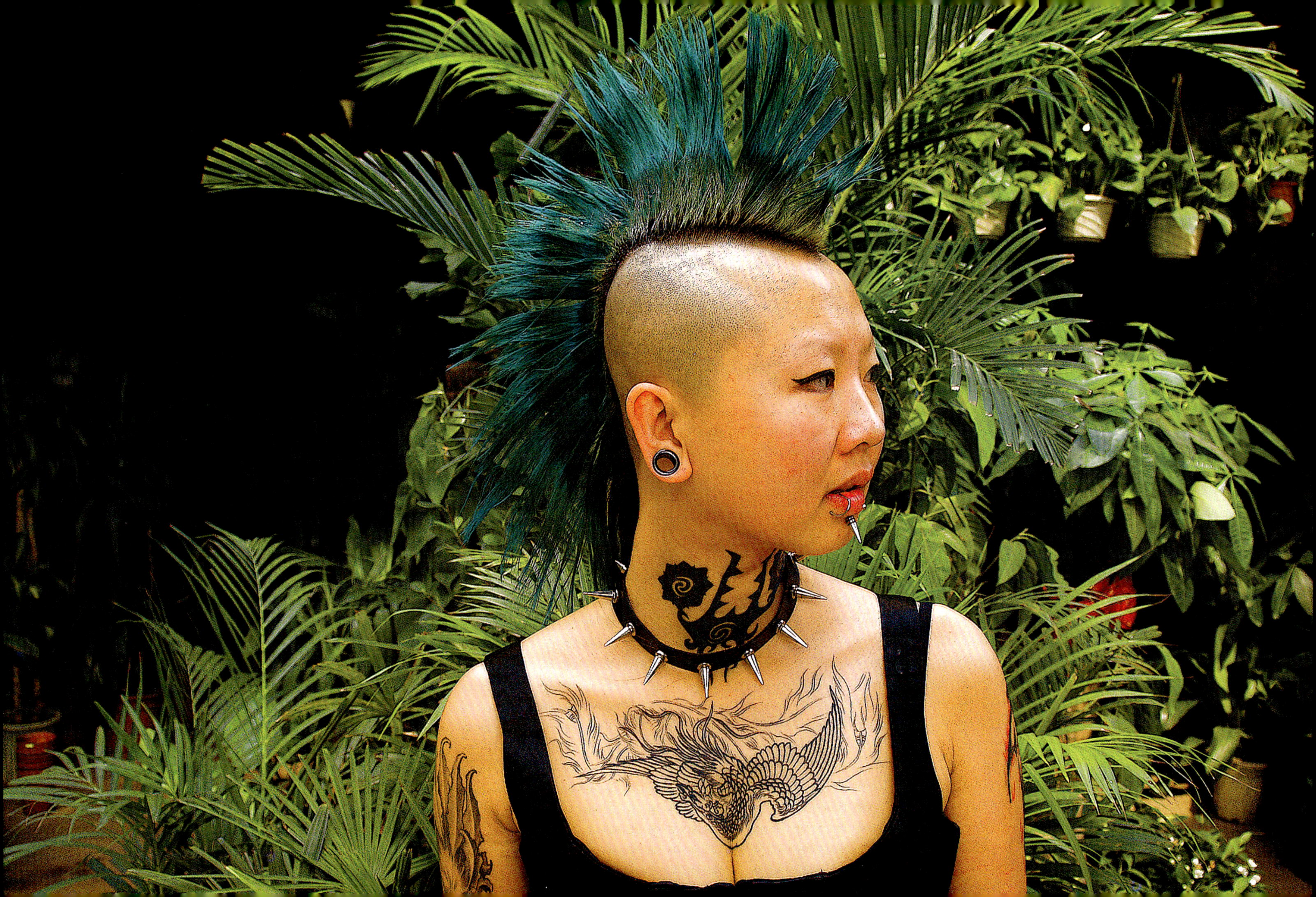

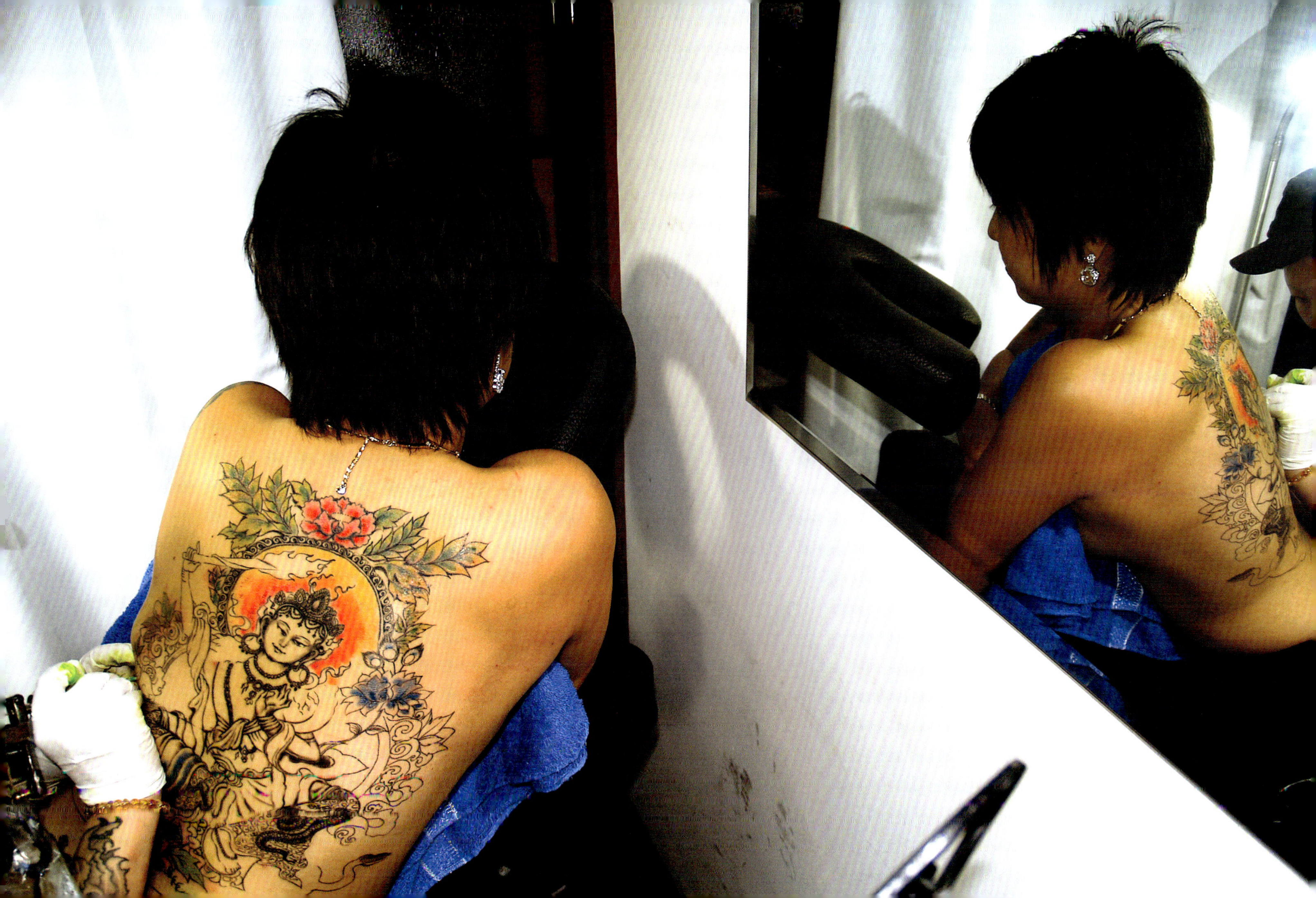

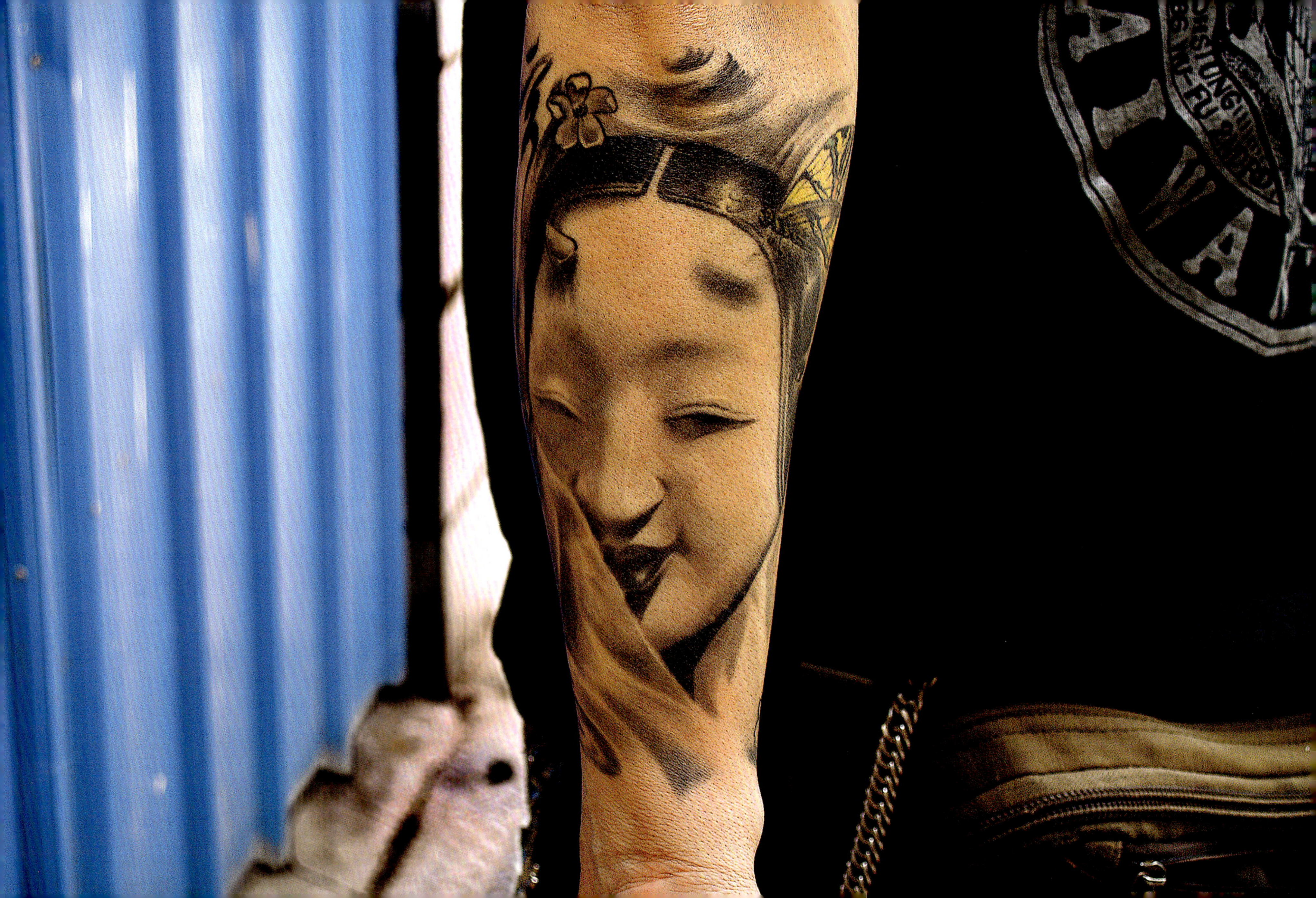

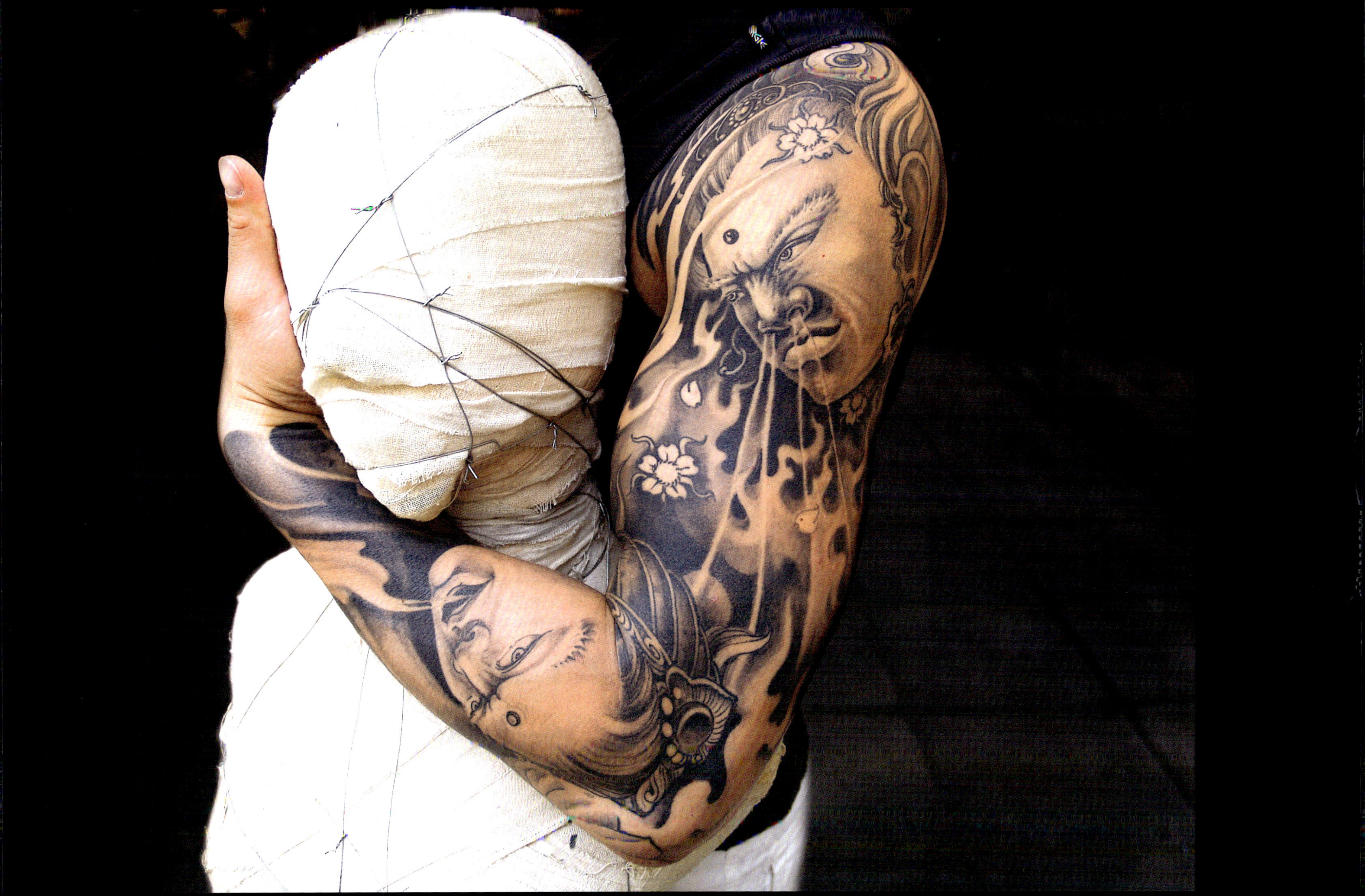

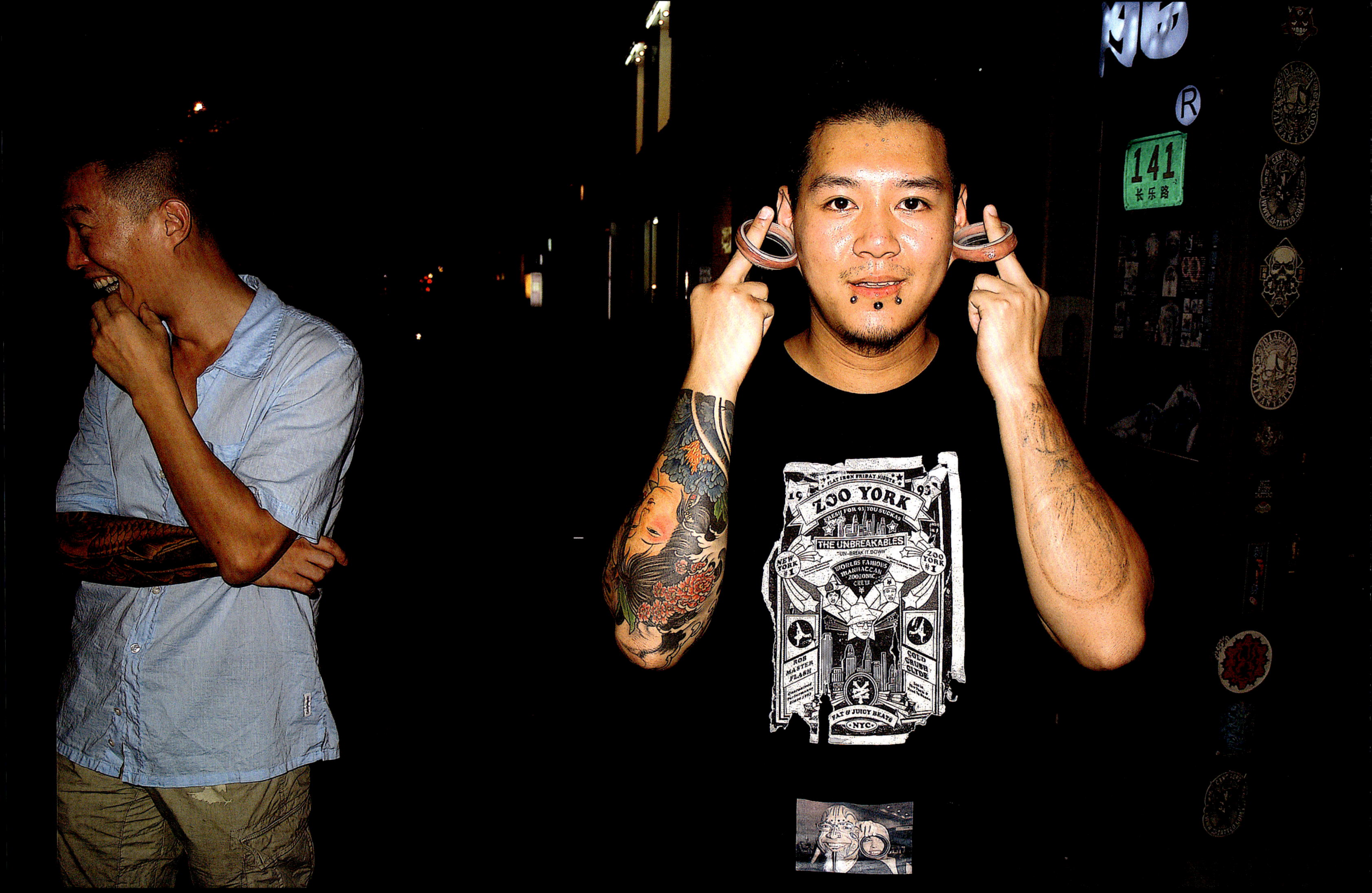
141
长乐路
ZOO YORK
THE UNBREAKABLES
"UN-BREAK IT DOWN"
FAT & JUICY BEATS
NYC

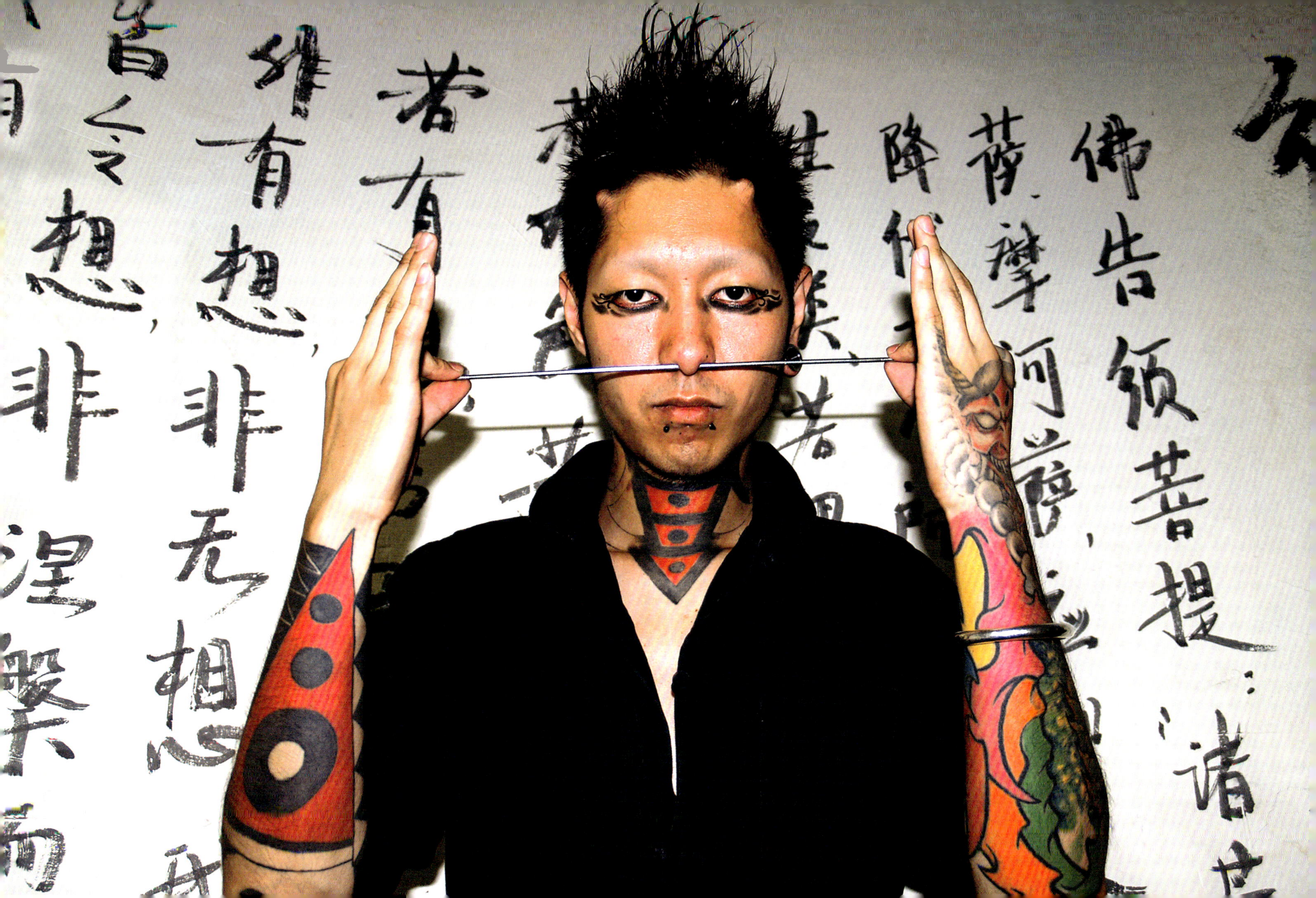

佛告须菩提：诸
菩萨摩诃萨
若有想，非无想

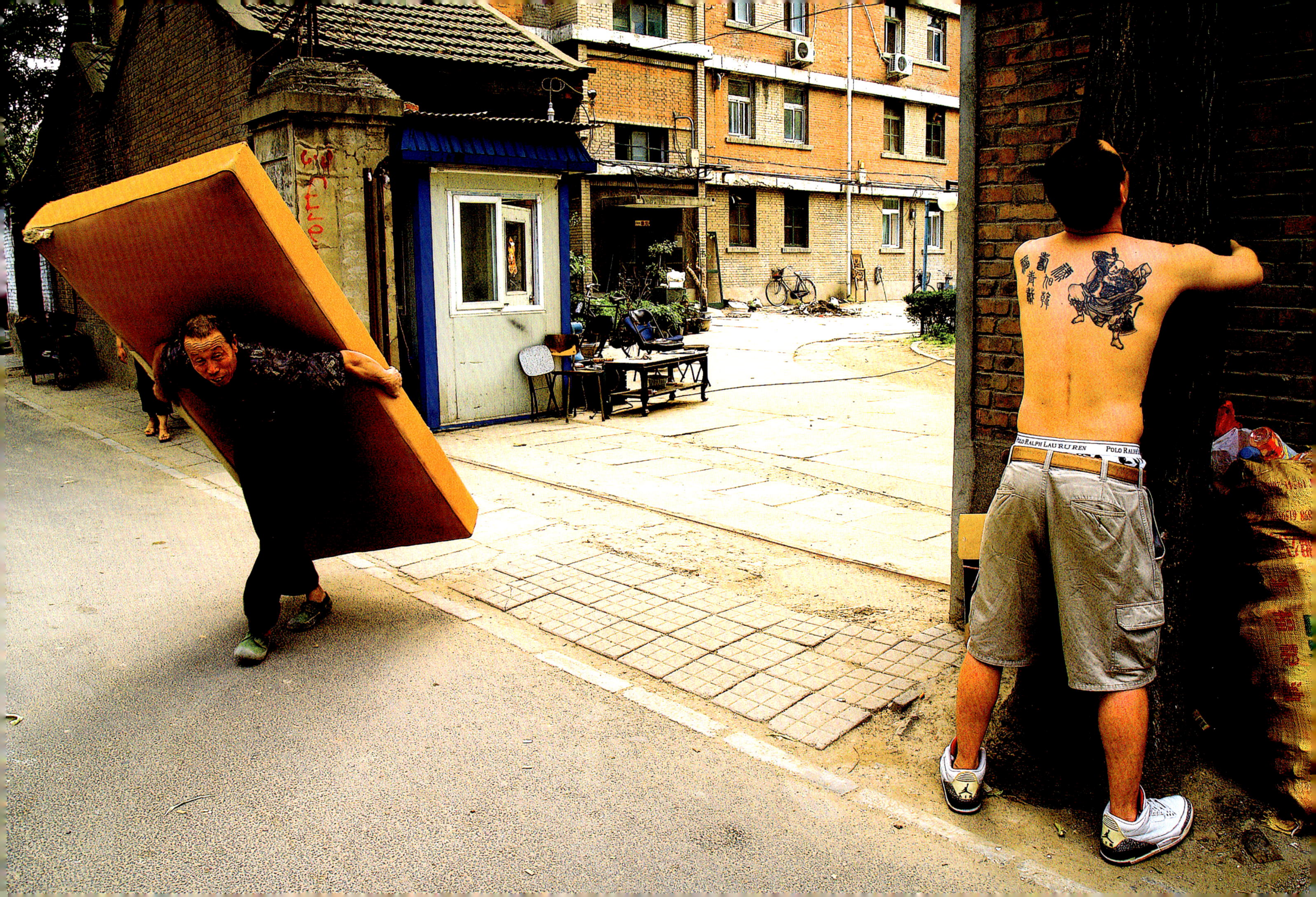
POLO RALPH LAUREN
POLO RALPH

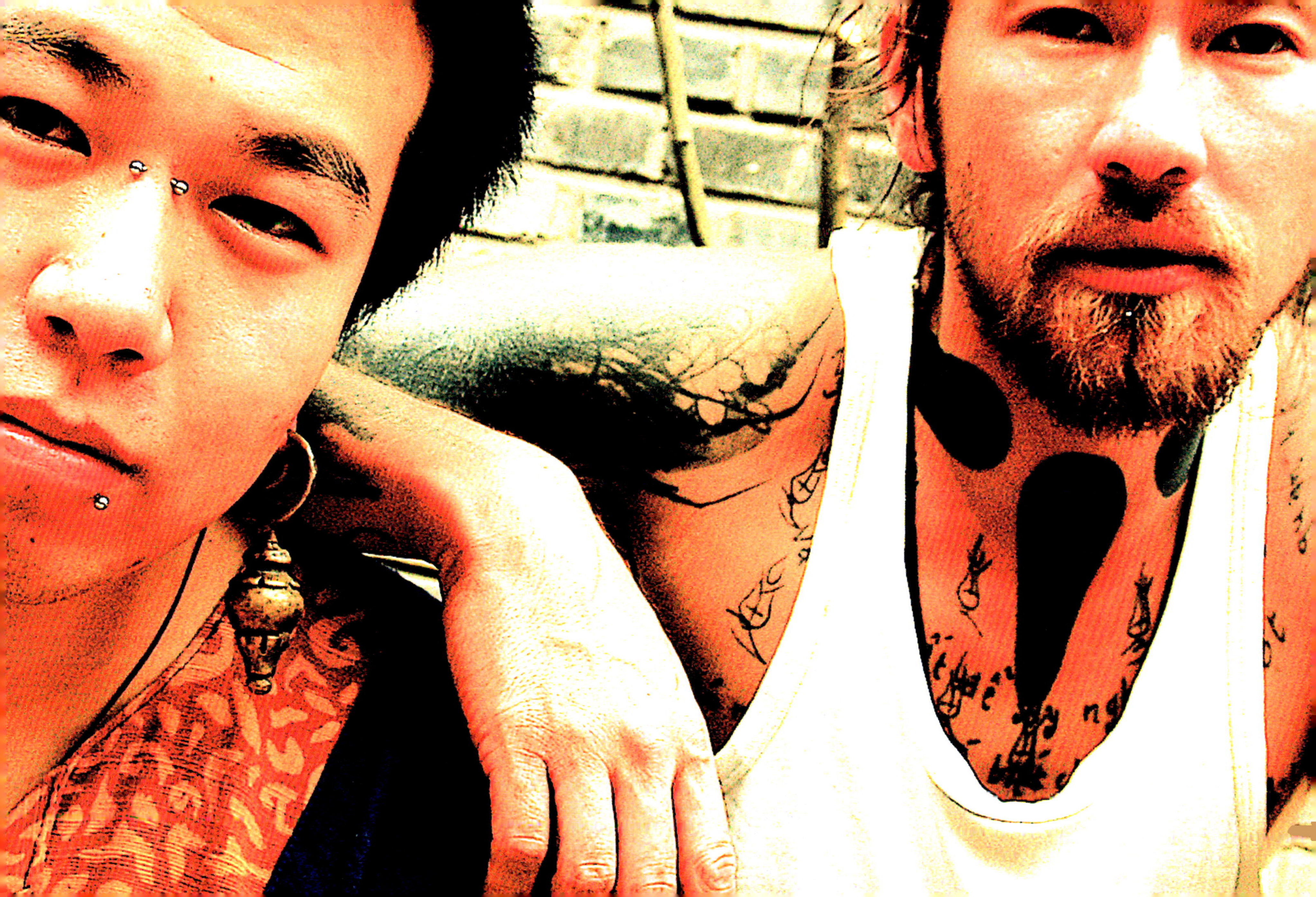

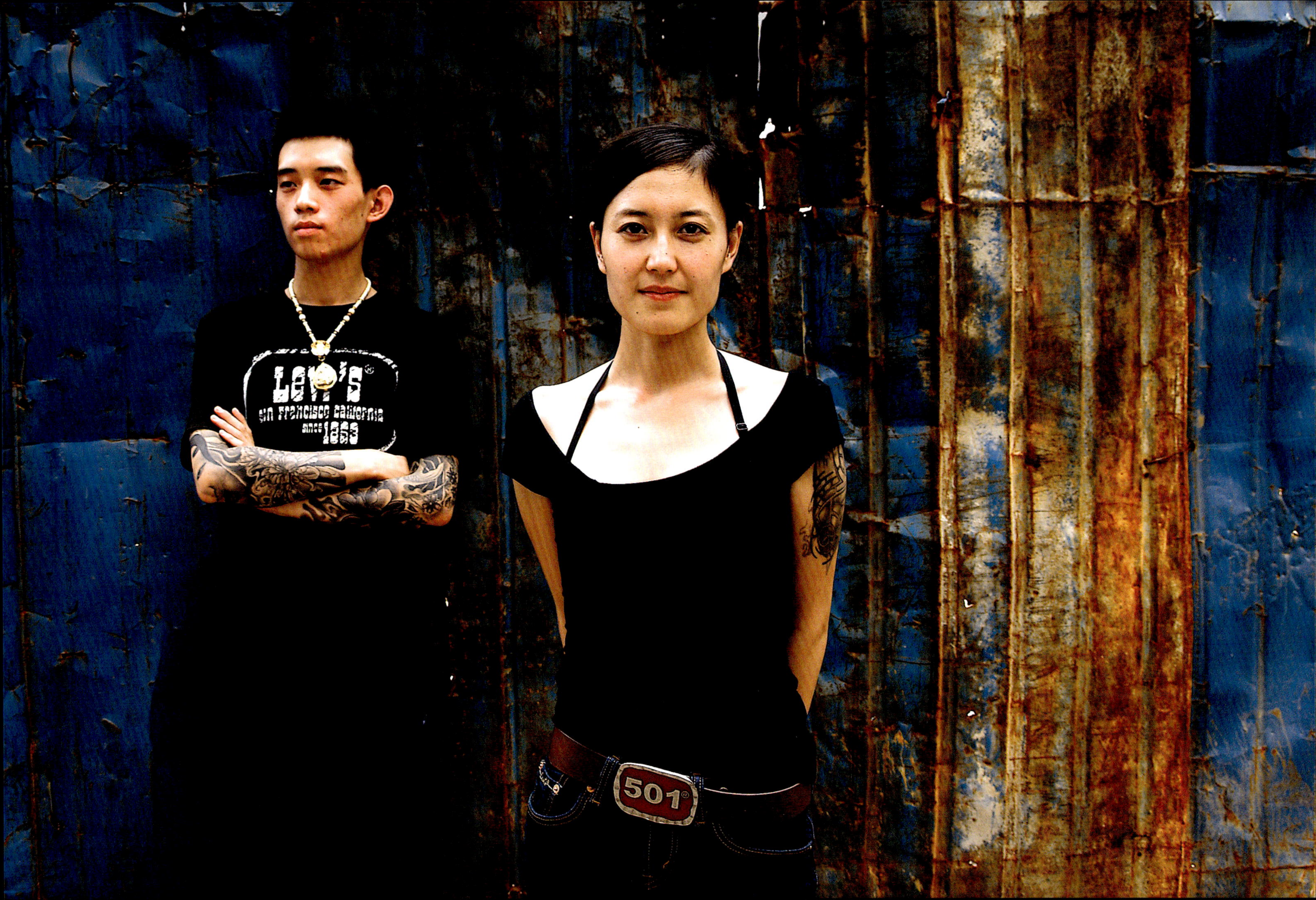
LEVI'S
San Francisco California
since 1853
501

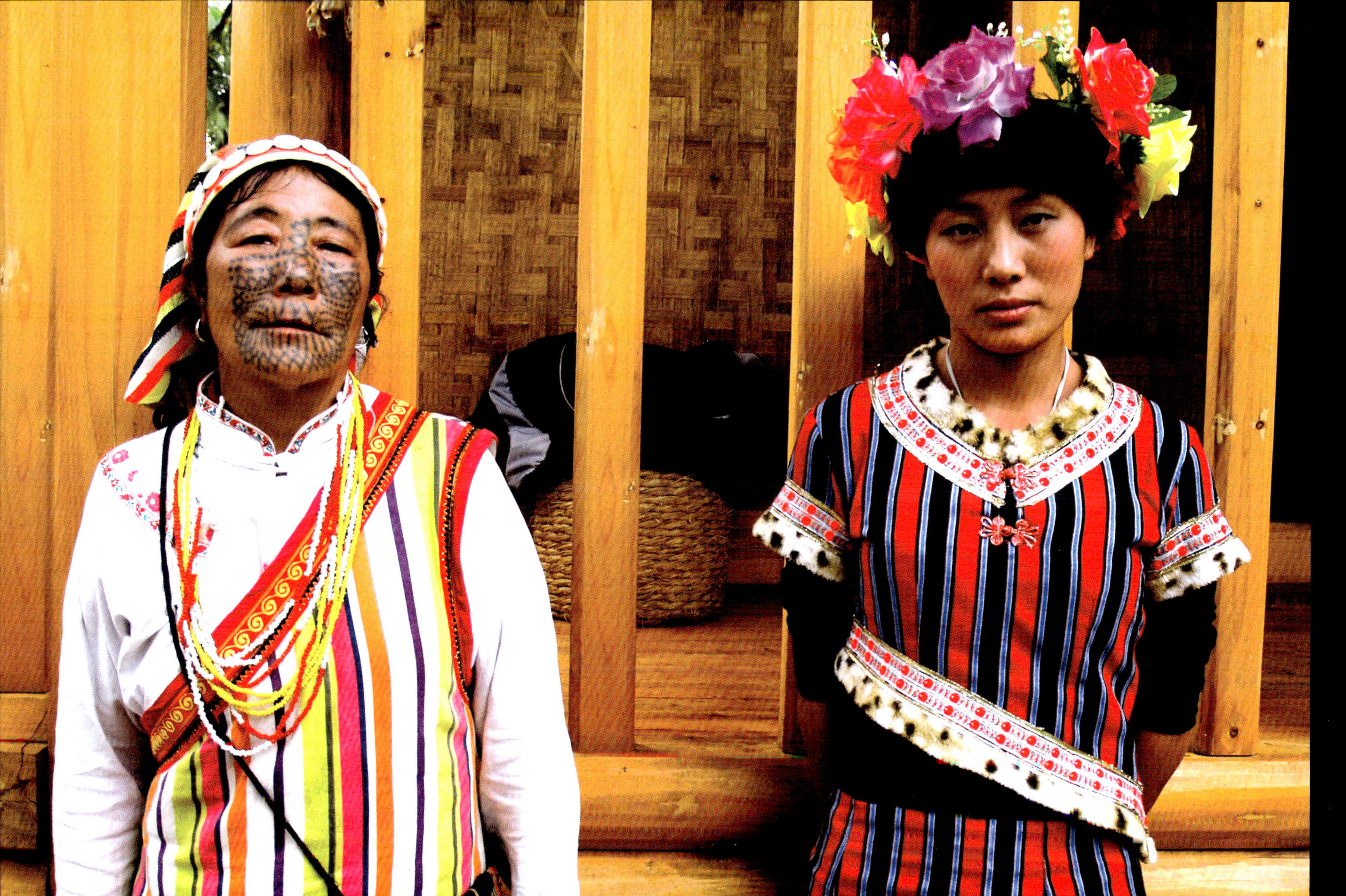

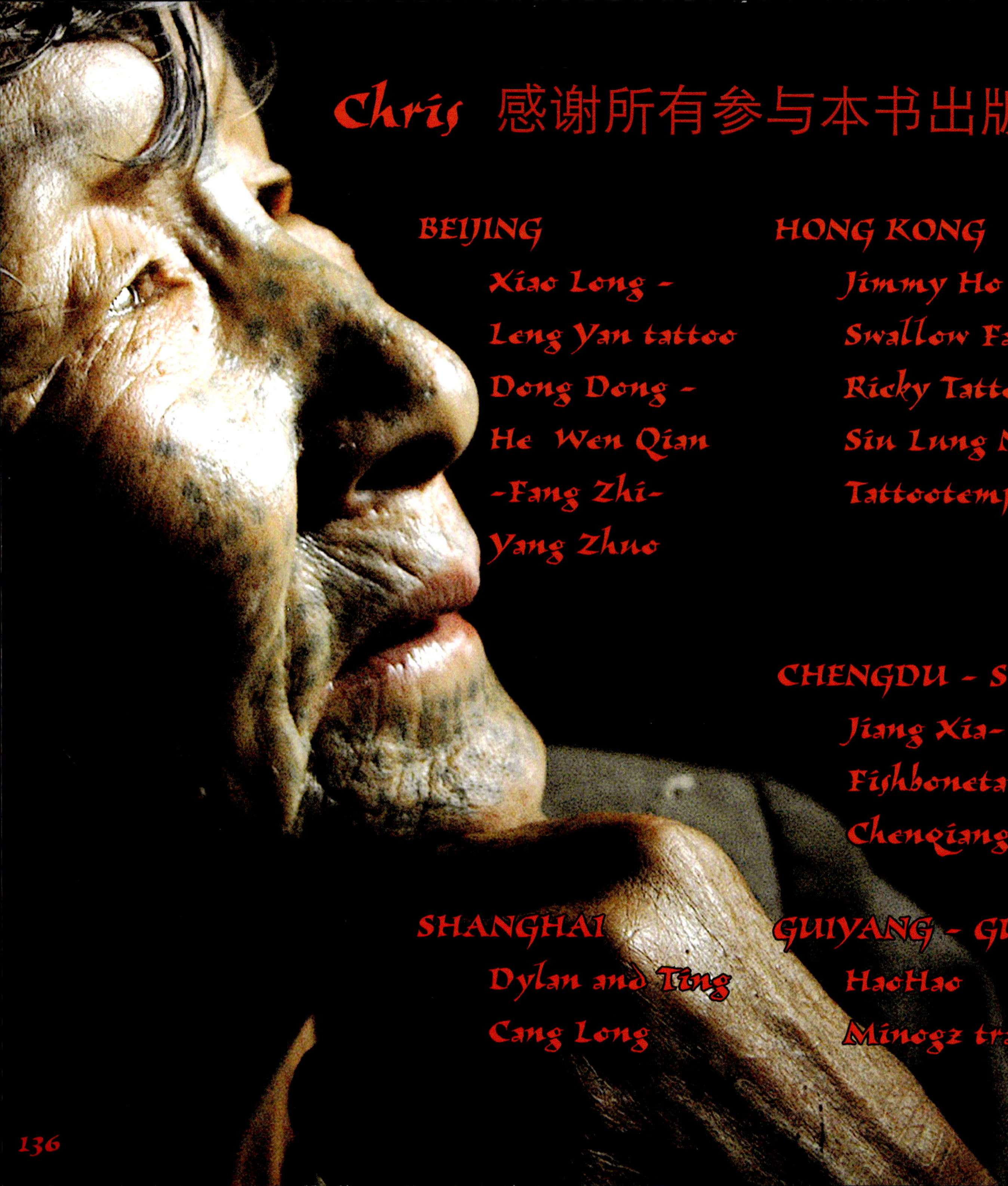

Chris 感谢所有参与本书出版的人

BEIJING

Xiao Long -
Leng Yan tattoo
Dong Dong -
He Wen Qian
-Fang Zhi-
Yang Zhuo

HONG KONG

Jimmy Ho
Swallow Family
Ricky Tattoo
Siu Lung Ng
Tattootemple

KUNMING - YUNAN

Stone Love tattoo
Dulong minority
Ma Hong Bo

QING DAO

Jin Ji
Zhu Hao Yu

CHENGDU - SICHUAN

Jiang Xia-
Fishbonetattoo
Chenqiang -

TIAN JIN

Xiao Jien
Lao Ke
Dong Hua

SHANGHAI

Dylan and Ting
Cang Long

GUIYANG - GUIZHO

HaoHao
Minogz travel

JINAN

Mr and Mrs Fu

Special thanks to everyone who made this book possible

GRAPHIC DESIGN

Paul Riley

UNITED KINGDOM

Nottingham Trent University

School of Art & Design

Richard Woodfield

Bob Easom

ADDITIONAL PHOTOGRAPHY

Mark Ning

Ma Hong Bo

ORIGINAL CONCEPT

Joey Pang and Chris Wroblewski.

TRAVEL INTERPRETATION

Leon Lam -Hien

PRE-PRODUCTION (CHINA)

Miss Xue

Dipper Studio Beijing

TRANSLATION

Ni Na

THIS BOOK WAS CREATED USING OLYMPUS E500 CAMERAS.

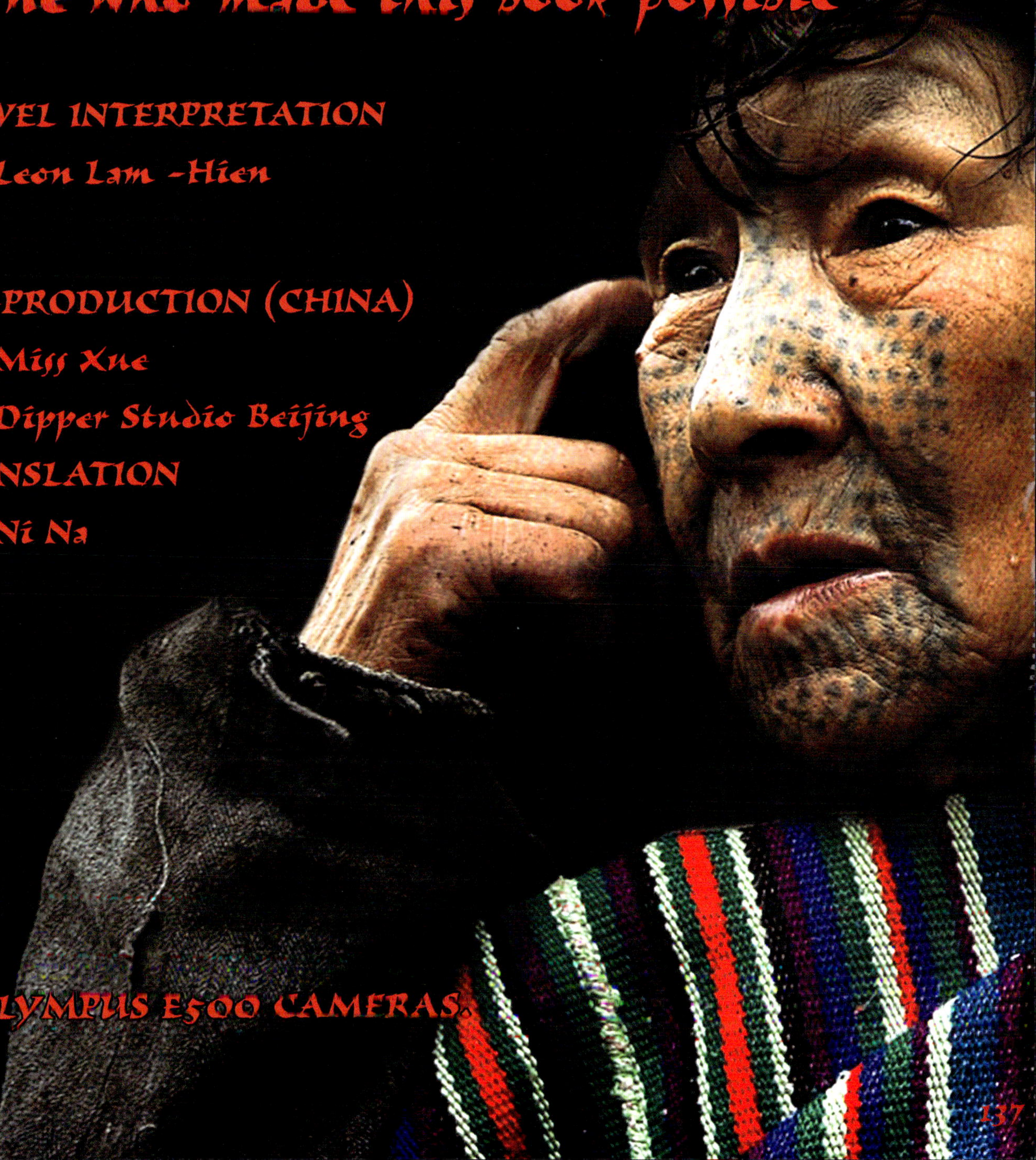

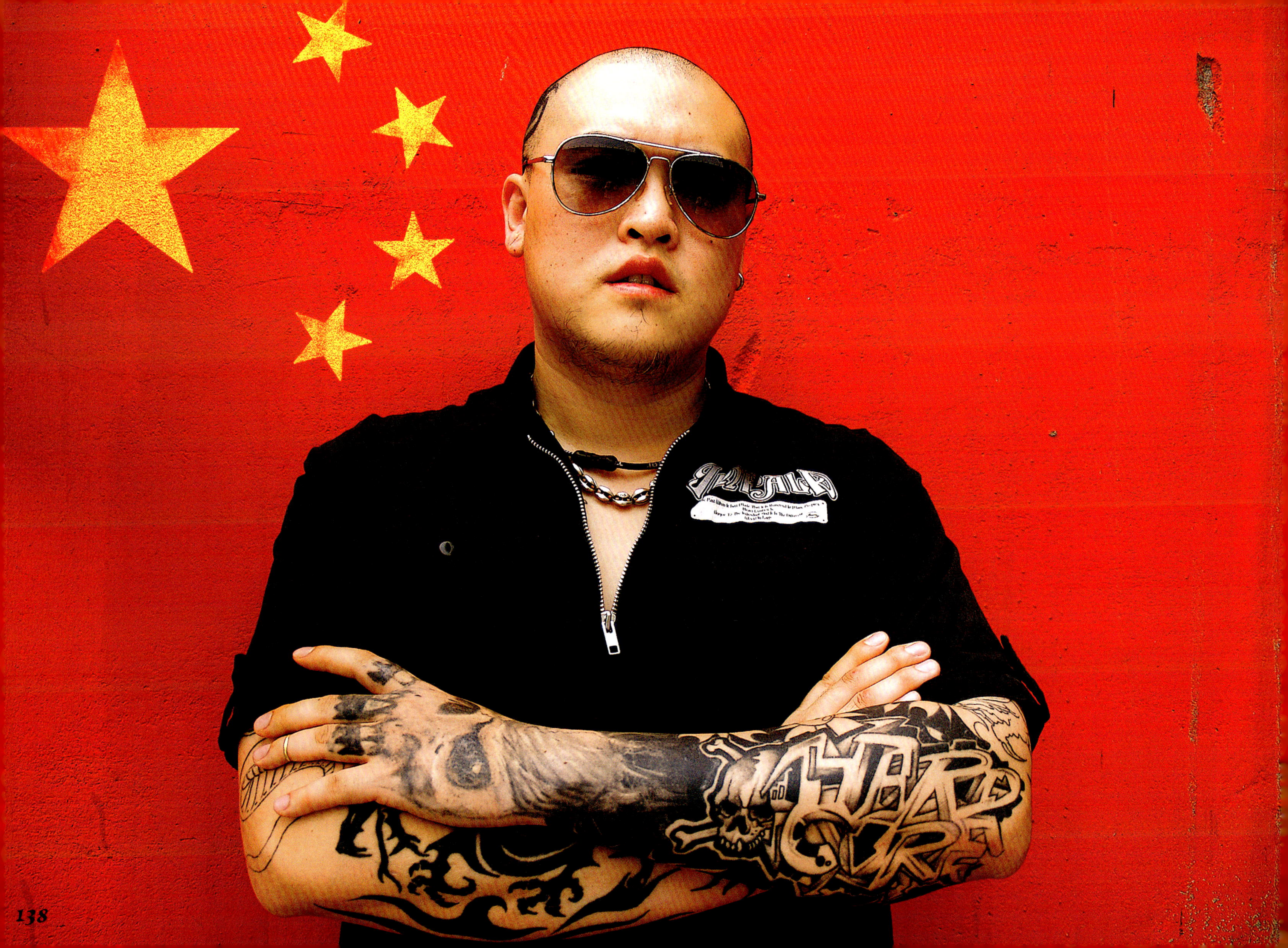

Chris Wroblewski:

世界上最著名的纹身花刺艺术摄影师，出生于英格兰并在英格兰受教育．年毕业于诺丁汉一所享有盛誉的艺术学院(特伦特工艺学校1974 - 1977).自那以后，他一共出版了20本书籍，其中包括最畅销的作品《SKIN SHOWS - THE TATTOO BIBLE》．除了他的国际出版物和国际展览之外，Chris也拍摄文献影片．他在法国拥有一家纹身花刺博物馆和画廊，并在香港中心的纹身花刺殿堂现任画廊理事。

Chris Wroblewski was born and educated in England.
He became interested in photography during travels to India in 1974.
Three years later he graduated, from Trent Polytechnic, and Derby college of art and design where he studied creative photography.
In 1981 he published his first book; Skin Show-The art of tattoo.
Since then he has produced several original portfolios on body art and photography.
His new book and short film 'Tooth Mechanics' is a documentary about Indian street dentists.

Titles by Chris Wroblewski

Skin Shows – The art of tattoo –1981
City Indians –1983
Tattoo art on women –1985
Skin Fantasies –1986
Die Sinnlichkeit der steine (The Sensuality of Stones)–1986
Pigments of Imagination –1987
Modern Primitives –1988
Skin Shows – the art of tattoo –1989
Skin Shows 2 –1990
Tattooed Women –1991
Skin Shows 3 –1993
Tattooed Women 2 –1994
A Head of His Time –1994
Skin Shows 4 –1995
Classic Skin Shows –1995
Skin Shows 5 –1996
Skin Shows 6 –1997
Cosmic Zoo – Portraits of Brasil -2000
Smudgers- Street photographers- Olympus Optical.co.uk -2003
Skin Shows- The Tattoo Bible, Collins and Brown -2004

CREDITS TO PHOTOS

Front cover- inspired by 2000 year old Chinese Bronze vase-tattoo by Xiao Long- worn by Chen Tian Jiao.Beijing

Page 2- Dulong woman-Kunming -Photographs by Ma Hong Bo.
Illustrations on English text pages by Dong Dong-Mummy Tattoo-Beijing
Illustrations on Chinese text pages- John White (1577-90)-Courtesy of British Museum, London
Page 20- Leng Yan tattoo studio, 798 Arts complex, Beijing
Page 21- Young tattoo fan, Sunshine gallery,Beijing
Page 22- Liu Ming,Beijing
Page 23- Hu Yang, Beijing
Page 24- Sunshine gallery tattoo exhibition, Beijing
Page 25- Laye-Sunshine gallery tattoo exhibition, Beijing
Page 26- Jeremy Johnston-Tattoo by Yang Zhuo-Beijing
Page 27- Yang Zhuo-Tattoo by Xiao Long-Beijing
Page 28- Binghe- Beijing
Page 29- Tattoo by Xiao Long-Beijing
Page 30- Left-Beijing tattoo show, Right-Lang Fang tattoo show
Page 31- Left-Beijing tattoo show, Right- Wen Jun Tattoo
Page 32-33- Beijing tattoo show
Page 34- Left-Jinan-, Right-Shanghai-tattoos by Cang long
Page 35- Left-Beijing tattoo show, Right-Lang Fang tattoo show
Page 36- Left-Chen Yang, Right-Tian Tian-Beijing tattoo show
Page 37- Left tattoo by Xiao Long, Right Kunming
Page 38- Sanlitum-Beijing
Page 39- Left-Stone Love-Kunming, Right-Beijing
Page 40- Tian Jin tattoo party
Page 41- Left-Tian Jin tattoo party, Right- Beijing tattoo show, tattoo by Qian He Zong
Page 42-43-Xiao Long studio Beijing
Page 44- Lang Fang tattoo show-Dong Dong
Page 45-Lang Fang tattoo show-Sun Wen Bo
Page 46-47-Leon Lam-Hien, Tian Jin Tattoo party-Chest tattoo on Xiao Jian
Page 48- Zhang Bo-Tian Jin tattoo party
Page 49-Xiao Long tattoo studio, Beijing
Page 50-Left-Lang Fang tattoo show, Right-Tian Jin tattoo party
Page 51-Left-Tian Jin tattoo party, Right-Zhang Qi-Beijing
Page 52-Left-La Fang tattoo show, Right-Tian Jin tattoo party
Page 53-Left-1XT studio,Beijing, Right-Tian Jin tattoo party
Page 54-Kowloon,Hong Kong studio-Jimmy Ho
Page 55-59-Tattoo flash by Swallow-Hong Kong-c 1960's
Page 60-James Ho business card and tattoo machines-c 1950's
Page 61-1st tattoo studio in Hong Kong, and tattoo machines
Page 62-63- Swallow tattoo studio- Hong Kong-1989
Page 64-67-Tattoo flash by Swallow-Hong Kong
Page 68- Gabe, with David Beckham and Ursula-Ace and Dragon tattoo studio, Hong Kong
Page 69- Tattootemple studio. Joey Pang tattooing Eric, Hong Kong
Page 70-Left-Cang Long-Shanghai, Right-Ji Nan-tattoo by Fu Hai Lin
Page 71-Left-Shanghai studio, Right- Ji Nan-Mr and Mrs Fu Hai Lin
Page 72-Left-Tian Jin studio, Right- studio-Chengdu
Page 73-Left-Kunming studio, Right- Beijing studio
Page 74-5-Kunming studio
Page 76-Qing Dao-studios
Page 77-Left-Studio-Gui Yang, Right -studio-Qing Dao
Page 78-81-Street tattooists- Gui Yang
Page 82-Qing Dao
Page 83- Studios-Gui Yang

Page 84-Tian Jin. Right-Beijing.
Page 85- Left Beijing, Right-Tian Jin tattoo party
Page 86-87- Lang Fang tattoo show
Page 88- Left-Lang Fang tattoo show
Page 89- Left-Tian Jin tattoo party, Right-Lang Fang tattoo show
Page 90- Left-Lang Fang tattoo show, Right-Tian Jin tattoo party
Page 91- Liang Liang-Tattoo by Lao He-Beijing, Right-Lang Fang tattoo show
Page 92- Left- Yan Wei, Right-Yang Wei-Beijing
Page 93- Left –Lin Lin-Music festival Beijing, Right-Beijing tattoo show
Page 94- Beijing tattoo show
Page 95- Tian Jin tattoo party
Page 96- Chen Tian Jiao-tattoo by Xiao Long
Page 97- Top-Lin Lin-Bottom –XLT studio Beijing,
XLT studio-Beijing
Page 98-99- Dong Dong-Mummy tattoo, Chen Cheng-Beijing
Page 100-101- Studio and artwork by Leng Yan-Beijing
Page 102-7- Tattoo by Leng Yan-Beijing
Page 108 -9- Shufa by Cheng Zhi Cheng-Beijing
Page 110- Ling Dian Wa Wa -Lang Fang tattoo show
Page 111- Wen Hua Ren-Lang Fang tattoo show
Page 112- Tattoo by Chen Xin Long
Page 113- Tattoo by Dong Dong-Beijing
Page 114- Qiang Zi-Lang Fang tattoo show
Page 115- Left-Lang Fang tattoo show, Right-Tattoo by Lao He-Beijing
Page 116-Tattoo by Yang Zhuo-Beijing
Page 117- September'-Beijing
Page 118- Mu Wa Wa –Lang Fang tattoo show
Page 119- Da Bian-Lang Fang tattoo show
Page 120- Left Beijing tattoo show -Right Shanghai Ting
Page 121- Left Cang Long studio Shanghai- Right -Beijing tattoo show
Page 122-3 -Stone love studio-Kunming
Page 124- Mrs Fu Hai Lin-Lang Fang tattoo show
Page 125- Left-Tian Jin tattoo party, Right-Xiao Long-Beijing
Page 126-7- Ting portrait, and at work in her studio Shanghai
Page 128- Kunming –tattoo by Xiao Long
Page 129- Tattoo by Dong Dong –Beijing
Page 130- Yu Li-Shanghai
Page 131- Jin Ji-Qing Dao
Page 132- Tattoo by Zhang Xin-Beijing
Page 133- Mark Ning and Leon Lam-Hien-Beijing
Page 134- Zhang Xin-Beijing
Page 135- Dulong women-Kunming
Page 136-7- Dulong women-Kunming
Page 138- Yan Wei-Beijing
Page 143- Da Fei,tattoo by Xiao Long,Beijing
Back cover- Shufa (calligraphy)-Wenshen(tattoo) by Cheng Zhi Cheng-Beijing

Selected Reading

The Len Family's Family Iron by Fabio Paleari: Trolley Books, London, 2003.

Stewed, Screwed and Tattooed by Madame Chinchilla: Triangle Tattoo and Museum Press, USA 2003.

The History of Hair by Robin Bryden: Phillip Wilson publishers, 2000.

The Illustrated Man by Ray Bradbury: Doubleday books, 1951.

Escape Velocity – Cyberculture at the end of the century by Mark Drey: Hodder and Staughton, 1997.

The Electronic Disturbance by The Crtical Arts Ensemble: Autononmedia, 1994.

Wrapping in Images – Tattooing in Polynesia by Alfred Gell: Clarenden Press, 1996.

The Body in Parts, Fantasies of corporeality in early modern Europe, edited by David Hilman and Carlo Mazzio: Routledge books, 1997.

Dancing on the Grave – encounters with death by Nigel Barley: Abacus books, 1997.

L'argot et le tatouage des criminals by Jean Craven: Switzerland, 1962.

Marks of Civilsation; Artistic transformations of the human body, edited by Arnold Rubin: Los Angeles Museum of cultural history, 1988.

Future Primitive and other essays by John Zerzan: Autonomedia, 1994.

The Hidden worlds of Polynesia by Robert C. Suggs: Cresset press, 1962.

Pierced hearts and true love by Hans Ebenson: Derek Verschoyle Ltd, 1953.

Die Marquesaner und ihr Kunst by Carl Von Steinen: Berlin, 1925.

The History of Tattooing and its Significance by W.D.Hambly: London 1925.

Guns, Germs and Steel by Jared Diamond: Jonathan Cape, 1997.

The Voyage of the Challenger by Eric Linklater: John Murray books, 1972.

Body marking in South East Asia by Henry Field: Peabody museum, 1958.

Tattooing amongst civilised people by Robert Fletcher: Anthropological society of Washington, USA, 1882.

Polynesian researches, 4 vols, 2nd rev. edition, London: Fisher, Son and Jackson, 1831.

Moko or Maori tattooing by Major H.G.Robley: London, 1896.

Irezumi; The pattern of dermatography in Japan by W.R.Van Gulik: Leide –E.J.Brill, 1982.

Sex and repression in savage society by B.Malinowski: Kegan Paul books, 1927.

Tatowieren, Narbenzeichen und koperbemalen by W.Joest: Berlin, 1887.

Skin Deep; The mysteries of tattooing by R.Scutt and C.Gotch: London 1974.

Pierced hearts and true love –A century of drawings for tattoos –the drawing center: Hardy Marks, 1995.

Pushing Ink by Spider Webb: USA, 1976.

The Language of Ornament by James Trilling: Thames and Hudson books, 2001.

Written on the Body –edited by Jane Caplan: Reaktion books, 2000 (info reaktionbooks.co.uk).

Stoney Knows How –Life as a Tattoo Artist –Leonard St Clair and Alan B Govenar: The University Press of Kentucky, 1981.

The Tattoo Baron –A novella of Tragedy and Comedy, by Carol Nightingale: USA, 1979.

Forever The Land Of Men –An account of a visit to the Marquesan Islan by W.C.Handy: Dodd and Mead and Co, 1965.

Fragments for a History of the Human Body –Volumes 1, 2, 3, edited by Michel Feher with Ramona Nadoaff and Nadia Tazi: Zone, 1989.

Tattoo in early China by Carrie E.Reed, Journal of the American Oriental Society, 2000.

The Tattoo Club of Great Britain can be contacted for certain rare and limited editions at: http://www.tattoo.co.uk.

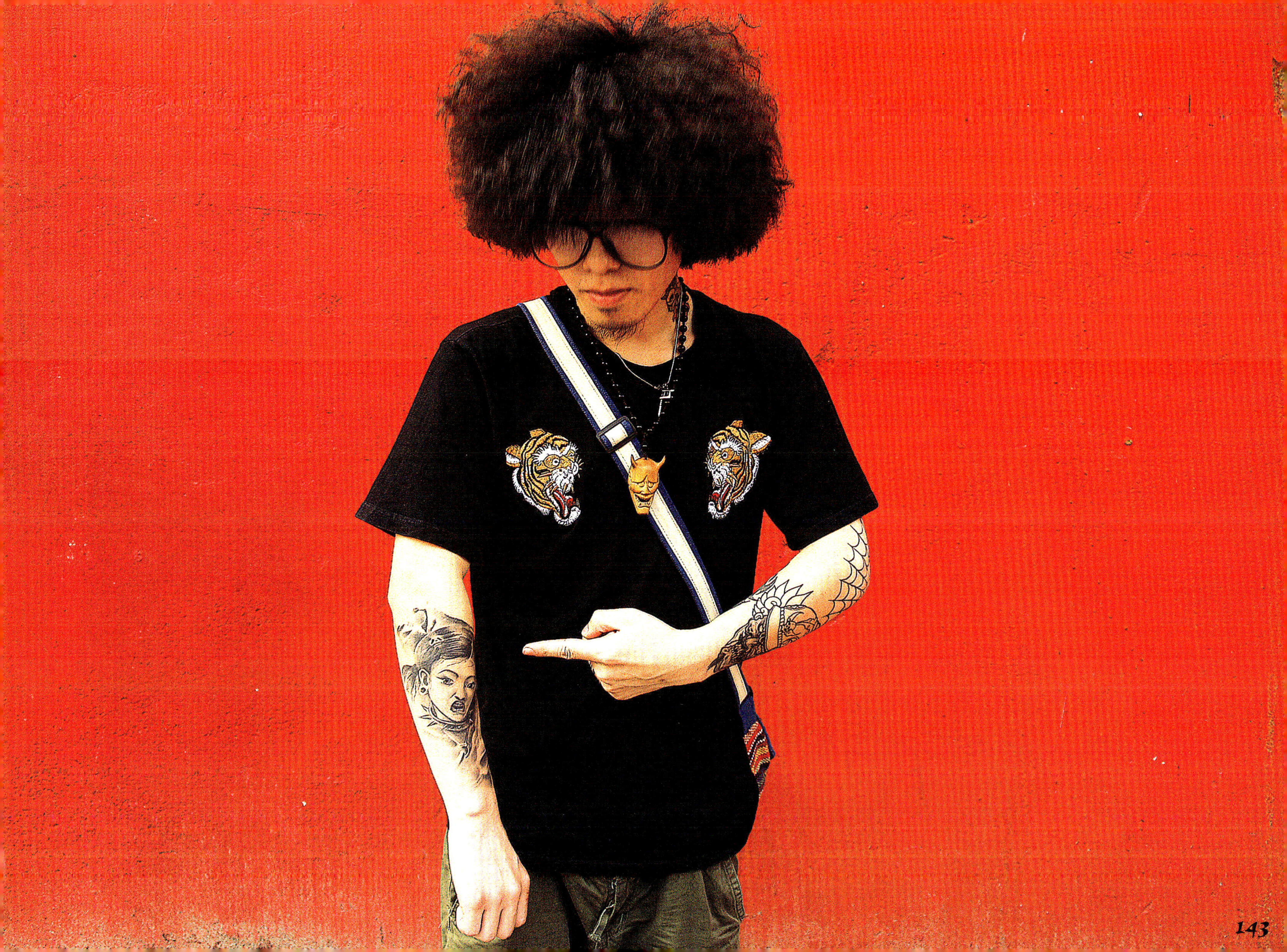

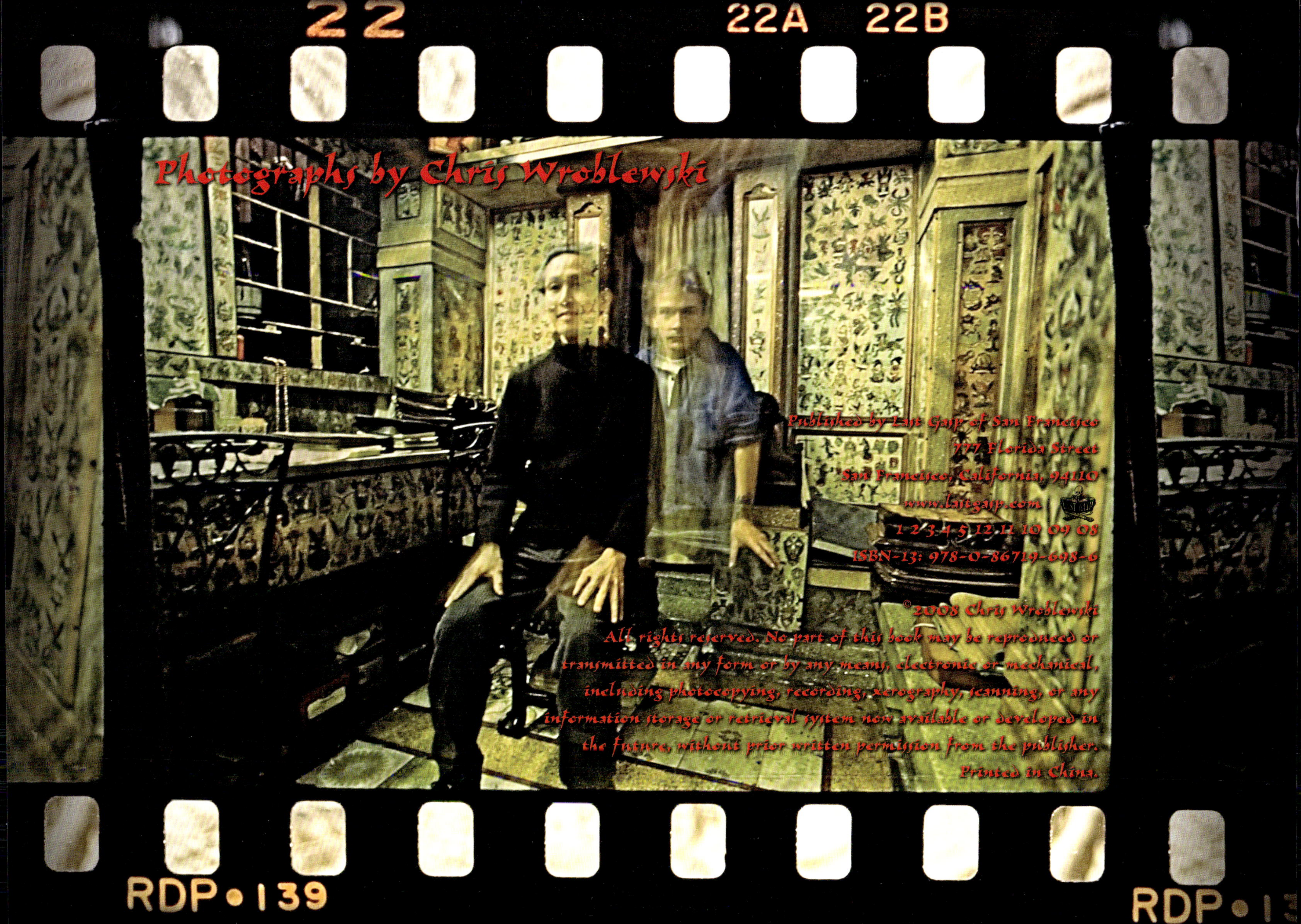

Photographs by Chris Wroblewski

Published by Last Gasp of San Francisco
777 Florida Street
San Francisco, California, 94110
www.lastgasp.com
1 2 3 4 5 12 11 10 09 08
ISBN-13: 978-0-86719-698-6

Preface

Tattooing has only recently emerged as an art form in China. Previously it was always regarded as a demeaning activity or taboo to a self-respecting citizen. Although it was widely practiced by many tribal groups in the central kingdoms of China it was never regarded as a mark of civilized behavior. In fact the colorful and sometimes extreme examples of many tribal customs were officially ridiculed and used to epitomize how 'barbaric' people behaved.

The moral teachings of Confucius (551 BCE – 479 BCE) stressed the idea that the body was sacred, a gift from one's parents, and not to be transfigured in any way: "filial piety is the root of all virtue, and the stem out of which grows all moral teaching. Our bodies - to every hair and bit of skin are received by us from our parents, and we must not presume to injure or wound them". The tattoo was even less welcome in the years of the Cultural Revolution. Throughout Chinese history the tattoo was often used as a form of punishment that could result in either ostracism or permanent exile.

Nevertheless, in spite of official condemnation, there have been many recorded instances of citizens ignoring such taboos and enthusiastically embracing the tattooist's use of the needle. The tattooing of women's eyebrows and beauty spots has been practiced for centuries, and many people chose to have poems and legendary designs etched onto their bodies. In the Tang period Duan Chengshi (c.800-863), wrote in his Youyang zazu that quite a few citizens from varying ranks of society eagerly pursued tattooing. He mentioned several instances of tattooing, in particular that of a street patrolman who had his body covered with poems and finely executed pictures. His texts further reveal dramatic accounts of tattoos being applied to high-ranking women as well as concubines and slaves. Another popular account of tattooing that captured the public's attention was the story of how the famous Song general, Yue Fei, (1103-41) was given tattoos by his mother. Using an embroidery needle and rubbing the ink into his fresh wounds, she inscribed on his back the words 'Serve the nation with absolute loyalty'.

Centuries later the popular novel, Shuihi zhuan (Water Margin) vividly portrayed the tattoos on five of its heroes. One of these heroes, Shi Jin, was known as the nine-patterned dragon. His arms, shoulders and upper torso were immaculately decorated with dragons that his father had commissioned from a skilled tattooist. The other four characters were less dramatically decorated but it seems that their tattoos as well as their daring adventures gained the public's admiration. It is doubtful whether this novel greatly influenced tattooing in China. Officials went so far as to have all copies of the book destroyed on penalty of punishment. However, when the text was translated into Japanese as Suikodon in the 18th century it certainly had a great impact and influence on tattooing in Japan. For the next 300 years in China tattooing continued as an underground activity, irrevocably associated with the exploits of outlaws, soldiers or sub-cultures existing outside the moral fabric of society.

Now that China is beginning to interact more openly with the West and allow its people to engage freely in the frivolities of fashion, music and art, tattooing has once again made its presence felt. This time it is no longer linked with stigma or opprobrium. Many Chinese artists have now become enthusiastically involved in the practice of permanent body art. Although this discipline is still in its infancy, Chinese tattooists have certainly inspired a huge following in their own country as well as impressing the rest of the world with their amazing skills.

This book, which is the first publication ever to reveal the contemporary scene of Chinese tattooing, illustrates the growing enthusiasm and dedication towards one of the oldest and most inspirational art forms known to mankind. It sets an example for others to follow.

前言

纹身直到最近才作为一种艺术形式在中国出现。从前人们认为纹身是一种有损尊严的禁忌活动。尽管在中国的许多部落中纹身也广泛流行，但它从来不被当作是一种文明的行为。事实上许多部落中光怪陆离的习俗和有些比较极端的例子常遭到人们的耻笑，而且正好用来说明这些人有多么“野蛮”。

孔子（公元前551—479年）的道德教条强调身体的圣洁，他说：“夫孝，德之本也，教之所由生也。身体发肤，受之父母，不敢毁伤，孝至始也。”因为身体是父母所赐，所以绝不能以任何方式污损。在文化大革命期间，纹身更是受到了前所未有的批判。纵观中国历史，纹身通常被用作一种惩罚的形式，而被惩罚的人可能会受流放之刑。

不过，虽然官方对此持反对态度，但还是有许多史实记录下许多人置禁忌于不顾，反而对纹身师的针法痴迷不已。许多世纪以来，妇女热衷于纹眉和点美人痣，还有很多人选择将诗歌或传奇故事纹在身上。唐朝的段成式（公元800—863年）在他的《酉阳杂俎》中描述了当时社会中各个阶层的市民争先恐后纹身的场景。他提到了一些例子，其中一个是说在一个巡街的人身上刻满了诗歌，并且还配有精致的图画。他在书中进一步说明了当时纹身的对象不但有贵妇、姬妾同时也有奴隶。另外一个特别引人关注的例子是宋代岳飞元帅（1103-41）岳母刺字的故事。岳母用绣花针将墨渗入皮肤，在他背上刻下了“精忠报国”几个大字。

几个世纪之后，在通俗小说《水浒传》中，生动地描绘了五位绘有纹身的英雄。其中之一是“九纹龙”史进。他的父亲请纹身高手在他的胳膊、肩膀和后背纹上了九条龙。其他的四位人物身上没有这样漂亮的装饰，但是他们的纹身和勇敢的举动同样受到人们的崇敬。我们不清楚这部小说是否曾对中国的纹身产生重要的影响。官府采取惩罚措施，将这本书所有的刻本都销毁了。不过当18世纪这本书被翻译成日文并介绍到日本后，它无疑对日本的纹身起了很大的作用。在那之后的300年中，纹身在中国继续其地下活动的命运，一成不变的与囚徒、士兵为伍，只存在于社会道德网络以外的亚文化中间。

今天中国开始更多地与西方接触，这使得中国人能自由地欣赏花样翻新的时尚、音乐和艺术，人们再一次感受到了纹身的魅力。而如今人们不再把纹身和刺字、耻辱联系在一起了。许多中国艺术家也开始积极地探讨永久人体艺术的实践。尽管这门艺术在中国仍然方兴未艾，但是中国的艺术家们不但在自己的国家中造就了一大批热衷于此的追随者，而且用他们的精湛技术让世界赞叹不已。

这本书是有史以来第一本展现当代中国纹身艺术的出版物，它刻画了今天人们对世界上最古老、最富灵感的艺术形式不断增长的热情和奉献精神。它也为后来者树立一个可供效仿的榜样。

INTRODUCTION - *"WRITING ON BODIES"* - A SLIPSTREAM ANTHROPOLOGY OF TATTOOING

"MY INTENTION IS TO TELL OF BODIES, CHANGED TO DIFFERENT FORMS". Ovid –Metamorphoses.

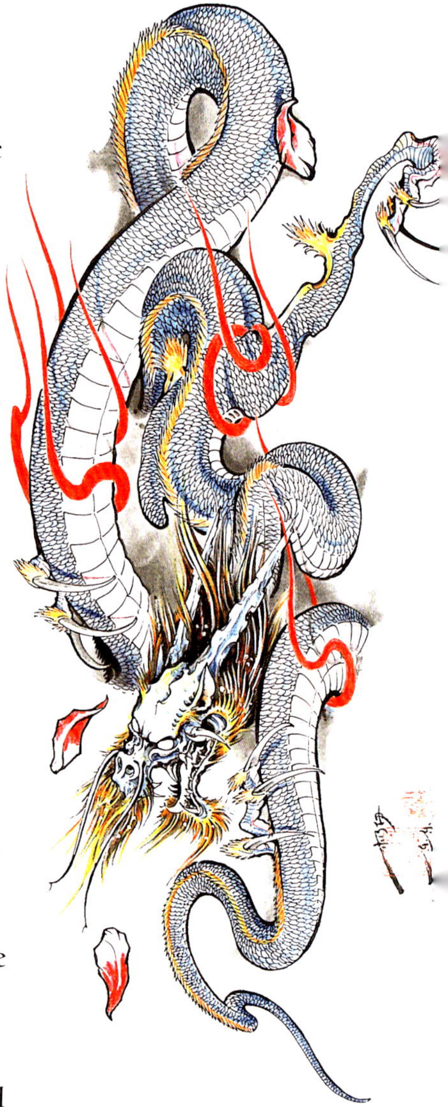

Tattooing by puncture probably found its origin in the deliberate intention of an unknown genius who saw in it a way of making magical-religious colourings more permanent, since man's early attempts at puncturing the body were undoubtably crude and bewildering rituals, designed to appease a multitude of spirit entities and demons of pain.
In the beginning, priests had nothing to do with tattooing. They involved themselves when they realised what advantages could be drawn from the imposition of a religious ceremony into the rituals, monopolising the practice in order to suppress any competition. The high payment for the art was then connected with an "offering", with the obvious implication that poorer members of the tribe were ignored or simply used for practice by novices.
The priests knew very well how to appease the powerful in this world to their own advantage, and dispensed their services to chieftains and the ruling classes, who obtained a receipt for their 'deliverance", in clear and beautiful writings on their bodies.
Practically every tribe in recorded history is thought to have engaged in some form of contractual 'wounding' ceremony, whether on himself or on sacrificial others. The release and manipulation of blood became a fertilizing and binding ingredient that sealed a pact between man and his creator.

It is possible to imagine the use of blood as the first form of human currency, which was traded as a down payment to alleviate suffering in this world and also to assure safe passage to join the ancestral spirits in the afterlife. However, before the body could be transformed and the person subjugated with these divine inscriptions, the soul first had to be cleansed, or wiped clean, then subjected to a set of imperatives, allowing for the transmission of the supernatural to become codified and embedded in the profane flesh, which then became a sacred body.
Another important function of tattoo ceremonies would be the re-construction of a person, and the creation of a principle of citizenship. It was a practical way of distinguishing the slaves and prisoners, by prominently branding them on their foreheads. Other citizens would have been spared this ordeal or marked with less drastic insignia, as befitting their rank and superiority. In many ancient civilisations, tattooing was used as a convenient technology of hierarchical inscription.
Futhermore, the language and dramaturgical scenes of these 'holy transactions' eventually began to evolve into more dramatic and sinister ceremonies; trepanation, castration and genital mutilation were just a few associate vectors along which the body was often forced to engage so as to be dramatically reinvented.
It is reasonable to imagine that primordial rituals of body wounding - by scarification and tattooing - had originally started out as simple totemic and therapeutic rites with decoration being an afterthought. Body marking rituals then became invested with divine mystery and what had once been totemic was now taboo; the tattoo technician became a member of a hierarchic cult rather than an itinerant craftsman.
We know that preliterate tribal societies had not only devised elaborate and complex body marking rituals, but had also established extremely bizarre burial techniques, together with a host of superstitious legends and mythologies, which accompanied them throughout the world, thousands of years ago during the great leap forward.
The migration of peoples from the Asian mainland into Oceania certainly introduced a profound cultural memory into the scattered islands of the Pacific Ocean. These new colonising migrants were left undisturbed for thousands of years, resulting in a

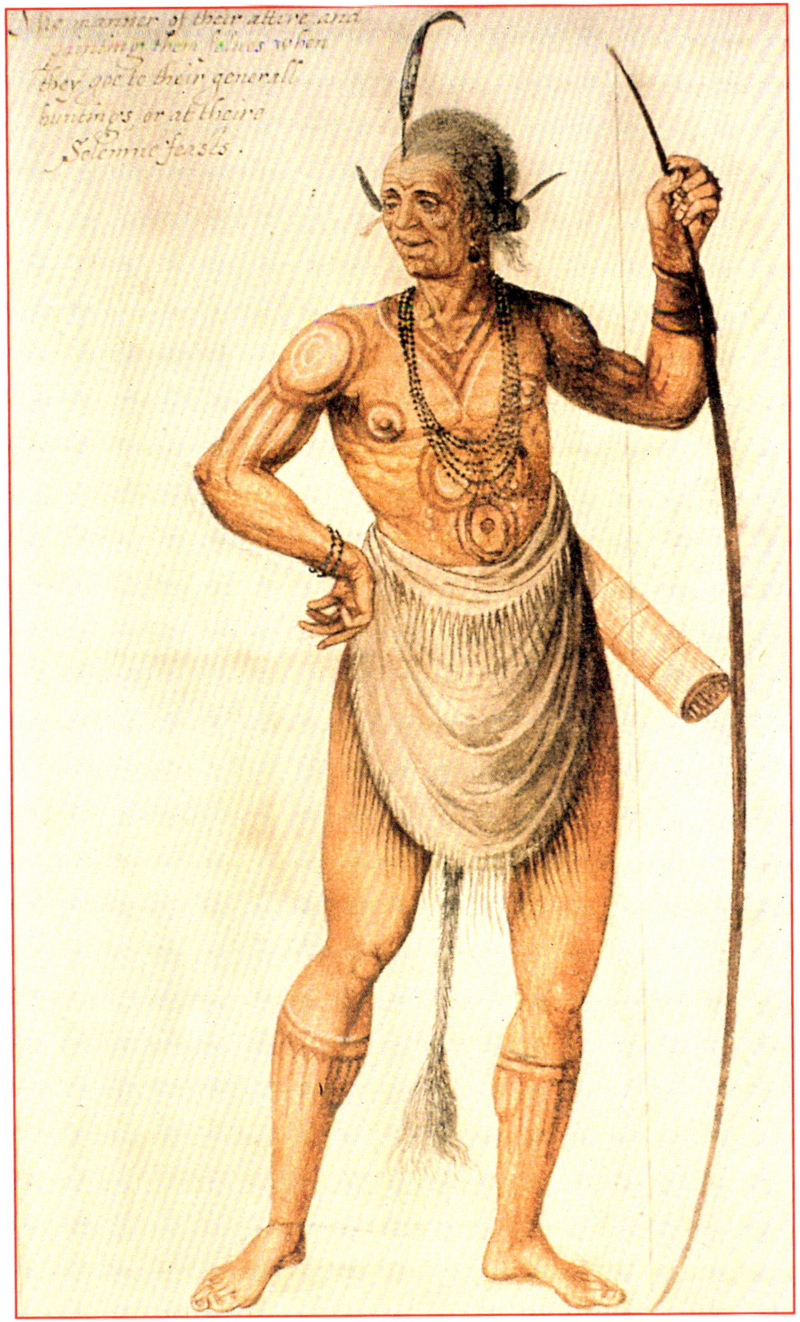

引言

“在身体上书写”

纹身的人类学演绎

“我的意图是讲述身体变成不同的形式”——奥维德《变形记》

针刺纹身也许起源于某个无名天才的精心意图，即用这种方式让魔法和宗教的色彩能留存得更为长久。在人类早期，对身体针刺无疑是一种为取悦众多精神实体以及痛苦之魔而设计的粗暴且怪异的仪式。

最初，司祭们与纹身并无关系。不过当他们发现可以利用这种仪式来安排宗教典礼并谋求好处时，他们就参与进来了。而且他们还垄断了这项业务以打压竞争对手。

这种艺术的高回报于是便和“供奉”联系到了一起，很明显，这背后的含义是部族中贫穷的成员无足轻重，且常常成为新人练手的工具。

司祭们很懂得如何取悦这世上的强者来为自己谋求好处。他们向酋长和统治阶层提供这项服务，而这些权贵则通过在身体上留下清晰漂亮的花纹来为司祭们带来收入。

人们认为，自有历史记录以来，实际上几乎每一部族都存在某种合约式“创伤”仪式，这仪式的对象既可以是部落成员也可以是用作牺牲的其它东西。放血成为一个人和他的创造者之间订立盟约的促进及结合因素。

我们不妨将如此使用的血液想象成人类货币的最初形态。它被当成一次性付款来交易以减轻人们今生的痛苦，并且可确保死后有一条安全通道能与先祖的灵魂结合。

虽然身体可变形，人也屈从于这种神圣的刻印，然而在此之前，人首先需要将灵魂洗涤或将其擦拭干净，然后再遵从一套必要的规则，使得超自然力得以传递，成为法典，最后嵌入世俗的身体里，这时身体才能成为圣洁的肉体。

纹身仪式的另一个重要功能是人的重塑，以及公民身份原则的创立。在额头上烙印是区分奴隶和囚徒的实用方法。其它成员则可免去这一痛苦，而用其它较轻的标志与他们各自的等级和地位相对应。在许多古代文明中，纹身是显示等级印记的便捷手段。

另外，这些“神圣交易”中使用的语言和戏剧般的场景最终演化成更为戏剧性和狰狞的仪式。额窦环钻、阉割和切掉生殖器只是几个把戏，身体常常被迫接受这种刑罚，以促使其戏剧性地重生。我们可以想象，原始的身体创伤仪式（牺牲和纹身）开始只是一种简单的图腾和治疗性仪式，其装饰功能是后来才有的想法。

身体标志仪式慢慢地被神话占据。之前的图腾功能现在被禁忌取代，而纹身画师不再是居无定所的匠人，而成为等级信徒的成员。

我们知道在有文字历史之前的氏族社会不仅设计了详密而复杂的身体标志仪式，千百年来，在文明的跃进中，他们还建立了极为奇异的丧葬习俗。这些与大量的迷信神话传说一起，伴随着他们贯穿整个世界的历史。

myriad of customs, languages and ceremonies being formulated in pristine isolation before being re-exported to neighbouring islands and continents. In the Americas, prehistoric settlers had also introduced shamanic beliefs and wounding ceremonies that became widespread amongst the Indian nations. Many tribes believed in the apotropaic function of cutting rituals, in which the spirit forces would enter and cleanse the body. These rituals varied from sublime to terrifying. Teeth marks of ancestral spirits would be imprinted during initiation rites for protection. Warriors would often cut their bodies before entering a sweat lodge to dispel evil spirits and some tribes designed elaborate suspension techniques, in which the chest was cut open and hooked up to ropes, then lifted into a divine embrace with powerful gods.
Sometimes these dramatic encounters resulted in bloody and gruesome spectacles of human sacrifice. The Spaniards who conquered the Aztec empire merely replaced one bloody regime and ritual with another. At first, the Conquisadors were astonished to witness the bloody public ceremonies in which human hearts were ripped out of living bodies and children slaughtered during times of harvesting. According to Aztec beliefs, life itself had to be killed, and before a person decomposed, his energy was taken out and re-harnessed.
The equally grotesque sight of crucifixtions was soon to become commonplace in Latin America during periods of colonialist genocide; this collision of worlds would result in the disintegration and collapse of entire societies and traditions. The age of exploration had just introduced one bunch of savages to another.

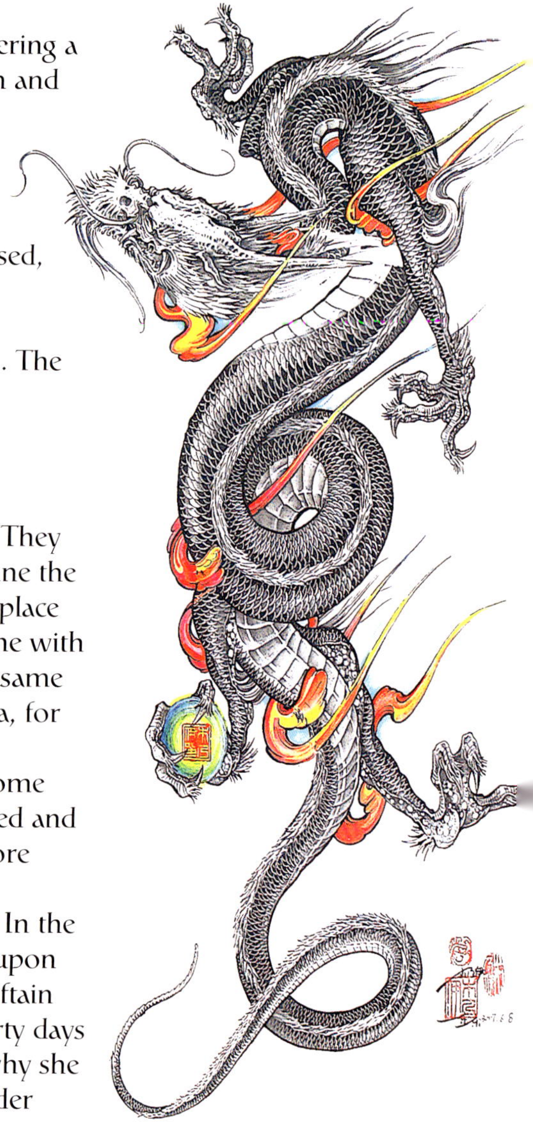

As the Inca and Aztec empires collapsed, other explorers such as Sir Walter Raleigh, made a number of famous voyages to Roanoke island, Virginia, America. On board was the artist,cartographer, John White, whose stay amongst the Algonquin Indians allowed him to witness and paint many of their customs, which he duly reported to the incredulous Elizabethans: "They lai the dead corpses of their cheefe lordes theruppon in the followinge. First the bowells are taken forthe.then layinge downne the skinne,they cutt all the flesche clean from the bones,which they drye in the sonne,and well dryed they enclose in matts,and place at their feete. Then their bones (remaininge still fastened together with ligaments whole and uncorrupted) are covered agayne with leather, and their carcase fashioned as yf their flesh was not taken away. They lapp each corps in his ownne skinne after the same is thus handled, and lay yt in his order by the corpses of the other cheef lordes, By the dead bodies they set their idol Kiwasa, for they are persuaded that the same doth keepe the dead bodyes of their cheefe lordes that nothinge may hurt them".
Discoveries of tattooed Eskimos and tribes' people from Brazil and Indonesia were also providing spectacular evidence of some distant pagan identity. These "poor creatures" were abducted and brought to Europe where they were studied, probed, traded and finally placed on public view like freaks. In fact they were the first bunch of human curiosities to hit the headlines, long before Barnum Bailey and other circus acts got in on the business of exploiting oddities.
In Polynesia, other explorers encountered intriguing and gruesome rituals taking place on many of the island communities. In the Marquesas they discovered that the natives had not only created the most incredible expression of tattoo art ever seen, but upon death, they began a process of reversing this ornate and painstakingly produced artwork. After the death of the famous chieftain Iotete, in 1844, a French missionary, Aimable Petithomme, went to visit the Queen who had been occupying herself for thirty days since the death of her husband in - "taking off with her fingers the skin of the deceased, as it came away, and when asked why she did so, she said it was in order to efface the tattooing, as it was necessary that her husband's body should be stainless, in order that the great goddess, Oupu take him to live on her land and bathe in her lake... the slaves and poor people went to a gloomy land which was never lighted by the sun, and where there was only muddy water". There were many more astonishing accounts of barbarism and savagery being reported throughout the south seas which inevitably ended once the new settlers arrived, but these were not whimsical gestures or something bestial as initial observers imagined.

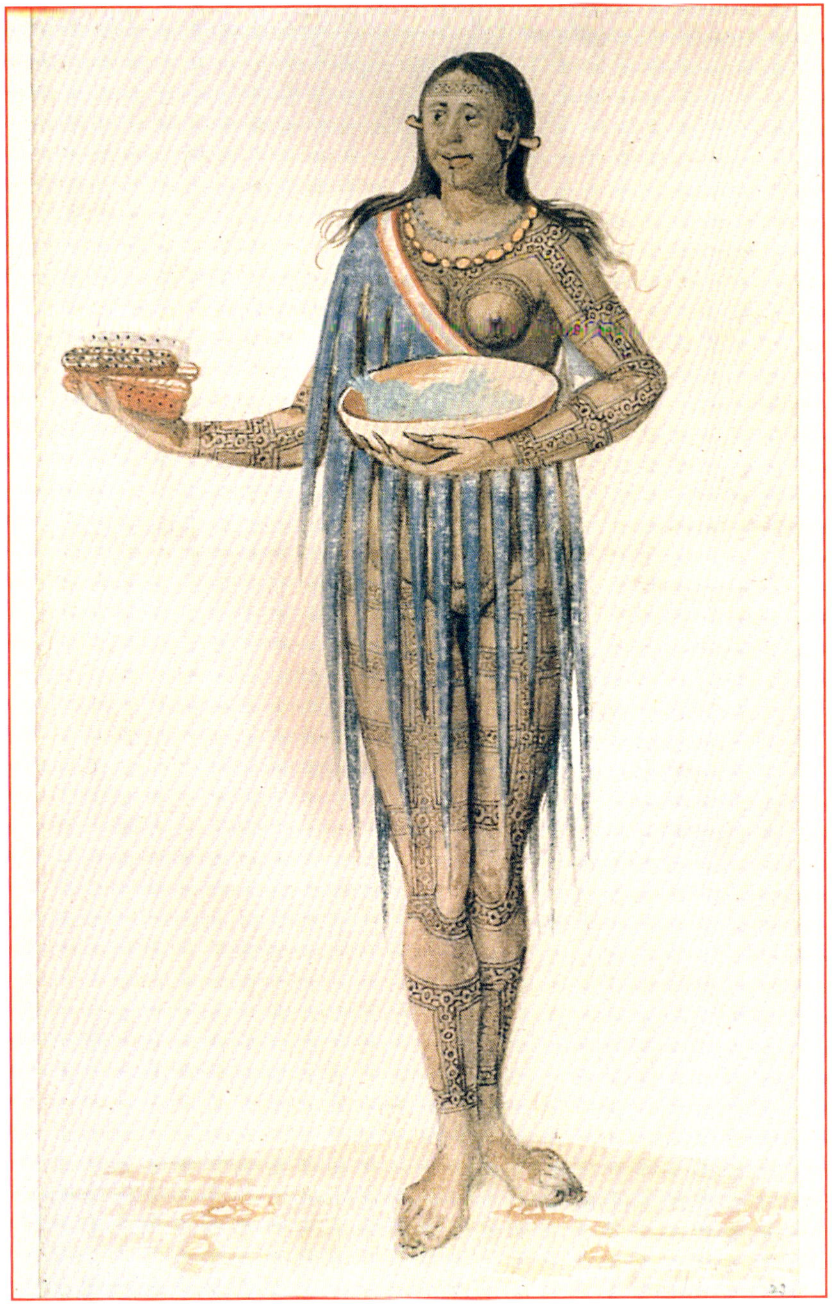

从亚洲大陆迁移到大洋洲的先人们将深刻的文化记忆保留在了那些太平洋星罗棋布的岛屿上。

这些新移民在无外界干扰的状态下生活了数千年，而在重新向临近的岛屿和大陆迁徙之前，他们已经在与世隔绝中形成了无数的习俗、语言和仪式。

在美洲，史前居民也引进了萨满式的信仰和创伤仪式，并在印第安各个民族间广泛流传。

许多部落认为割体仪式具有驱邪的功能，在这个过程中，精神力量能进入身体中，并清洗身体。这些仪式有些十分虔诚，有些令人恐惧。象征祖先精神的齿印将在初始仪式过程中被印下来作为保护。

武士在进入蒸汗屋之前会割破他们的身体以祛除附体的恶灵。有些部落设计了十分精巧的悬吊技术，他们将人的胸膛割开，然后钩在绳索上，接着高高地升起和万能的神做一次拥抱。

有时这些戏剧性的遭遇将引发血腥和恐怖的人殉场景。西班牙人在征服阿兹特克人时不过是将一种血腥的制度和仪式换成了另外一种而已。

最初西班牙征服者们在看到公共仪式上血腥的剖腹挖心，以及在收获季节屠杀孩童时都震惊不已。而根据阿兹特克信仰，生命本身就是要杀灭的。在一个人的身体解体之前，他的能量须被拿掉并被得到重新装备。

很快，一个同样血腥的基督徒被钉在十字架上的场景，就随着殖民主义者的种族灭绝迅速成为拉丁美洲随处可见的景观。世界之间的冲突带来的是整个社会和传统的崩溃和消亡。探索时代只不过让一群野蛮人见识了另一群野蛮人。

在印加和阿兹特克帝国陷落之后，其他的探险家，像Walter Raleigh 爵士曾在几次著名的航行中前往今天美国弗吉尼亚州的罗阿诺克岛（Roanoke island）。船上还有一名艺术家和制图家John White，他曾和亚尔冈京印第安人（Algonquin Indians）共同生活，这使得他能够目睹并画下他们的习俗，并向将信将疑的伊丽莎白臣民们讲述他的见闻。

“先把肠子掏出来，然后把皮剥掉，接着把骨头上的肉都剔除干净，再把骨头放到太阳底下晒干。干了以后用垫子包好放在脚下。然后再把这些人的骨头（骨头上的韧带还没有腐烂而且很完整，仍然将骨架连在一起）用皮革裹起来，使得这个躯体看起来还是肉身。

他们将每副躯体用原来的人皮按照同样的手法包裹起来，再按照顺序和其他的酋长摆放在一起。在尸体旁边他们会放上Kiwasa像，因为他们相信这样可以保护他们的酋长的尸骸不受伤害。”

在爱斯基摩人、巴西和印尼的部落成员身上发现的纹身，同样也为相隔遥远的异教同一性提供了令人惊叹的证据。

这些“可怜的人”被诱拐带到欧洲，在这里他们成为研究、探索、交易的对象，最后他们被当作怪物一般向公众展出。实际上他们是第一批引起轰动的活人展品，比Barnum Bailey和其它马戏团利用展览畸形来赚钱要早得多。

在波利尼西亚，其他的一些探险家遭遇到发生在许多海岛部落中更为怪异和可怕的仪式。在马克萨斯（Marquesas），他们看到土著居民不但创造了他们前所未见的最惊人的纹身艺术，而且在死亡时他们还开始一个将这种华美和精心制作的艺术品恢复原状的过程。

In Melanesia, certain tribes engaged in endo-cannibalism, whereby at a funeral, female relatives ate the body in order that the spirit force was prevented from escape and also to reincorporate the person back - as a protective ghost. Among the Marind-anim of the New Guinea south coast, it was the cadaveric fluid of the corpse that facilitated divination; this fluid was drunk by a close relative as she or he lay next to the corpse in the grave. Some tribes mourned their dead by violating themselves during moments of grief in order to mollify the deceased spirit. Cutting off the tops of fingers, slashing earlobes and faces were just a few of the obligatory rituals What was happening was a total de-naturalisation, and disconnection, of the body and its fusion on earth.
The only thing that mattered was to return to one's creator as an original spirit, and these eschatological dramas were enacted for the sole purpose of 'de-conceptualising' the person, in preparation for the voyage to paradise. The tattoos, scars and other emblems, which had offered protection and prestige, had served their purpose. It was now time to regenerate the dead, by transferring human vitality to living things.

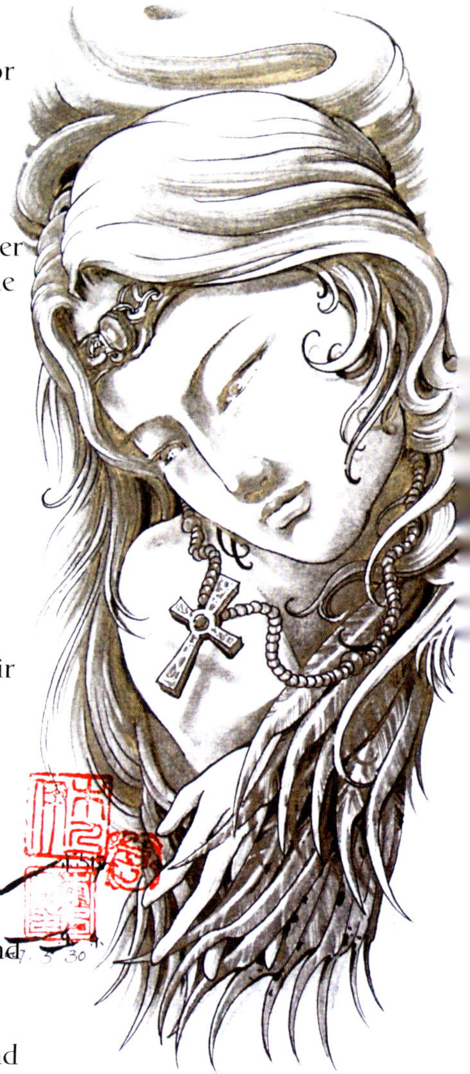

On other remote island societies, such as Japan and Borneo, tattoo inscriptions were integral to the soul's survival and were never to be removed. The ancient inhabitants, the Ainu, worshipped tattooed gods and had themselves heavily marked, like their divine protectors. The sacrement of tattoo was equally important in the next world. In Fijiian society, and for the New Zealand Maori. The absence of tattoos could result in terrible consequences when the soul reached the underworld, which was guarded by demons and witches who would prevent untattooed persons from entering. The Europeans who landed on the distant shores of the new world were well accustomed to images of torture and bizarre funeral enactments back home. For several centuries Europe had been devasted by plagues, long-running wars, and religious schisms, the sight of death was nothing new.
It had been a common practice in medieval times for monarchs, aristocrats and important religious dignitaries to leave money, and have their corpses dismembered then transported to different monasteries and holy sites. The idea was to multiply the number of sacred employees in the service of the souls salvation, and thereby ensure its release from purgatory. The powerful dead were laid out in grand mausoleums, with their sacred hearts and other organs carefully preserved and exhibited. To add to this surreal spectacle, other forms of corporeal dismemberment took place under the aegis of the church and monarchs who dispensed their divine judgements, through the medium of torture. The 'Guilty' were left rotting from scaffolds and gibbets, their heads stuck on spikes as reminders of acts of transgression. Public executions and crucifixions were accompanied by the application of a 'science of applied cruelty', in which eye gougers, thumb screw, spine rollers, and a variety of bone crushing gadgets began to inscribe different messages and texts onto bodies.
These gruesome writing machines would accompany the apocalyptic priests and missionaries as they landed in the new world. The body which had previously been viewed as a potential host of unholy and demonic alliances, now became divided into natural or unnatural states of being. The visible tribal scars, tattoos and necrophageous items adorning the bodies of Cannibals, Headhunters and Shamen, revealed unassailable evidence of a pagan and unnatural state of being which demanded God's intervention and purification. This divine justice was dispensed with incredible cruelty by Europeans when they began to settle and appropiate land from the natives.

Before entire societies were finally eradicated, collectors were busily shipping back human remains and collections of tribal art and artifacts to European musems. The trafficking of Maori tattooed heads reached such scandalous proportions, that eventually legal intervention was required to halt this trade and prevent a wholesale slaughter. One cultural virus emanating from Europe was about to lay waste to entire oceanic traditions, and other more deadly bacteriological ones were soon to follow. During the

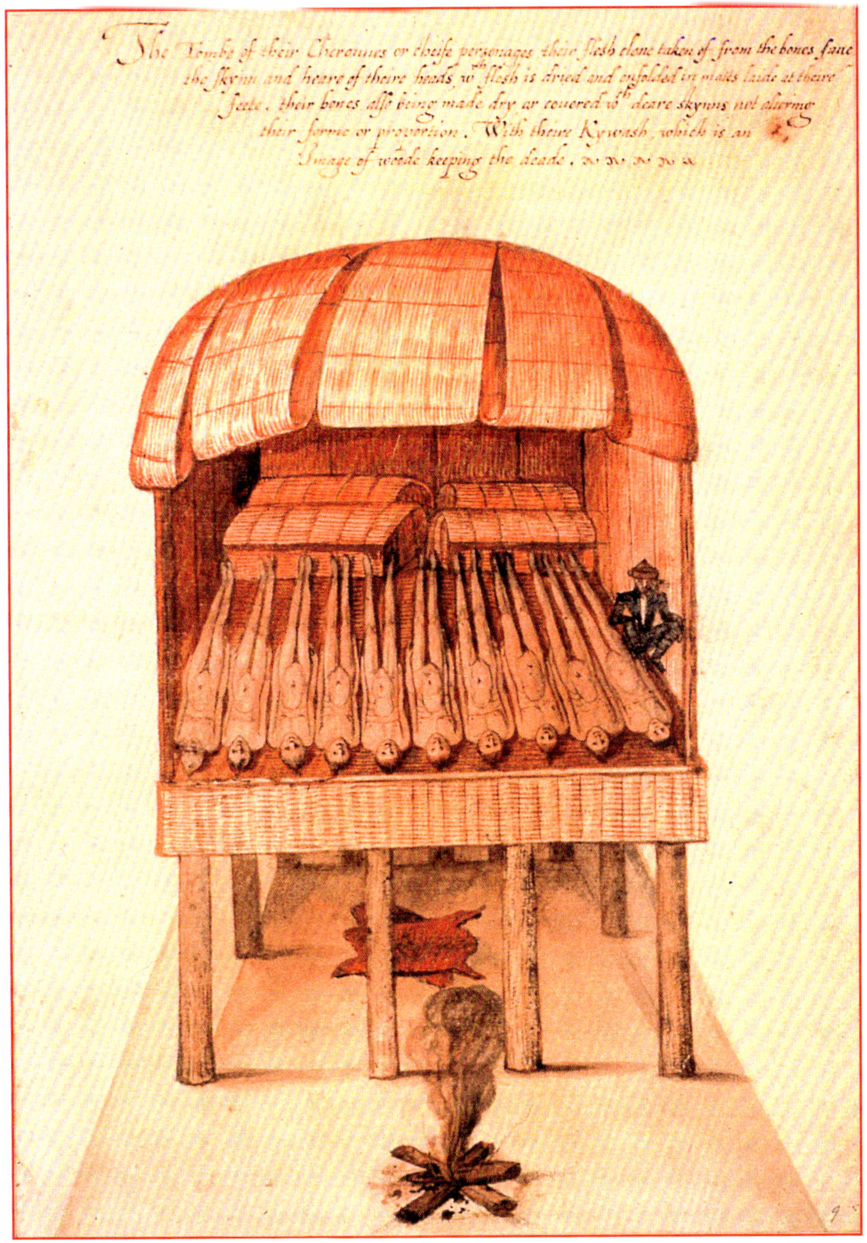

1844年在一个著名的酋长Iotete死去之后，一个名叫Aimable Petithomme的法国传教士前去拜访王后，她在她丈夫死后已经忙活了三十天。

“她用手将死者的皮揭下来，在皮被剥掉之后，当问她为什么要这样做时，她回答说要将皮上的纹身磨去。因为她丈夫的身体必须毫无瑕疵，才能在女神奥普（Oupu）的圣土上生活，在她的仙湖中沐浴……而奴隶和穷人只能去昏暗之地，那里终日不见阳光，只有泥浆浊水。”

在南海有关野蛮人的故事还有许多，这些故事在新移民抵达之后无可避免地消失了。这些故事并不是古怪的比划，或者如最初的探险家们认为的那样是兽类所为。

在美拉尼西亚，有些部落盛行一种称为“内群食人”（endocannibalism）的习俗。葬礼上死者的女性亲属要吃掉尸体以防止精神力量逃散，并将死者召回成为一个保护幽灵。

在新几内亚南部沿海的马林德－阿尼姆（Marind-Anim），尸身是用于占卜的利器。这种液体由在坟墓中和尸体并排躺下的男性或女性亲属喝掉。有些部落在哀悼死者时在悲痛的时刻鞭打自己来安慰死者的灵魂。

将手指尖割去，用刀切耳垂和面部只是这些强制性仪式的几种而已。实际的情况是身体和它与土地的融合完全异化和脱离。

唯一的重点是作为一个原始的精神，回归到创造者那里去，而这些末世学的剧情只不过是为了使人“去概念化”这一单纯的目的而编排，为搭建登天之途做准备。

这些提供了保护和声望的纹身、疤痕和图案已经达到了目的。现在要通过向活人传递人的精神让死者重生。

在其它一些遥远的海岛部落中，比如日本和婆罗洲，纹身是灵魂存续不可缺少的部分，并且永远不能去除。古代阿伊努居民崇拜绘有纹身的天神，并和他们的保护神一样全身都刺满了纹身。

纹身圣礼在其他地方也是同样重要的。在斐济的某些部落和新西兰的毛利人中，如果没有纹身，灵魂到达地下的时候会导致非常严重的后果，因为守护魔神和巫师会将没有纹身的人挡在门外。

当欧洲人到达遥远的新世界的时候，他们对发生的那些刑罚和怪异的丧葬场景早就习以为常，几个世纪以来的瘟疫、连绵不绝的战争、宗教分裂不断蹂躏着欧洲，所以在他们眼里死亡并不是什么新鲜的事情。

在中世纪，皇室、贵族、重要的宗教人物在死后习惯于留下钱财并将尸体分解，将各部分送到不同的修道院和圣地，目的是使参加灵魂拯救仪式的神职人员数量加倍增多，这样就能保证死后不至于堕入炼狱。权贵们死后尸体将安放在宏伟的陵墓中，他们的神圣的心和其它器官经过精心保存后对外展示。

为这些超现实画面增加一些色彩，其它形式的尸体分解也是在宗教和君主的庇护下进行的。他们通过刑罚为媒介执行了神的判决。“罪人”被砍头或被绞杀以后任其腐烂，他们的头颅插在尖刺上以警告违法者。公开的处决和钉在十字架上常常伴随着“实用酷刑科学”的使用。剜眼、剁拇指、抽脊和变换花样的断骨手法在身体上刻下了不同的信息和文字。

而随着世纪末牧师们和传教士纷纷踏上新世界的土地，他们也带去了这令人恐惧的书写机器。

massive displacements of human trafficking, tattooing was transmitted unwittingly back to Europe where it would once again appear as some form of curious inscription. For countless centuries and among differing civilisations the ceremony of tattooing has appeared then vanished, only to reassert itself in contrasting and distant cultures with entirely new rules and meaning.
In some undiscovered continent, deep inside a forest, tribal members were once incising the face of a warrior with the protective signs of his ancestral spirit that would guide and safeguard him during battle. Elsewhere, on the other side of the earth, advanced civilsations such as China , Japan and Europe, were commiting barbaric acts of punishment by publicly tattooing the faces of alledged criminals or dissidents. The Greek physician Aetius wrote how two monks who had reproached the emperor Theophilos, were imprisoned by his orders and had eleven iambic verses of satirical character tattooed on their heads, and in the early stages of the Christian empire, the tattooing of the face was a common punitive measure. Many condemned persons had their faces tattooed or branded as they were led off to work in mines or forced into exile.
This diabolical form of writing on the body was rigourously enforced by rulers and monarchs who sought total control over their subjects. The marking or branding of bodies with authoritative inscriptions, emitting signs denoting ownership, became an ideal tool for dehumanising a subject. In medieval Europe, during the various reigns of terror, a person could be forcibly detained and their body examined for signs of unholy transactions. Religious Inquistions resulted in grotesque verdicts, whereby a person could be condemned to death for having certain blemishes, warts or 'marks of the devil', secreted some place on their body. Witches were burnt at the stake on account of possesing magic tattoo marks and countless others were slaughtered simply because their skins were stained with birthmarks or signs that indicated heresy or linked them with satanic cults.
This phenomenon in which bodies are made to testify against their owners, is repeated throughout all civilisations. Ethnic hatred is just a by-product of this primordial fear of 'others'. The stranger or enemy was easily identified and classified by their cultural disfigurements, by their strange clothing, jewellery and hairstyles, and most importantly by their skin colour.
The Classical historians, travellers, naturalists and scientists who described nomadic tribes and primitive peoples, also added absurd speculation and fantasy to their accounts. Over a period of time many of these fabrications were taken as factual. The Greeks invented the term 'stigmata' to denote their disapproval of tattoo marks, which was passed on by the Romans and Christians and this negative connotation has been with us ever since. It didn't take long for criminologists to add their judgements and condemnations on the subject. Convicts skins were studied like ancient manuscripts for signs that the body was being possessed or predisposed to pagan and atavistic acts of self-wounding. What they failed to realise was, a convicts' skin is his only prized possession, and in the absence of freedom, provides the only opportunity and diary onto which he's able to transcribe his fears and obsessions.
The cult of 'stigmata' or 'pricking the skin', which had been popular traditions among numerous cultures, such as the Celts, Gauls, Picts, Vikings and ancient Britons, almost vanished from mainland Europe two thousand years ago. Very little is recorded about its practice, although there are scattered reports of the tattoo being used by religious pilgrims, adventurers and members of occult and secret societies. The prevailing political and religious forces usually reserved tattooing for use as a punitive measure and means of identifying the huge cargoes of human flesh, of convicts and slaves that were being traded and exchanged throughout the world.

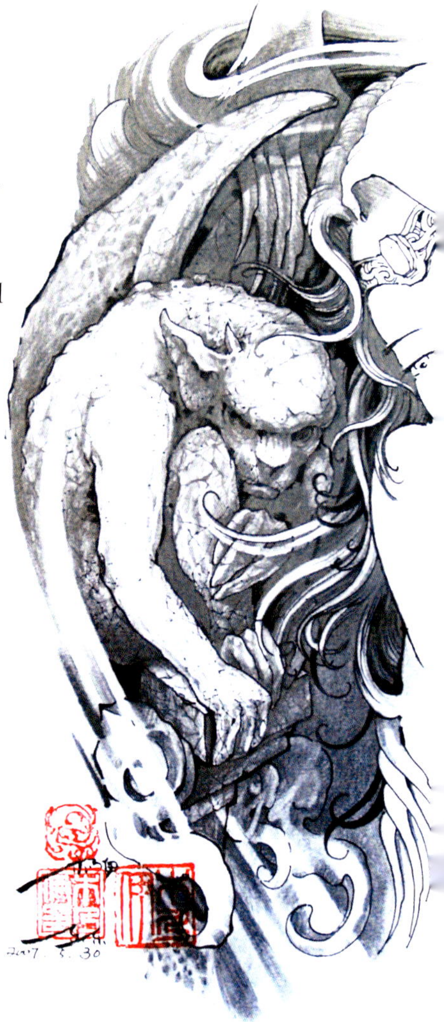

The great merchant and military expeditions of the Renaissance began to explore every corner of the world and uncover many strange customs and traditions which incidentally provided the sailors with the opportunity to acquire exotic and mysterious markings from the orient and south seas. The momentous discovery of Tahiti, by Captain Cook, considered by Europeans as a distant Eden, and his introduction of the word - tatau - added fresh impetus and value to the custom of tattooing. As more and

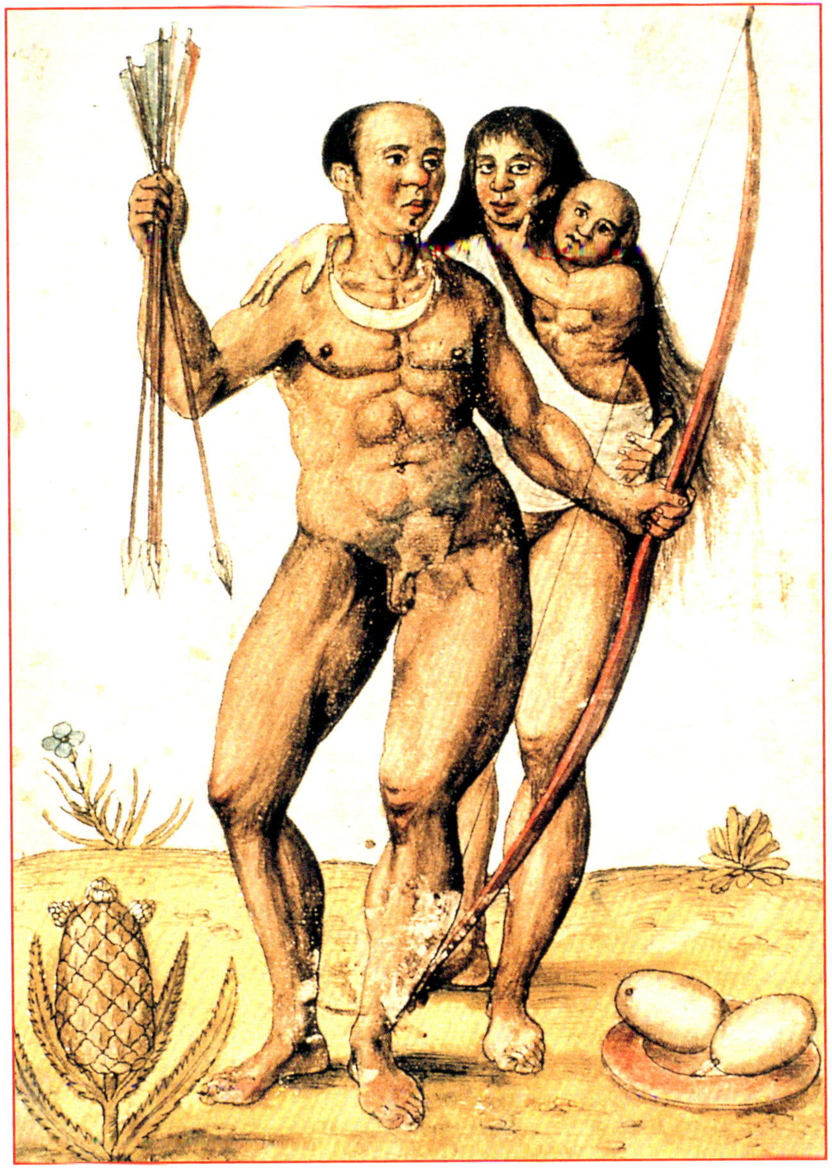

从前被视为不贞与魔性承载物的身体，如今却变成一种自然或非自然的存在状态。

食人族、猎头族、萨满族那些用来装饰族人身体的疤痕、纹身和死人饰物显示他们是处于非自然状态的异教徒，他们需要上帝的干预并对他们实施净化。当欧洲人开始在这些地方定居并且从土著人手里攫取土地时，欧洲人就用不可想象的残忍来执行着神的正义。

在部族被整个消灭之前，收藏家们在忙着往欧洲的博物馆运送着遗骸、部落艺术品和器物。他们走私毛利人绘有纹身的头颅，行径令人齿冷，以至于最后不得不由司法出面来阻止该项贸易并防止大规模屠杀。

一种源于欧洲的文化病毒即将破坏整个大洋洲的文明传统，而其他更多的致命病菌则很快会步其后尘。

在大规模人口贩卖引起的迁移过程中，纹身在不知不觉中又被传回到欧洲，在那里它再次作为某种形式的奇异的刻印而出现。无数世纪以来，在不同的文明之中纹身仪式或有或无，只是在与其它文化进行对比或将它们边缘化时，纹身才以全新的规则和含义重现自己的意义。

在一些不为人知的大陆上，在密林深处，部落成员曾一度在战士的脸上刻印花纹，那是他祖先精神的保护标志，可以在战斗过程中引导和保卫他。

在其它地方，地球的另一边，一些高级文明地区比如中国、日本和欧洲则采取在罪犯和持不同政见人士脸上纹身的野蛮方法以示惩罚。

希腊物理学家埃提乌斯（Aetius）讲述了两个和尚因咒骂皇帝提奥菲罗（Theophilos）而被下令监禁并在脸上纹下了十一行讽刺的抑扬诗的故事。在基督教帝国的早期，纹面是一种常见的惩罚手段。许多罪犯脸上刻着花纹或印记，被迫在矿场劳作或流放。

这种对身体书写的形式是那些统治者和君主为了对他们的臣民实行完全的控制而严厉实施的残暴行径。在身体上用权威性的刻印打上标记和烙印，显示的是一种所有权，并成为将所属者非人化的理想工具。

在中世纪欧洲不同方式的恐怖统治下，一个人可能被武力拘留，其身体会被检查是否存在某些不洁交易的标志。宗教裁判所制造了荒诞的判决。一个人可能因为身体的瑕疵、疣子或者在身体某些隐秘部位有“魔鬼的标记”而被判处死刑。女巫因为有神秘的纹身而被大量烧死。数不清的人仅仅因为皮肤上的胎记或标志，被认作是异端或邪教而遭到屠杀。

在整个文明过程中身体是对他们的所有者不利证明的现象都在不断重复着。种族仇恨只不过是这种原始对“他者”恐惧的副产品。对于陌生人或敌人，他们的文化异态、奇装异服、珠宝、发式，最重要的是他们肤色，使得对他们的辨别和划分变得十分容易。

古典历史学家、旅行者、博物学家和科学家在描述游牧部落和原住人民时，也时常在他们的记述中加入荒唐的幻想，在一段时间内，这种加工出来的故事被当成了事实。古希腊人创造了“stigmata”这一术语来表现他们对纹身标记的反感，这一单词经由罗马人与基督教流传至今，它的负面含义从那时起就留存在我们的语言中。不久犯罪学家就将他们的裁判与惩罚加在他们的对象身上。

他们像研究古代手稿一样仔细端详犯人的皮肤，希望找到异教徒和返祖行为的自伤身体标记，不过他们却忘记了囚犯的皮肤也仅是他自己的战利品。在失去自由的岁月中，他只能通过书写日记来表达他内心的恐惧和妄想。对“stigmata”或“刺伤皮肤”的崇拜原本是在许多文化比如凯尔特、高卢、皮克特、维京和古代不列颠人流行的传统，但是在两千年前它

more sailors, servicemen and adventurers acquired their inky souvenirs in distant ports, and brought them back for the admiration of folks back home, a gradual and simple nomenclature was being created from these 'significant' images and motifs.
Tattoo Albums containing mysterious eastern symbols and talismans, together with images of demons, dragons, snakes, religious motifs, and lewd dancing girls began to attract the curious public who could now obtain some of these exotic and permanent charms, without the discomfort of long voyages. Even though Westerners were accustomed to seeing the continuous parade of 'tattooed oddities' being brought back from Africa, the Arctic and the Far East, whose entire bodies were emblazoned with fascinating pictures and marks, they weren't prepared for the brilliant and shocking style of Japanese tattooing, discovered at the end of the 19th century. In spite of a long tradition of using tattooing to distinguish and punish criminals - Ire Zumi (to mark). The Japanese established an aesthetic of permanent body art only ever equalled by the Polynesians.
The style they created within the space of one hundred years was known as Horimono - which now signified decoration instead of punishment... An unlikely alliance was forged by Western tattoo enthusiasts and Japanese tattoo masters. British sailors, officers and dignitaries visiting the cities of Tokyo and Yokohama were able to acquire spectacular and colorful Japanese works of art and then re-introduce them into the newly established tattoo salons of Europe. The impact was almost immediate and the craze for exotic tattooing reached all classes of society at the end of the 19th century.

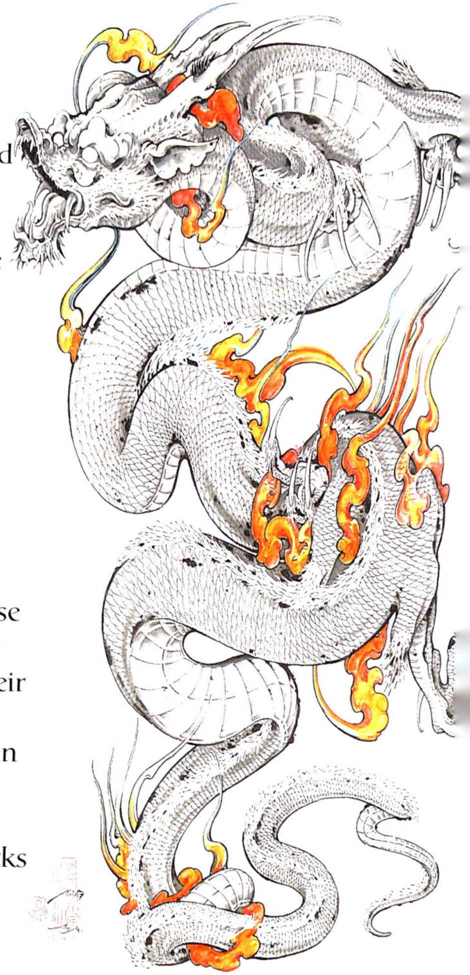

British artists such as Sutherland Macdonald and George Burchett were to have an ernormous influence on tattooing in the following decades, especially as they happened to be illustrating the aristocracy. The term 'tattooist' was coined by Macdonald who wanted the public to respect tattooing as an art form rather than as a simple craft. George Burchett wanted to reassure the public that his methods were scrupulously clean. His shop resembled a doctor's surgery and he wore a white coat to work.
But the idea of permanent body decoration would still have to contend with the moral strictures of polite society, who placed a cultural quarantine over the vulgar act. It seemed to belong to the spectacle of carnival amusement rather than the art salon. The problem for the critics was that the tattooed person was barely able to articulate the motivations behind the artwork, which appeared as haphazard and unconnected. The frivolities of the flesh and the fabricated histories got in the way of serious discourse which left the spectator more bemused than intrigued. For most of the 20th century tattooing was considered to be a quaint and amusing irrelevence. The media enjoyed the endless parade of spectacular freaks and tattoo celebrities who tried to cash in on their fake savagery. The public was further confused when biker gangs, skin heads and an assortment of disenchanted kids started to pick up on the craze and provoke further sensational news coverage. Laws were passed prohibiting the tattooing of minors and in many American cities tattooing was banned on health grounds. The image of tattooing was generally perceived as a seedy backstreet activity on par with an abortionist.
Tattooists were basically an itinerant bunch of carnival showmen, gypsies and vagabonds who preferred the lifestyle of the barracks or the travelling circus. They made their nests in the backwaters of great port cities, amidst the brothels and drinking dens. These self-taught artisans boarded ships and trains and followed the battalions of soldiers and pilgrims who needed protective charms and amulets, or just a girl's name, to remind them of their odyssey. Tattooists camped outside military centres in their mobile homes, and set up studios in tents. They worked in barber shops, in amusement arcades and at popular seaside resorts. They weren't used to settling down and giving up their lifestyles and it took some time before they adopted professional habits and stricter discipline in their working environment.

The famous port cities such as San Diego, Singapore, Hong Kong, Liverpool, Honolulu, Yokohama, Hamburg, Copenhagen, were to become the centres and academies of tattoo education in the '50s and '60s... and a number of well-established tattoo

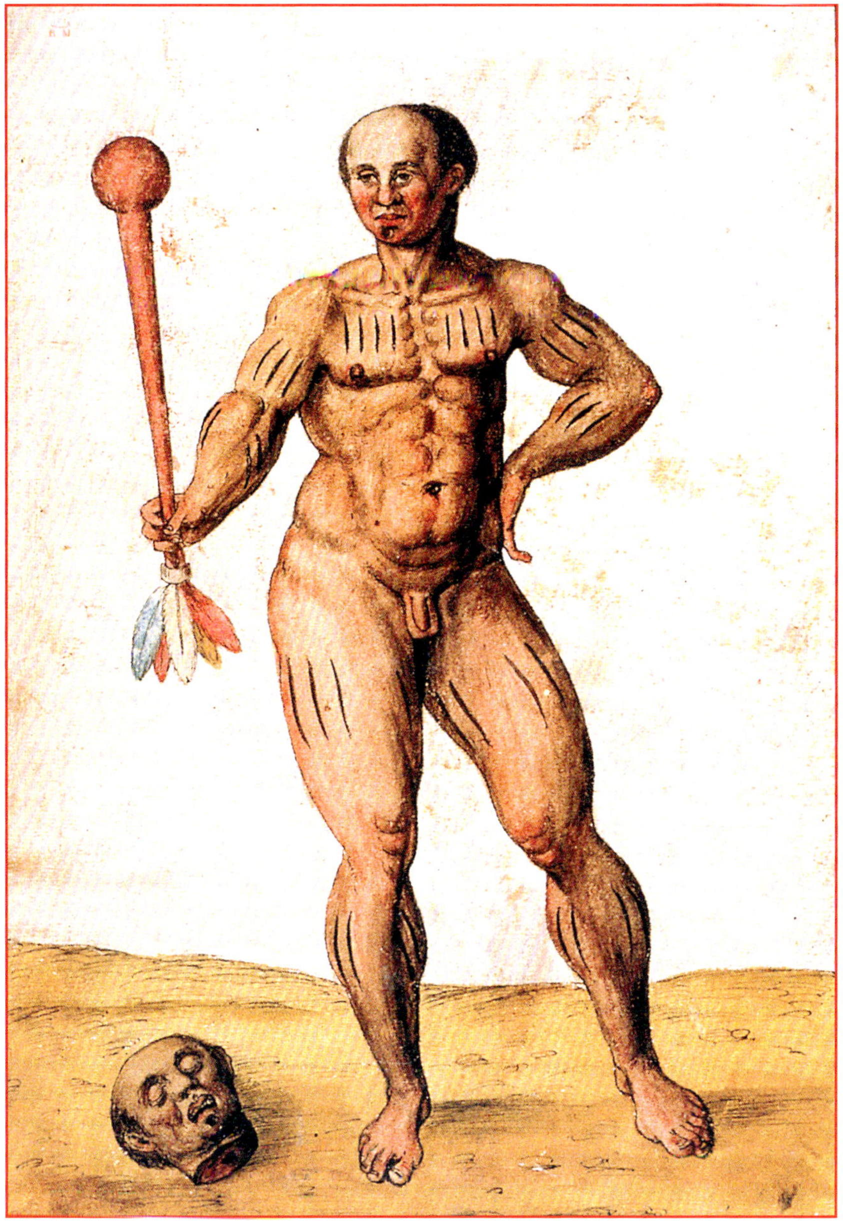

们却几乎完全消失了。尽管还留着朝圣者、探险家和密教或神秘社团使用过纹身的零星记录，但是有关纹身活动的记载却已经十分罕见。

当权的政治和宗教势力通常将纹身保留作为一种惩罚措施，同时也用作对在全世界范围内交易和买卖的肉体货物、囚犯和奴隶进行识别的方法。

文艺复兴时代那些伟大的商业和军事探险开始探索世界上的每一个角落并发现了大量的奇风异俗。这使得水手们偶然有机会获得东方和南太平洋的神秘标志。库克船长对塔西提岛（欧洲人相信那是遥远的伊甸园）的重大发现，以及由他引进的“tatau”一词，为纹身风俗加入了新的动力和价值。

随着越来越多的水手、士兵和探险家从远方的海港不断获得墨纹纪念物并将它们带回家呈献给民间文化管理部门，从这些“重要”的图案和花纹中逐渐产生了一种简单的命名法。

《纹身图册》包含了神秘的东方符号和辟邪物，同时还有妖魔鬼怪、龙、蛇、宗教文饰和放荡舞女的图画，它开始吸引充满好奇心的大众，而他们如今在旅途劳顿之后也能够获得某些充满异域风情和永久性的饰物。

尽管西方人对从非洲、北极和远东带回来全身绘满奇异文饰的“纹身异人”已经见怪不怪，不过当他们看到19世纪末发现的日本美丽惊人的纹身风格时，他们还是被震撼了。虽然长期以来纹身被用于识别和惩罚罪犯，日本人却将“*Ire Zumi*”（打印记）发展成一种永久性的身体美学，而这项艺术也只有波利尼西亚人才能媲美。

他们在一百年时间内开创的名为“*Horimono*”的风格，今天已经不再是惩罚性标志而被看作是装饰性艺术了。在西方纹身爱好者与日本的纹身大师不可能地冲撞在一起。英国水手、官员和贵族在造访日本的东京和横滨等城市时将购买的丰富多彩的艺术品引进到欧洲那些兴起的纹身沙龙里。随后迅速在19世纪末引发了社会各阶层追求异域纹身的潮流。

英国一些艺术家比如Sutherland Macdonald 和 George Burchett在后续的几十年中对纹身艺术产生了巨大的影响，这尤其应该归功于他们给贵族们的纹身。

“纹身师”一词是Macdonald 创造的，他希望公众将纹身作为一种艺术形式来尊重，而不仅仅将它看作是一种技艺。George Burchett 要让大众相信他的纹身方法极为小心而且十分干净。他的沙龙和医生的诊室很像，而且他工作的时候还穿上白大褂。

但是永久性身体装饰的理念却免不了要和社会的道德规则发生冲突，因为社会对低俗的行为会采取一种文化免疫措施。纹身看起来属于狂欢场面而非艺术沙龙里的情景。让批评家们困扰的问题是有纹身的人很少能清楚说明这件艺术品背后的动机是什么，这让它显得充满了偶然和无所关联。

肉体的轻薄和臆造的历史阻碍了对此的严肃讨论，并让观众感到更多的是茫然而不是发生兴趣。在20世纪的大部分时间里，纹身被看作是一种古怪和有趣的不相关东西。媒体无休止地播放那些想通过假冒蛮族来大赚特赚的奇异怪物和纹身的名人一族，而当飞车党、光头党、乃至一群光怪陆离的孩童也加入到这种风尚中来并引发新一轮新闻炒作之时，公众的反应是更加困惑了。禁止给儿童纹身的法律被通过了，而且在美国的许多城市出于卫生原因不再允许纹身。纹身于是普遍被看作与堕胎一样是一种在肮脏小巷中进行的活动。

纹身师基本上又成为了四处游荡的卖艺人、走江湖的和流浪汉，他们对棚屋或者流动马戏团的生活颇为钟情，他们在大型海港城市僻静处，在妓院和酒馆之间搭建自己的栖身之所。

shops took root in these places. Millions of people passed through these great harbours and many stopped long enough to acquire unforgettable personal souvenirs such as a hangover, a tattoo, or a dose of the clap. Back in those days such cities thrived on their notorious reputations. These were demanding and volatile places in which to work and it required a certain stamina and ability to resist the deluge of drama, drunkenness and nostalgia that accompanied the client as they staggered into the tattoo parlour. It wasn't a job for the weak minded or delicate.

Nevertheless, tattooing was beginning to attract a lot of interest and in particular a new breed of art trained tattooist entered the profession and changed everything around. The reintroduction of Japanese tattooing was again responsible for redefining Western tattoo art, which was definately stagnating in the '60s and '70s. The kimono style of Japanese tattooing effectively disguised the mistakes and blemishes that many people had tattooed on their skins which in time began to resemble some kind of luggage that had labels stuck on.

The concept of full and unified body tattooing provided the artist a new opportunity to collaborate with his client and instigate an idea on a blank canvas rather than continuing to fill in the empty spaces - 'tattooing by numbers' would be an apt description of the art before the '70s. Another radical improvement in tattooing was the experimental style of 'fine line' tattooing which provided realism, perspective and a third dimension.

Tattoos were brash and unimaginative affairs no longer, nor did they look like blurry, stuck-on transfers. For the first time, tattoos became realistic, inventive and colourful. Professional organisations were formed which attempted to introduce standard codes of practice and hygiene. They began closing their downtown shops and opening chic and well appointed studios in the centre of cities. Attitudes started to change and it became important for the public to see tattooing as clean and safe.

A number of tattoo conventions in the late '70s provided an open forum and live gallery space in which the public could view artists from all over the world working with highly professional techniques, pigments and better equipment. Tattooists started offering 'customised work' consultations and an appointment service which became instantly popular with new age clients, the yuppies, and fetishists.

The indelible mark was now sanitised, reappraised and ready for mass consumption. Tattoos became chic products, 'personal ornaments', 'cosmic jewellery', 'pigments of imagination' - not gaudy kitsch souvenirs - like the poor trinkets that the working classes collected on their various drunken excursions. Instead, the tattoo was to become a suitable ornament for all sectors of society, especially the Blank generation, who after creeping out of their surburban caves, found themselves unbranded and unprepared in the semiotic jungle of postmodernist culture.

Tattoos were a perfect excuse for erasing one's existential anonymity and realigning oneself to a new set of tribal beliefs and customs. People started dreaming up all sorts of concepts like 'exteriorizing one's inner self', or 'wearing one's dreams'. It didn't really matter as long as they were enjoying the pain and the results were good. Tattooing has proven itself beyond doubt as being a unique artform that requires great skill and patience and finally endurance, before the results can be fully appreciated.

Furthermore tattooing is probably the only primordial ritual to have continued since its inception, which is one of the principle factors that made 'tribal tattooing' so popular during the last decade, along with music and drugs, seemingly connecting us to a mythical past. The Bodyfetish also makes great drama out of the tattoo; erogeneous zones are clearly emphasised, rebranded, and tagged with a metal implant, which now places tattooing in the realm of the cosmetic industry, rather than that of a decorative art.

The present craze for tattoos has meant that whilst there are many brilliant new artists out there stretching the limits of our imagination - there are also thousands of body shops, trading in poor counterfeit 'brandmarks', that can best be described as human graffiti. It's no accident that there are equal numbers of untrained body redecorators offering their services in tattoo removal - It's worth recalling a time honoured adage - "Think before you Ink!"

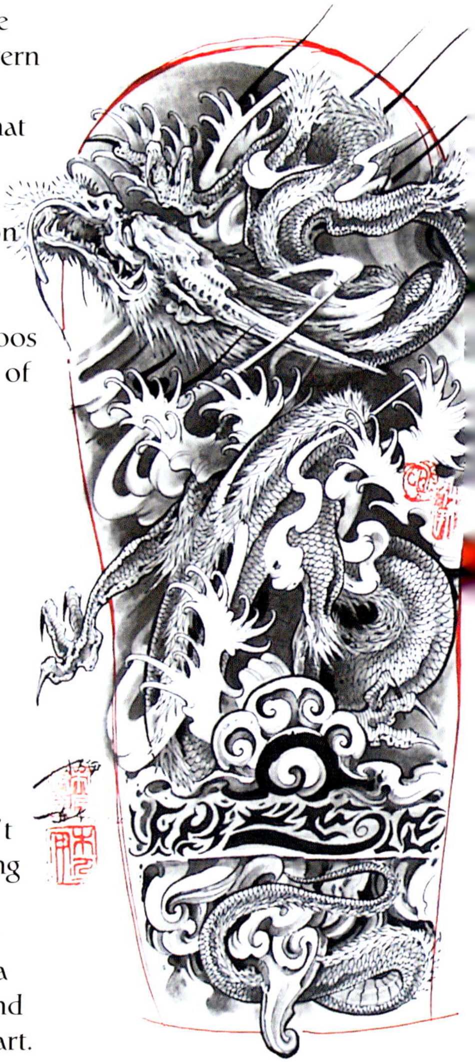

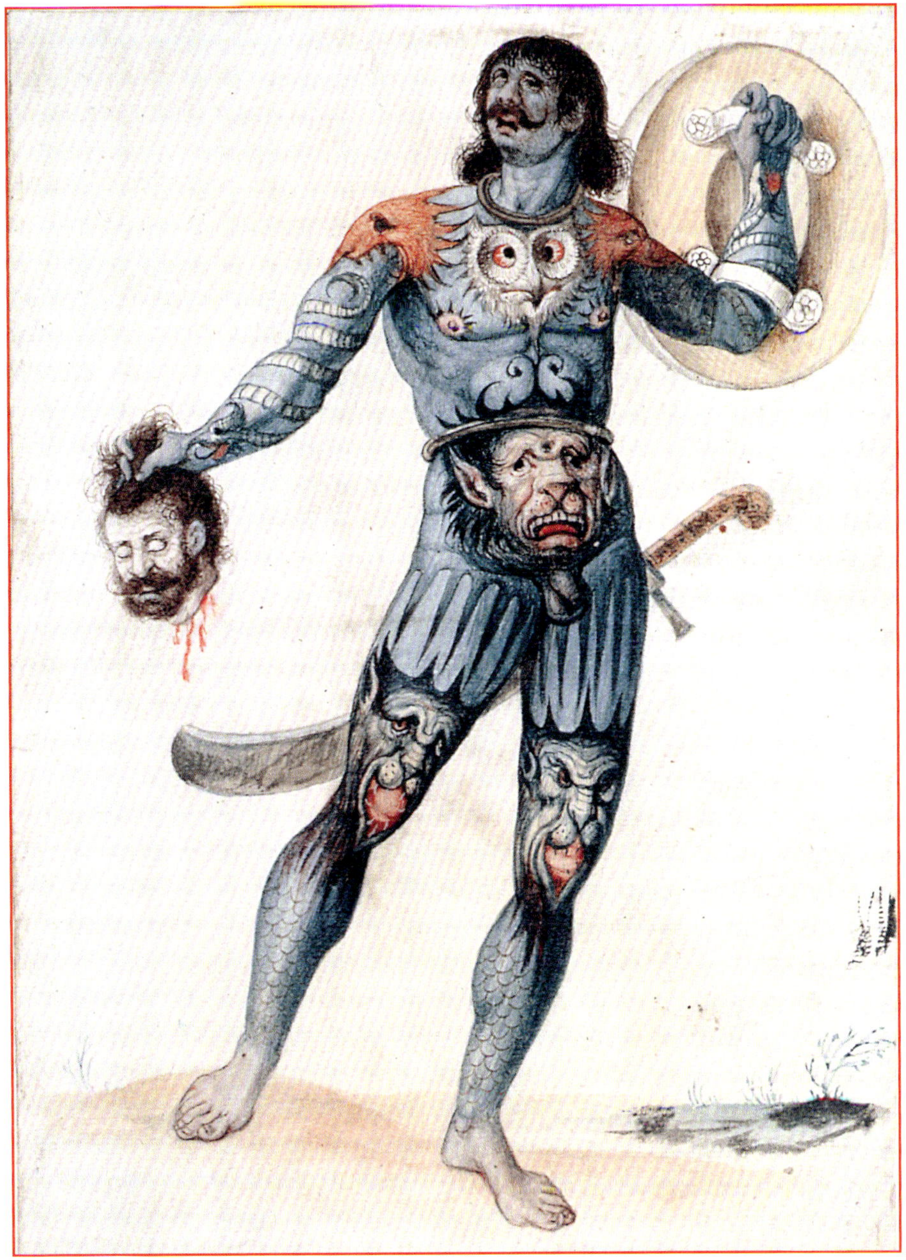

这些自学成才的艺人们或登上车船，或跟随开拔的军队，或加入朝圣者们的行列，为需要纹刻护身符的人服务，有时仅仅是刻上一个女孩儿的名字以聊慰他们的思乡之情。纹身师在军事基地外面安营扎寨，在帐篷里建起自己的工作室。在理发店、游乐场和公共海滨胜地都能见到他们的身影。他们不习惯安定的生活，也不愿放弃自己的生活方式，在接受职业习惯和在工作环境中培养更严格的纪律之前，他们还需要一段时间的适应。

在50-60年代，一些著名的港市如圣地亚哥、新加坡、香港、利物浦、檀香山、横滨、汉堡和哥本哈根成了纹身教育培训的基地，一些知名的纹身沙龙在这些地方扎了根。

数以百万计的人群在这些海港城市之间来来往往，其中许多人都驻足停留，为自己留个难忘的纪念，比如一场宿醉、一套纹身或者一次艳遇。在那些时日，这些城市因这美名而繁荣起来。在这些地方工作十分辛苦乏味，要求艺人们有足够的精神和能力来与跌跌撞撞闯进纹身沙龙的谩骂不休、满身酒气或思乡不已的客户们纠缠。这不是一个意志力差或者纤弱的人能做的工作。

不过纹身也开始引起很多人的兴趣，特别是随着新一代有艺术素养的纹身师加入到这个行业以来，情况发生了改观。对日本纹身的重新引进再一次对60-70年代停滞不前的西方纹身艺术进行了审视。和式纹身能有效地对皮肤上纹身的错误和疤痕进行掩盖，让它们看起来像是带着标签的文字。

完整和统一的纹身概念使得艺术家们有新的机会来与客户合作，让他们能够在一张白纸上描绘自己的理念，而不仅仅是继续填充空白之处。“人头纹身”是对70年代之前这项艺术的真实写照。

纹身艺术的另一个激进的革新是“细线”试验纹身风格的引进，它提供了现实主义、透视和三维风格。纹身不再是零碎且缺乏想象力的事务，它们看起来也不再是模糊和黏糊的转移。破天荒第一次纹身成了现实主义、原创性和色彩丰富的艺术品。他们成立了专业的机构为纹身活动设置相应的技术和卫生标准。而且他们还关闭了在闹市区的店铺转而在城市的中心地带建起工作室开门营业。人们的观念也转变了，他们逐渐将纹身看作是一项清洁和安全的艺术。

在70年代后期一系列纹身艺术大会为艺术家们提供了开放的论坛和直观的艺术空间，在这里公众可以观摩世界各地用高度专业的技艺、色彩和设备创造的纹身作品。纹身师们也开始提供“定制作品”，新一代客户、雅皮士和恋物者们很喜欢这种咨询和预约的服务。

不可磨灭的印记经过扬长避短，重新评估之后已经开启了大众消费之门。纹身成为了时髦的产品，成为了“个人饰物”、“化妆珠宝”、“想象力的色彩”，而不再是劳工阶层在醉醺醺的旅途中随手收集的那些俗气的饰品和纪念物。另外，纹身也称为社会各阶层合适的装饰，特别是那些空白的一代，当他们从远郊的洞穴中爬出来时，突然发现他们不再带有烙印并且已经置身于一片后现代文化的符号丛林中。

纹身是擦除一个人匿名存在以及重新按照新部族信念和习俗建立自我的绝好借口。人们开始梦想着各种各样的概念比如“内在自我的外化”或者“穿上梦想”等等。只要他们还能忍受痛楚并享受结果的话，也没有什么问题，而实际上他们正享受着这种结果。纹身已经证明是一种独特的艺术形式，在人们欣赏到作品之前，艺术家们需要有完美的技巧和耐心以及最后的忍耐。

此外，纹身也许是从开始一直流传至今的唯一的一项原始仪式，这也是为什么过去10年中“部落纹身”会如此广受欢迎，伴随着音乐和药物，似乎将我们与遥远的过去联系起来。

In this posthuman society where bodies are continually being traded remodelled and artificially rejuvenated, the tattoo mark may lose some of its' allure and mystique, once everyone gets in on the act. Celebrities of every rank and persuasion who once paraded their inky acquisitions now hide them or seek removal, once the glamour of youth and rebellion recedes. The authenticity of tattooing as a mark of distinction, or as a credible sub cultural activity has practically vanished.

It's ironic that, not so long ago, society was outraged at the idea of permanently altering one's skin. Now we are confronted with new writing machines that can probe and re-arrange every intimate part of our bodies and minds. New technology allows us the opportunity to swap body parts and even duplicate ourselves after death. Those in fear of cloning, DNA realignment, or the paranoid pro-life movements, are attempting to intervene in matters of personal choice and control in our lives! Worse still, the State has ultimate control on matters such as euthanasia, abortion, and how we ultimately treat our bodies. Perhaps the final irony, is the relentless reconfiguration that our minds and bodies are forced to undergo in order to participate in the global capitalist dream. Vast colonies of slaves or worker ants already exist, whether they are attached to their computers at call centres, or processing data as drones, in banks, media centres or confined to the repetition of industrial assembly lines. In this present charade of consumption and enslavement, we are continually being worn down; our bodies degraded by the necessities of work, play and finally by the widespread quest for oblivion, either through use of alcohol or dope. This has led to the creation of other redecorating industries that eagerly seek to cater for our downgraded selves – we are constantly being reminded of the undesirability of being overweight, or having wrinkly sagging skin and greying hair. Beauty-salons, plastic surgery units, together with health and rehabilitation clinics have become nothing more than reprocessing centres, in which we trade in our depleted bodies for one with a new expiry date. It's a bizarre and sobering thought, that mankind seems to be abandoning it's humanity by placing its future in the hands of technology. Films such as, the Matrix, may soon become documentaries instead of sci-fi entertainment.

In the foreseeable future, Cyborgs and Clones will dramatically alter our sense of identity and purpose, by replacing us entirely. Right now, high-tech alchemical laboratories are forcing newly adapted bodies to undergo ballistic streamlining in order to become amplified and accelerated post-evolutionary projectiles. A new set of explorers and adventurers are probing and examining the universe for signs of life. In this new form of voodoo, astronauts enter decompression chambers, realign their minds to computer terminals, connect their bodies to epidermal data suits of electrodes and sensors, and take a high velocity ride into outer space, hoping to make contact with ancestral spirits, just like the ancient shamanic priests robed in strange outfits, tripping on hallucinogenic substances once did. Nothing has changed, only the apparatus.

Chris Wroblewski

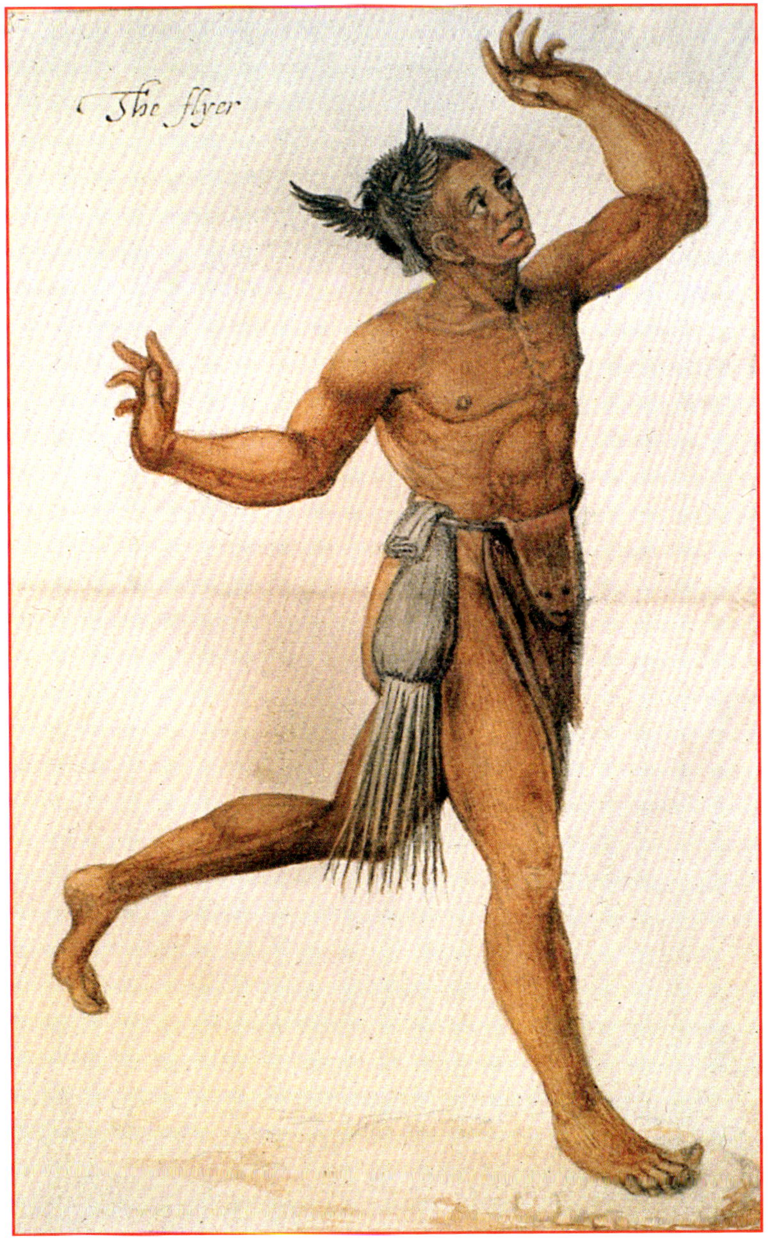

身体崇拜从纹身中还演绎出戏剧效果。性感区通过植入金属来获得强调、烙印和标记。这样使得纹身成为了化妆行业的一类，而不再仅仅是装饰艺术了。

当前对纹身追逐的风潮意味着新锐艺术家们正在扩充这我们想象力的边界，然而同样也存在着成千上万的美容店正在交易这各种品质低劣的假冒"烙印标志"。这些用"人体涂鸦"来描述再合适不过了。同时还有数量相等，没有经过培训的人体修饰人员在提供去除纹身的服务。因此我们有必要想想一句老格言："动手之前请三思"。

在这个后人文社会中，人的身体仍旧是交易、重塑和人造美化的对象。如果人人都参与这项活动，那纹身也会渐渐失去它的魅力和神秘。一度展示自己身体文饰的名人们今天却因为韶华不再或棱角消磨而悄悄地将纹身隐藏起来或将它们去除。作为一种等级分化的标记或作为亚文化活动的纹身已经销声匿迹。

具有滑稽意味的是，不久之前社会对于永久性改变一个人的皮肤还大为光火。而现在我们却遭遇到新的书写机器，它能够对我们身体和思想每一部分进行探查和改造。新技术可以使得我们更换器官，并在死后再造一个自我。那些对克隆、DNA重组或者那些妄想型反堕胎运动正试图介入个人选择的事务并控制我们的生活。更为糟糕的是美国对安乐死、堕胎以及我们处理自己身体的方式的控制得尤为严密。

我们的身体与灵魂将被迫加入到资本主义全球化的梦想中，也许这种残酷的重新控制才是终极的讽刺。由奴隶和蚁工组成的殖民地已经出现，不论他们是在电话中心里还是像工蚁一般在处理数据。他们在银行里、媒体中心或者被限制在装配线上做着重复的劳动。在这种消费主义和奴役的大合唱中，我们一天天被削弱。工作、游乐、以及通过酒精和毒品使我们忘却，让我们的身体堕落。

这种情况导致其它装饰行业的兴起，它们是为了满足我们自我堕落的需要。有人不断提醒我们肥胖、皮肤皱纹和白头发让你变得不受欢迎。于是美容院、整形外科、和健康修养诊所成为了再加工中心，在这里我们将已经被掏空的身体与另外一个有期限的身体进行交易。人类似乎在将自己的未来全部托付给技术，这种想法虽然古怪但不乏清醒的认识。《骇客帝国》也许不仅仅是一部科幻片，而很快会成为一部纪录片。

也许在不久的将来，赛博和克隆技术通过将我们完整地替换，将改变我们对身份和目的的感觉。当前高科技炼金实验室正在强制新型的适应性身体进行弹道流线试验，以开发放大和速度更快的发射物体。新的探险家在对宇宙进行探索以发现新的生命踪迹。在这种新形式的巫术中，宇航员们进入减压舱，将他们的思想与电脑终端重新校准，将身体与电极和传感器传输的数据相连，然后在高速下进入外层空间，希望能够与祖先的精神相遇。他们就像远古时代那些萨满祭司，身披奇怪的装束，施放这迷幻物质。除了装备变了以外，其它一切照旧。

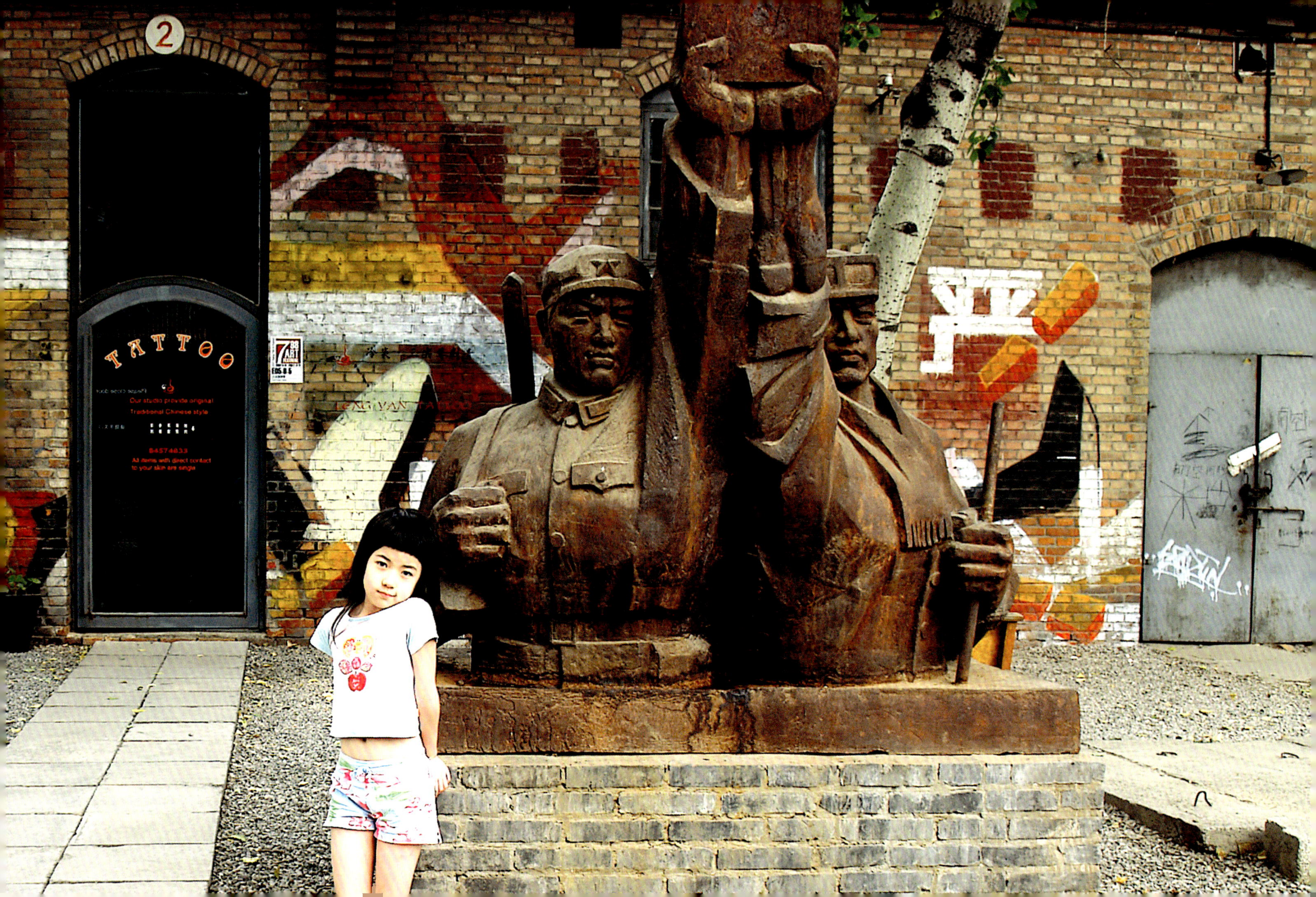
2
TATTOO

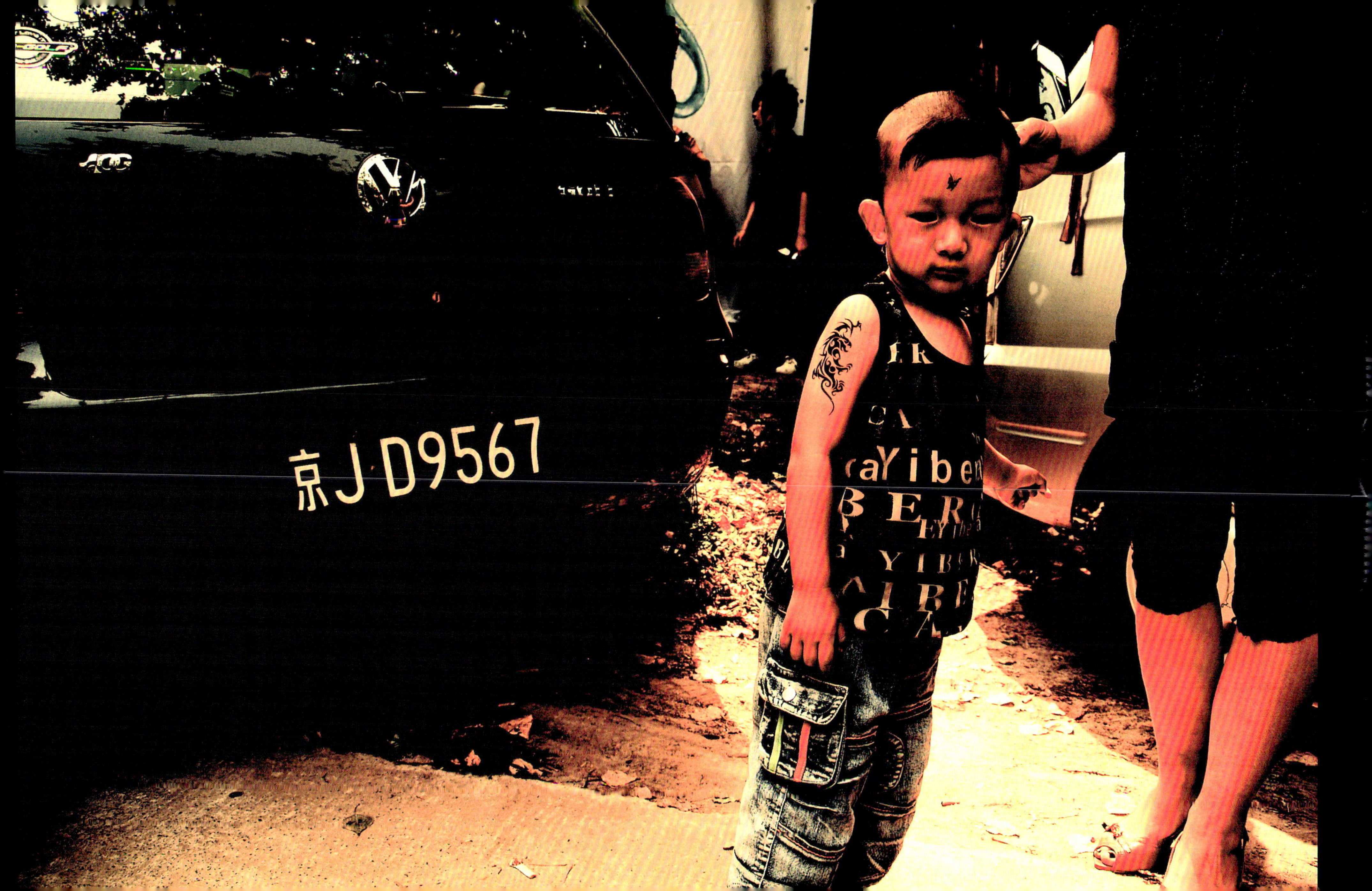
京J·D9567

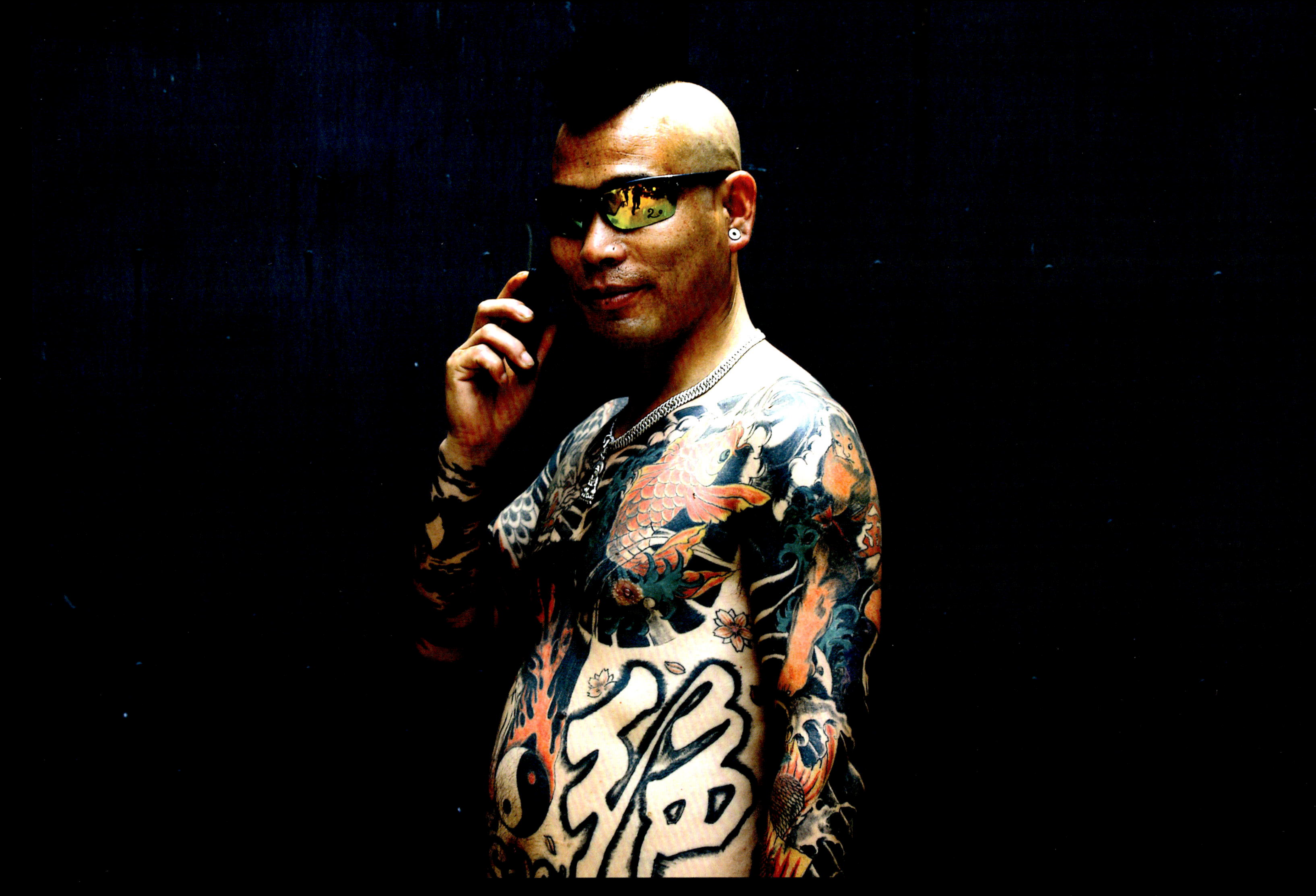

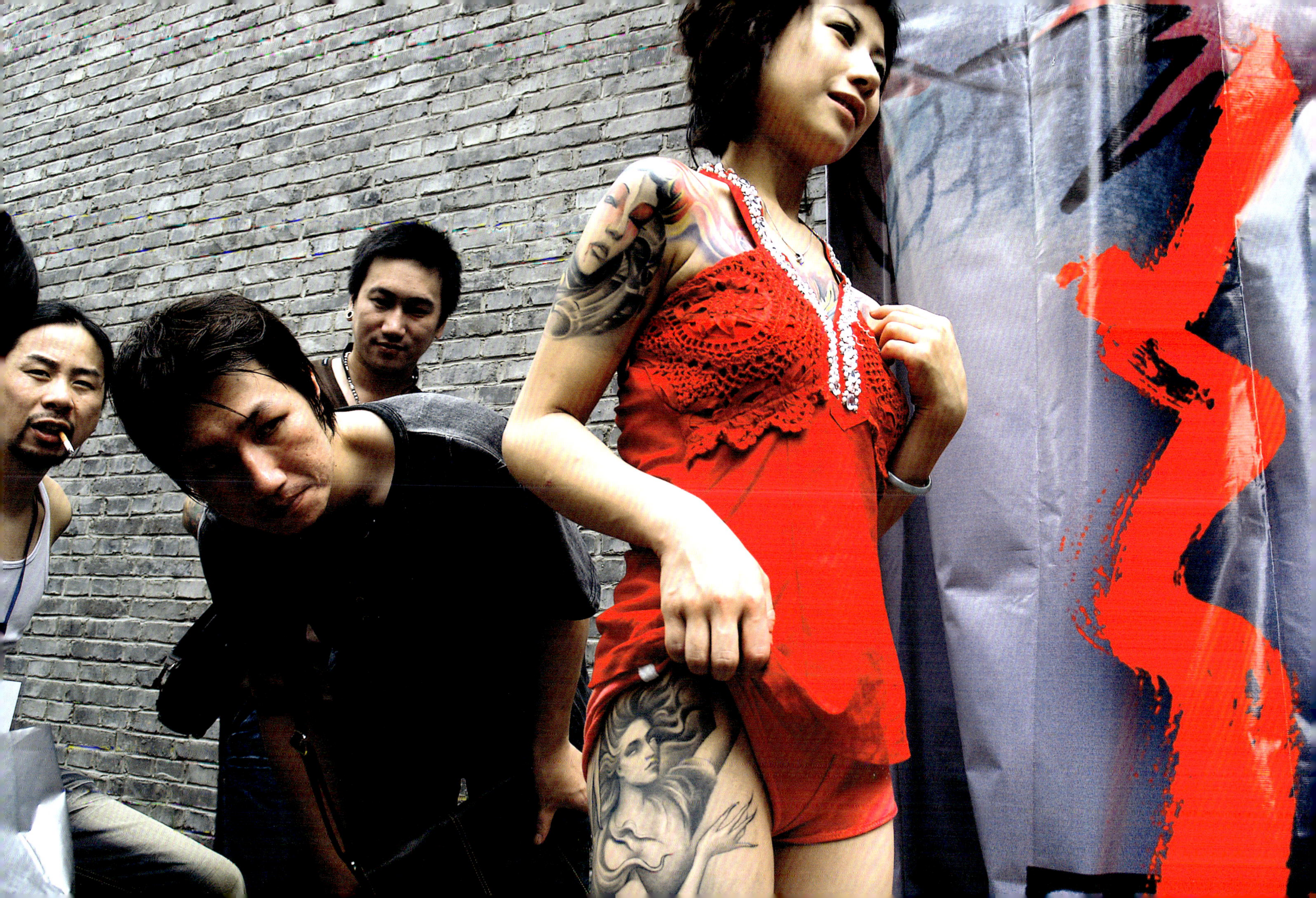

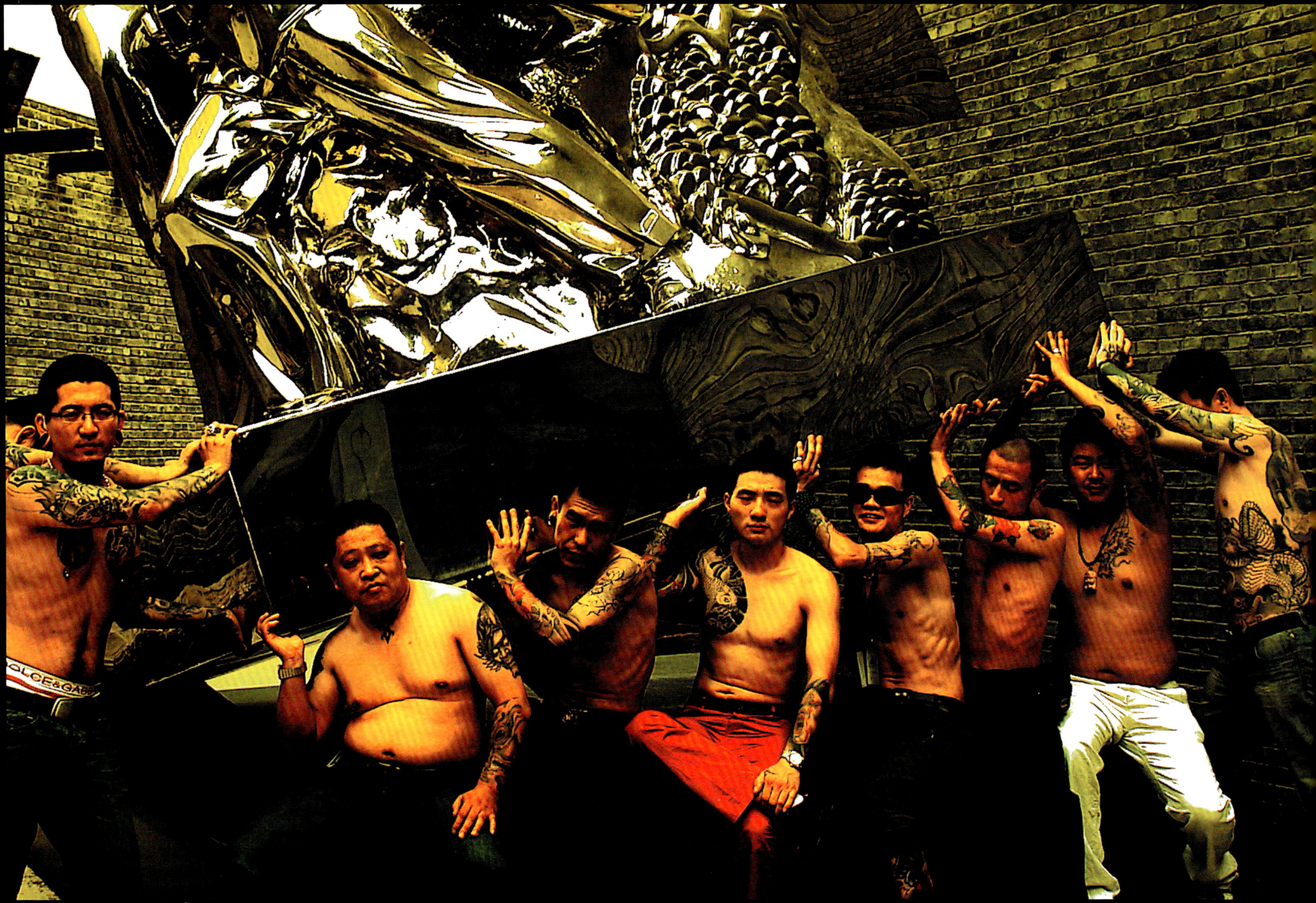
OLCE&GABB

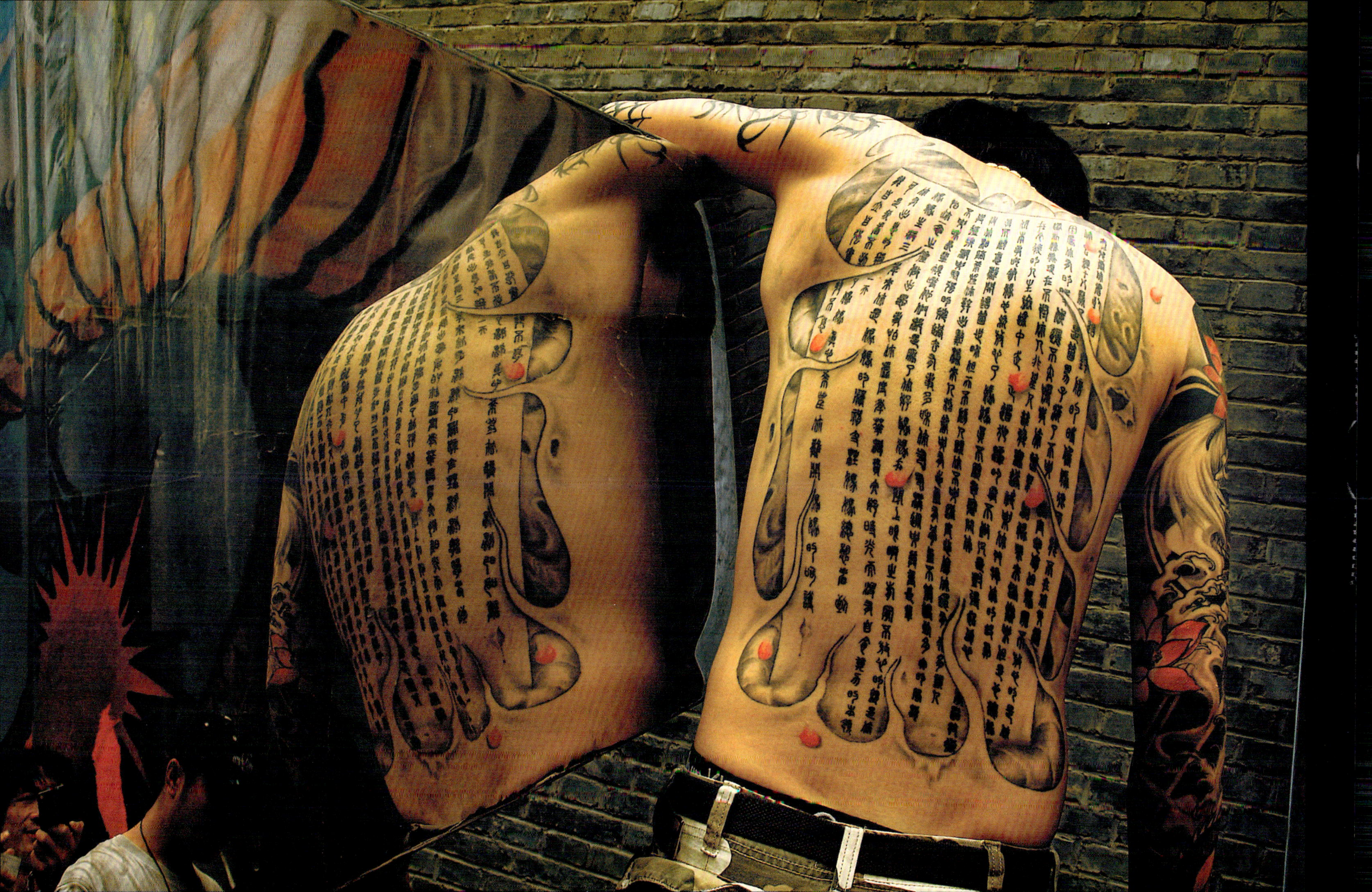

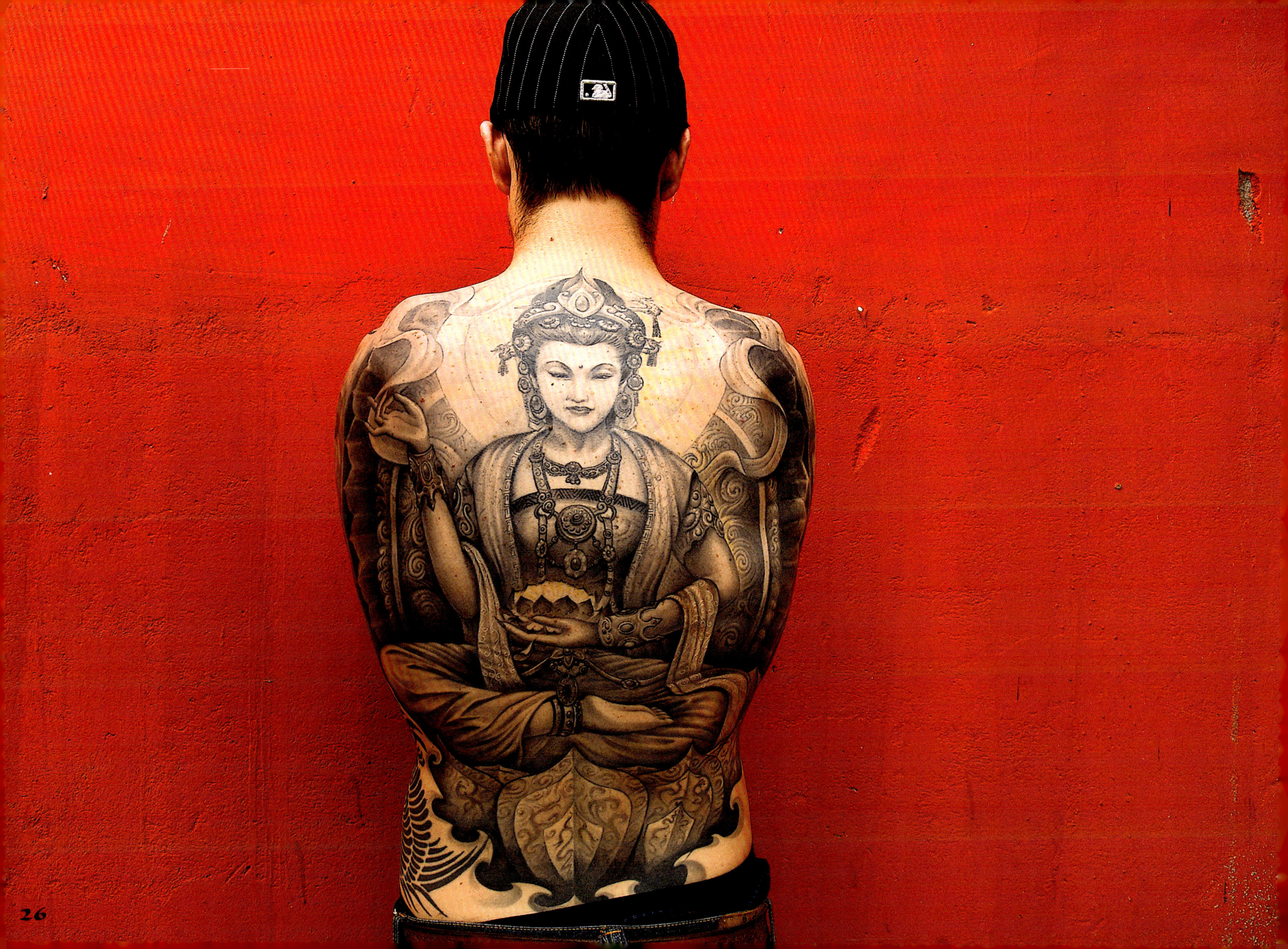

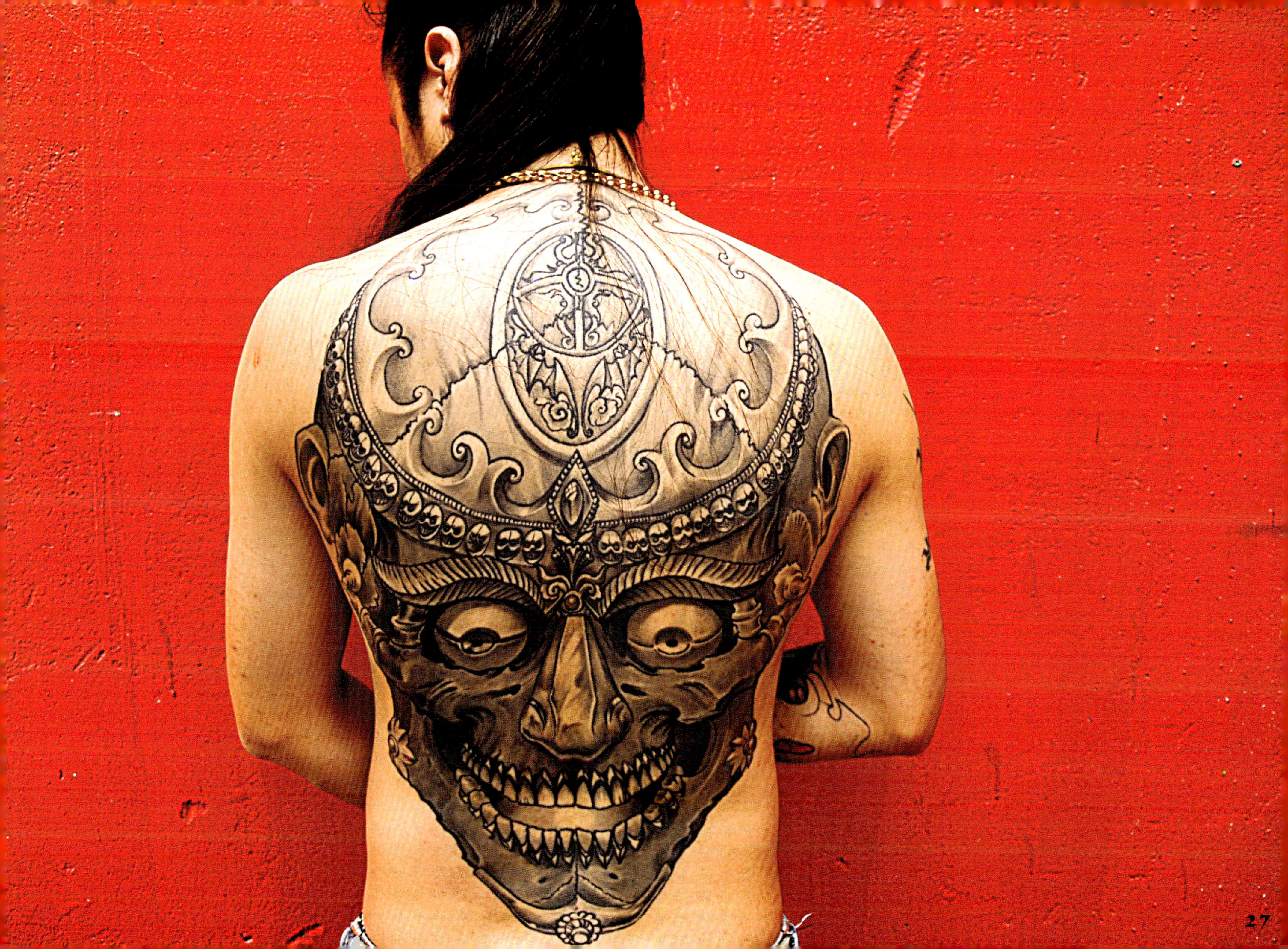

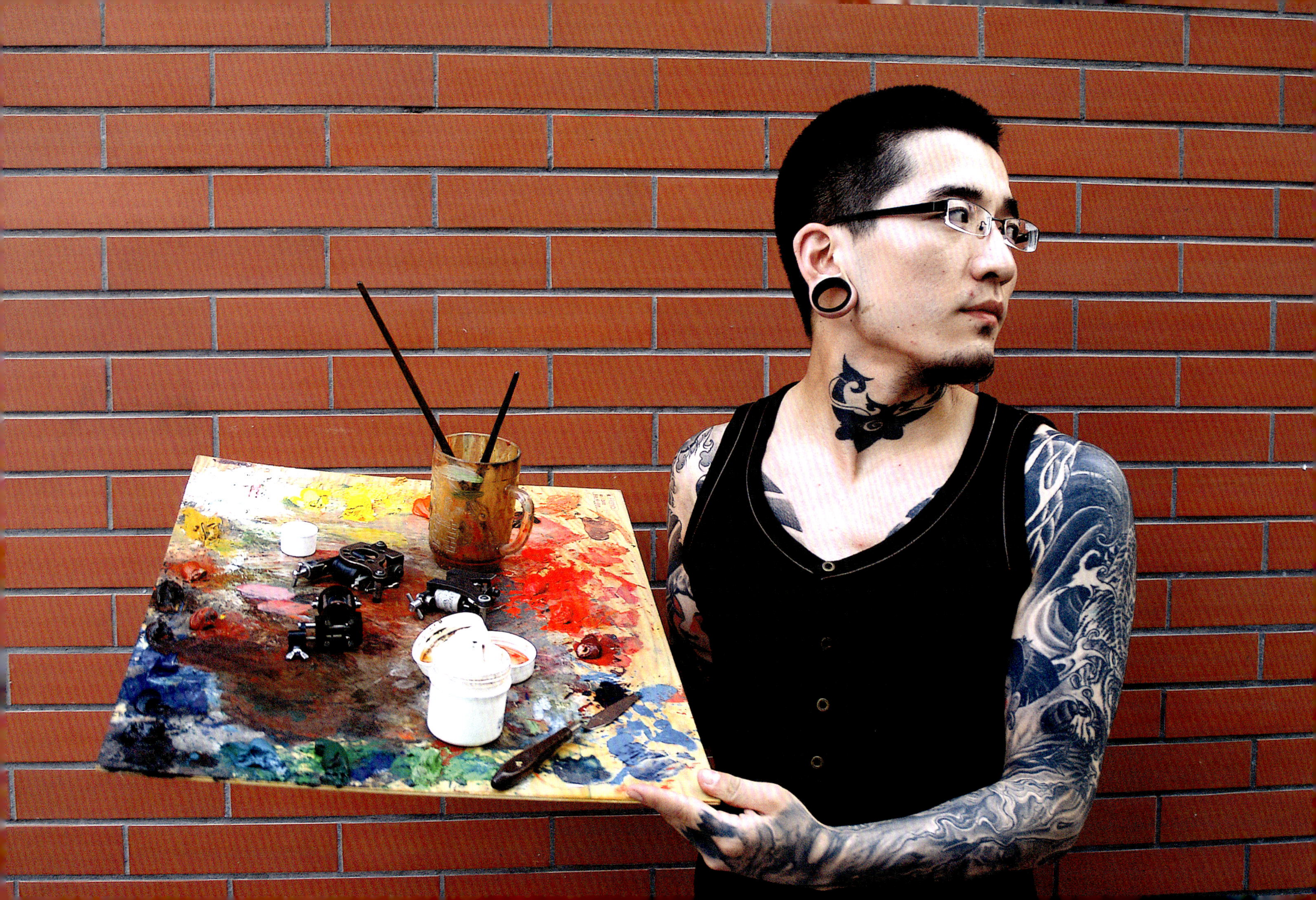

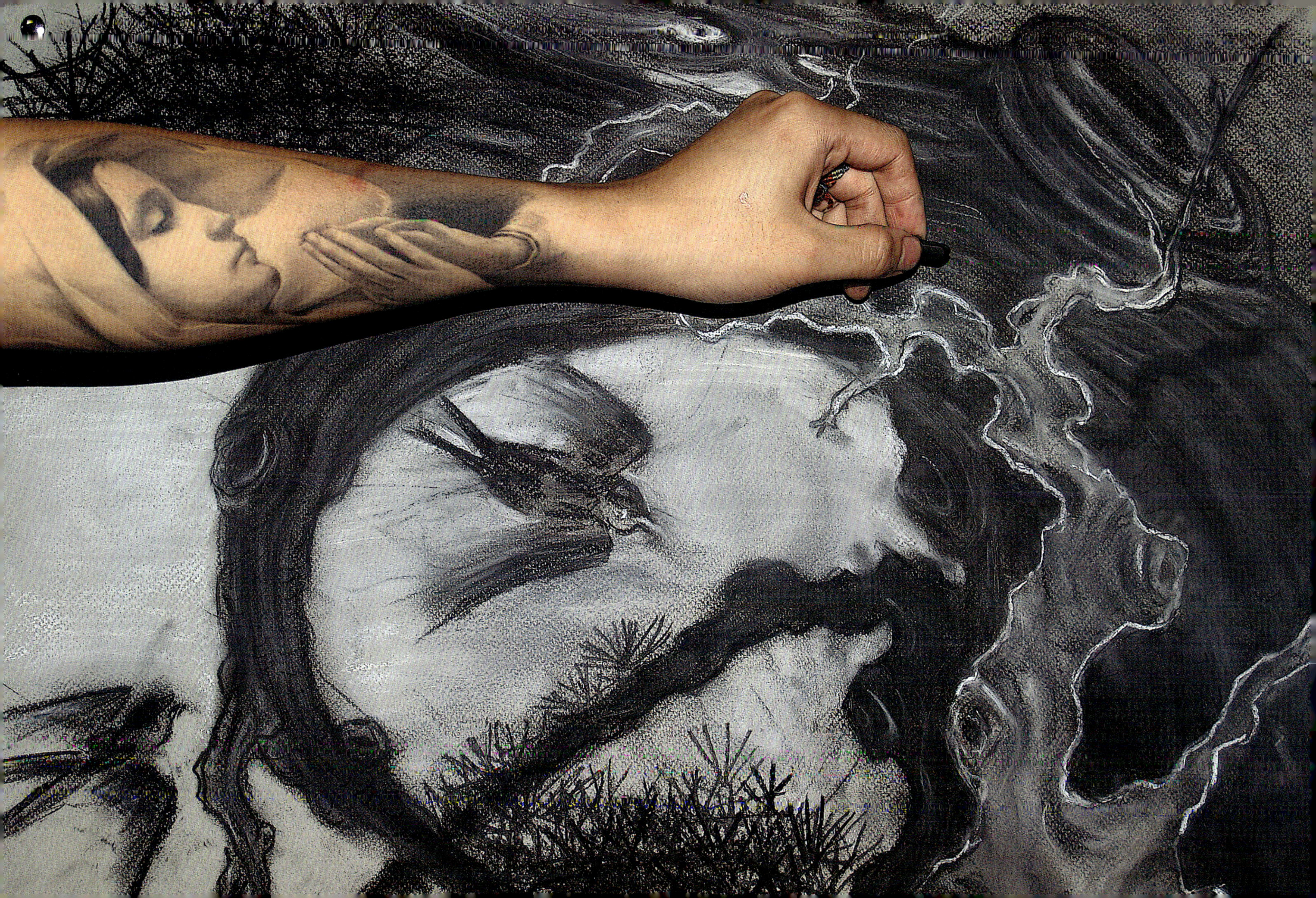

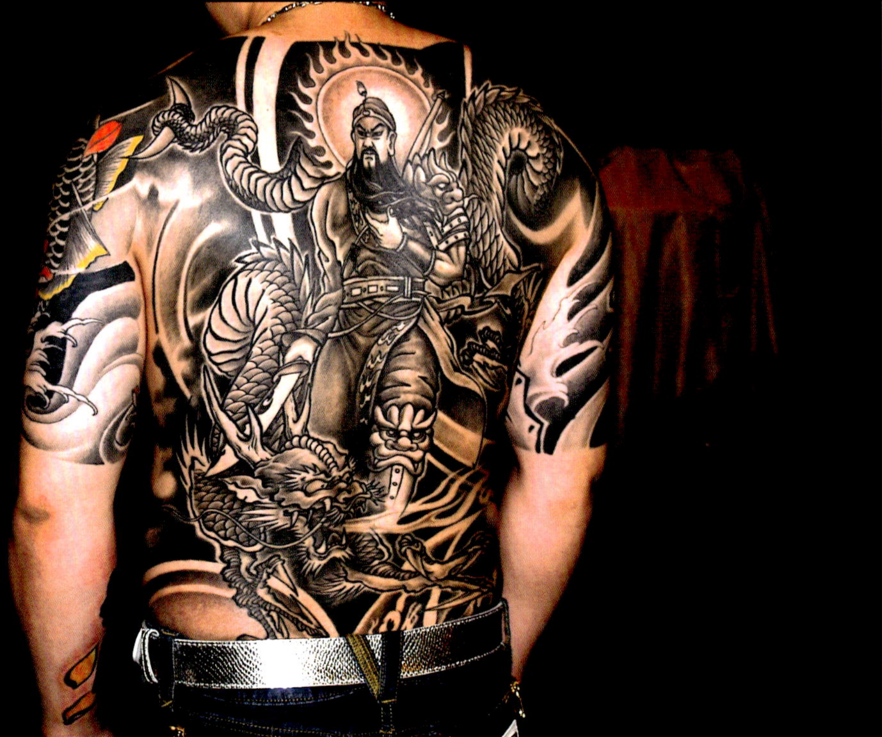

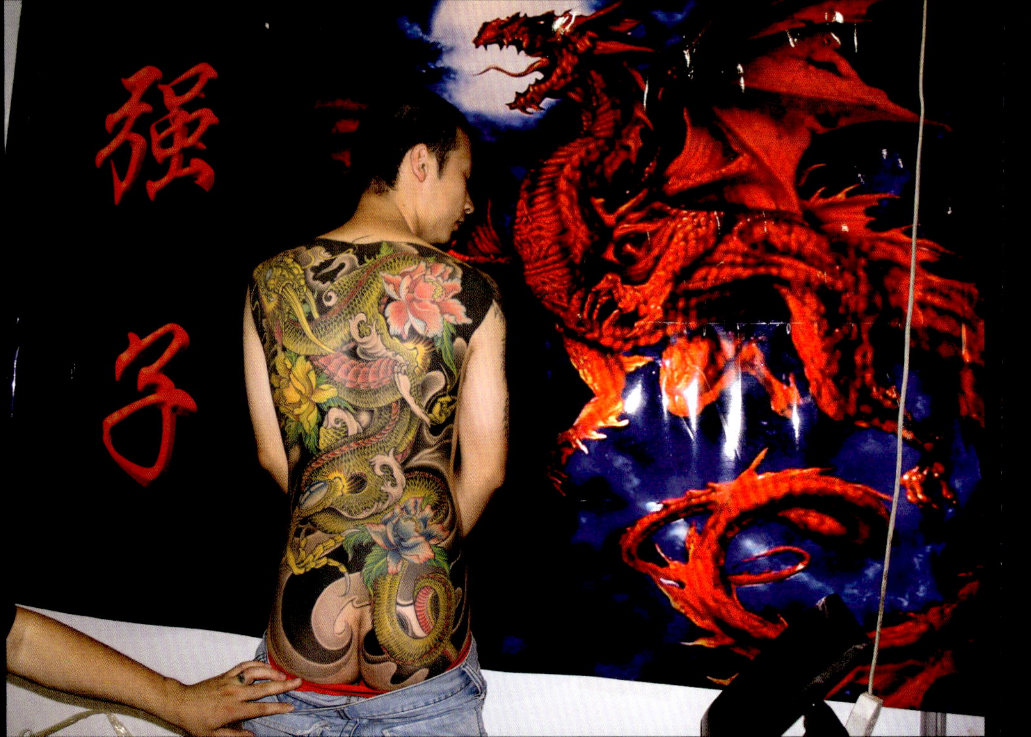
强子

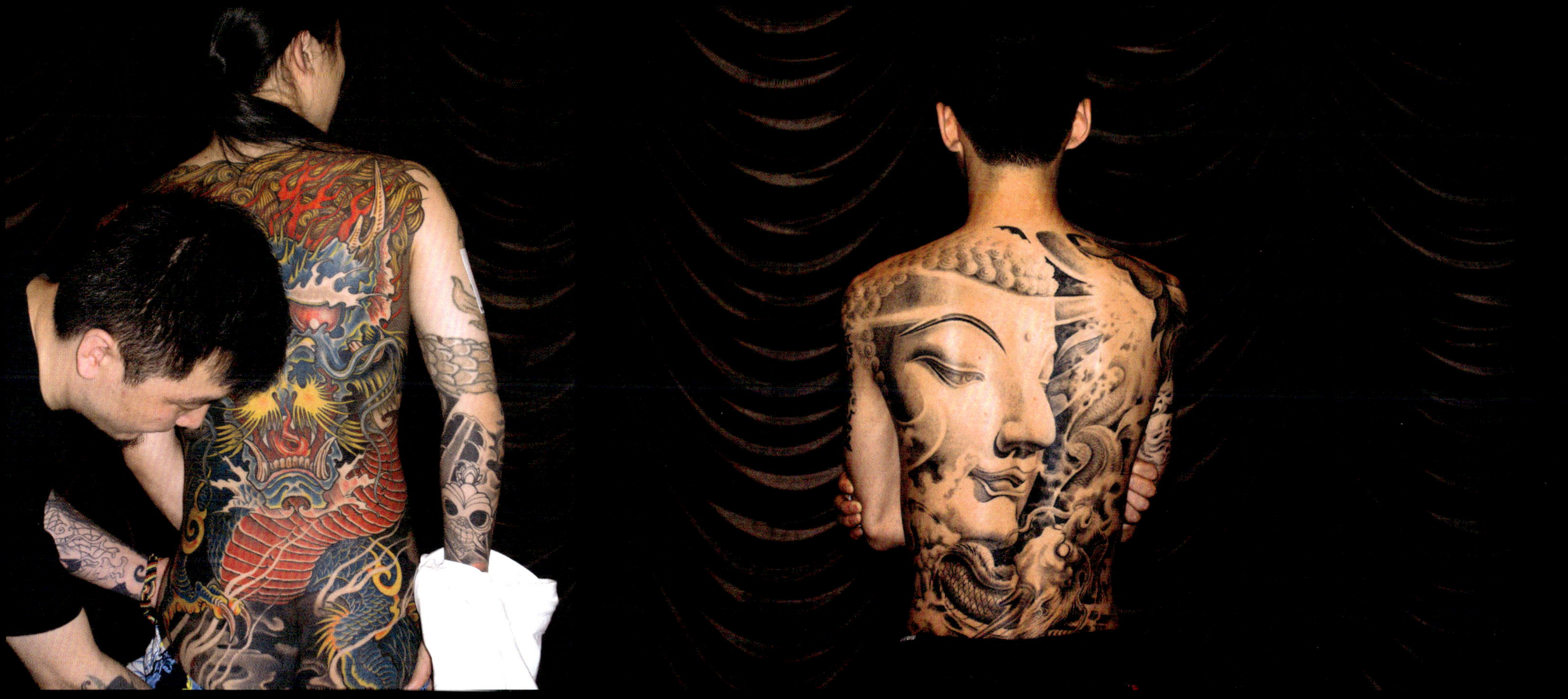

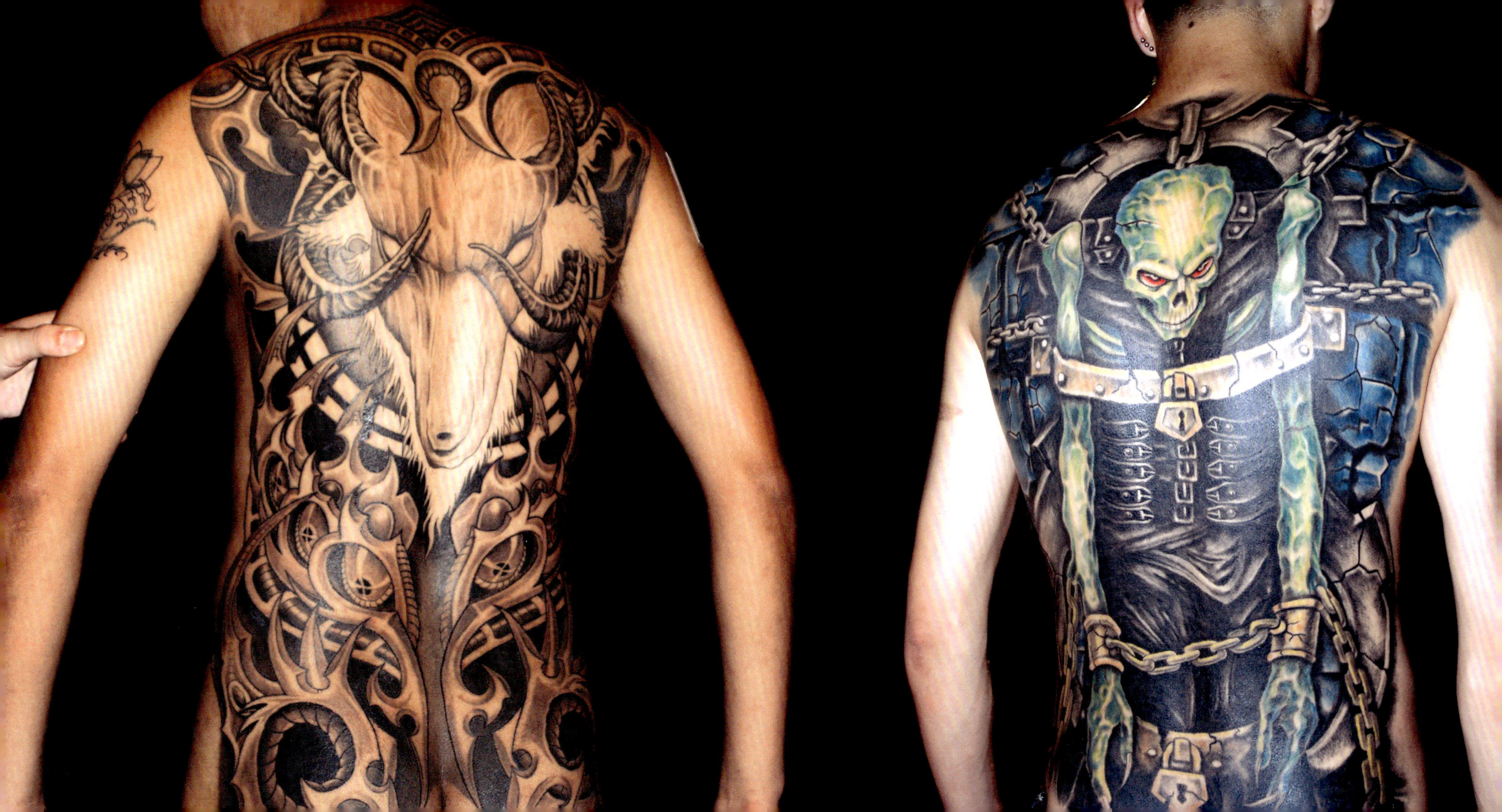

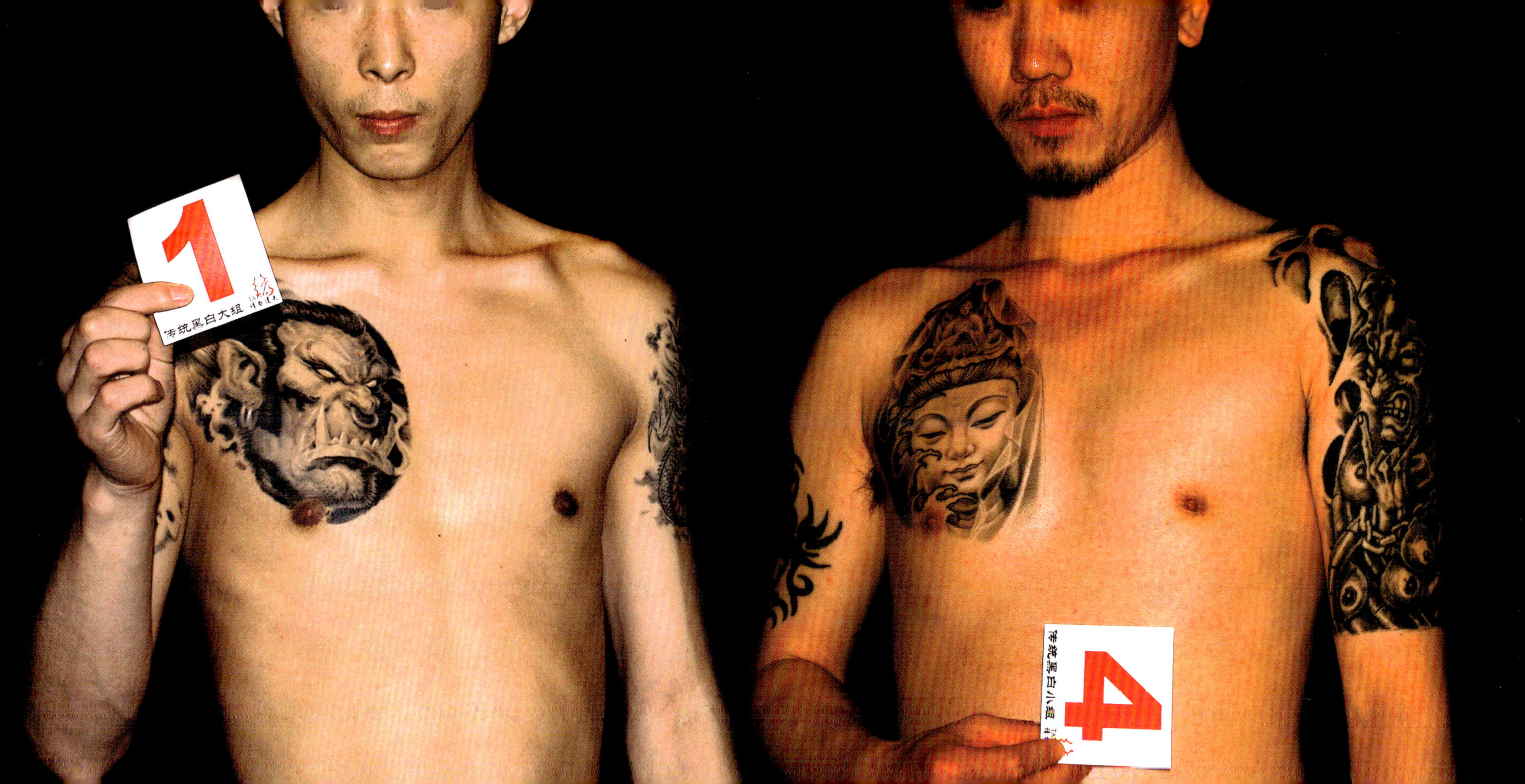
1
传统黑白大组
4
传统黑白小组

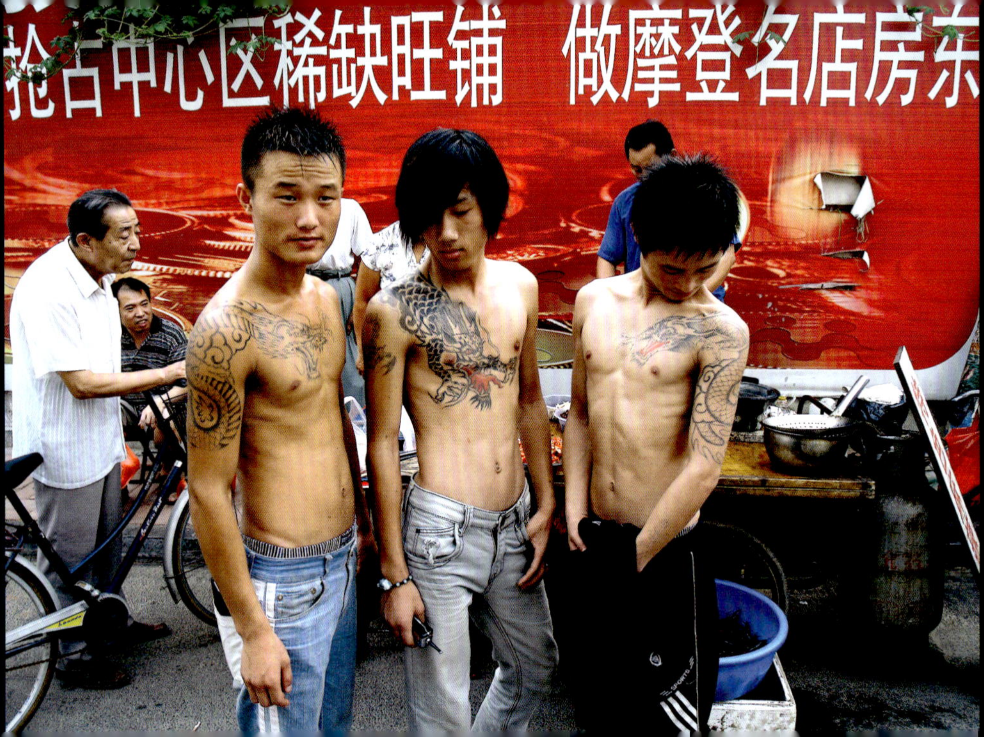
抢占中心区稀缺旺铺
做摩登名店房东

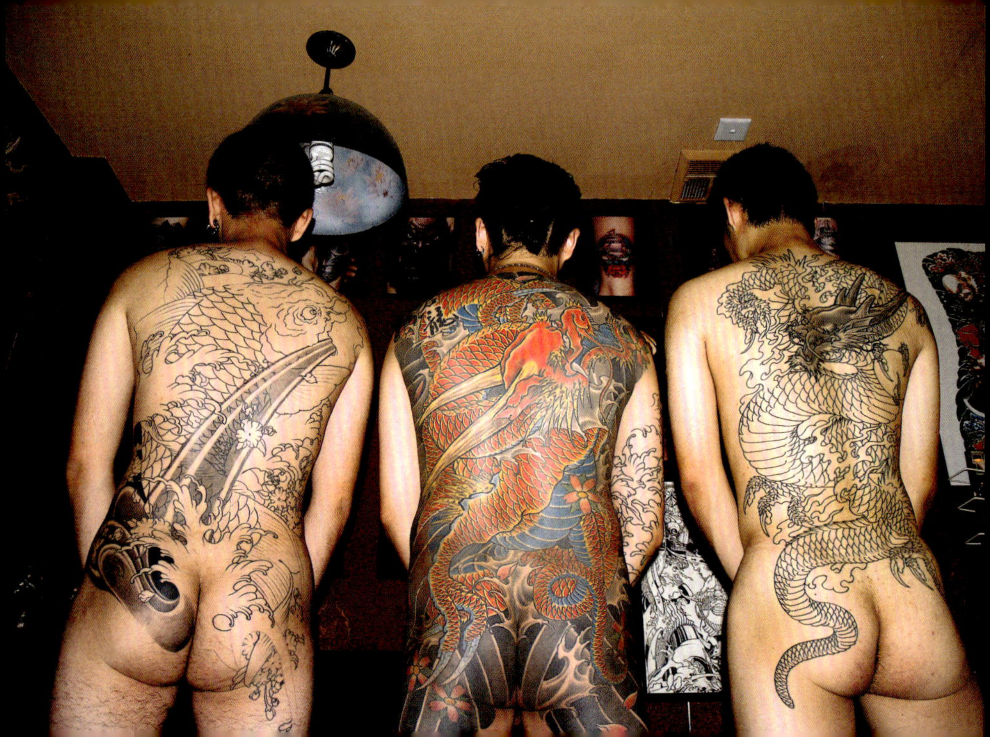

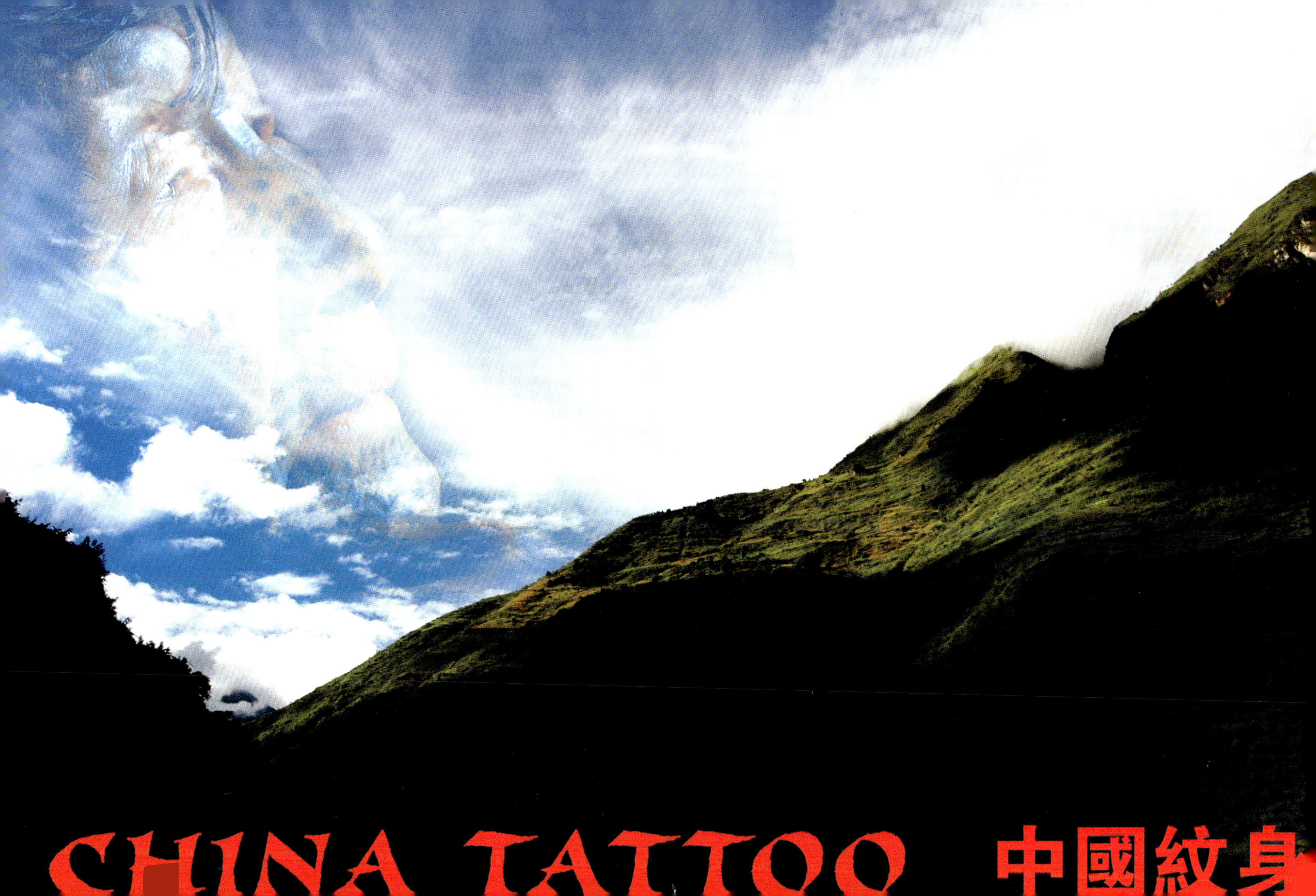
CHINA TATTOO 中國紋身

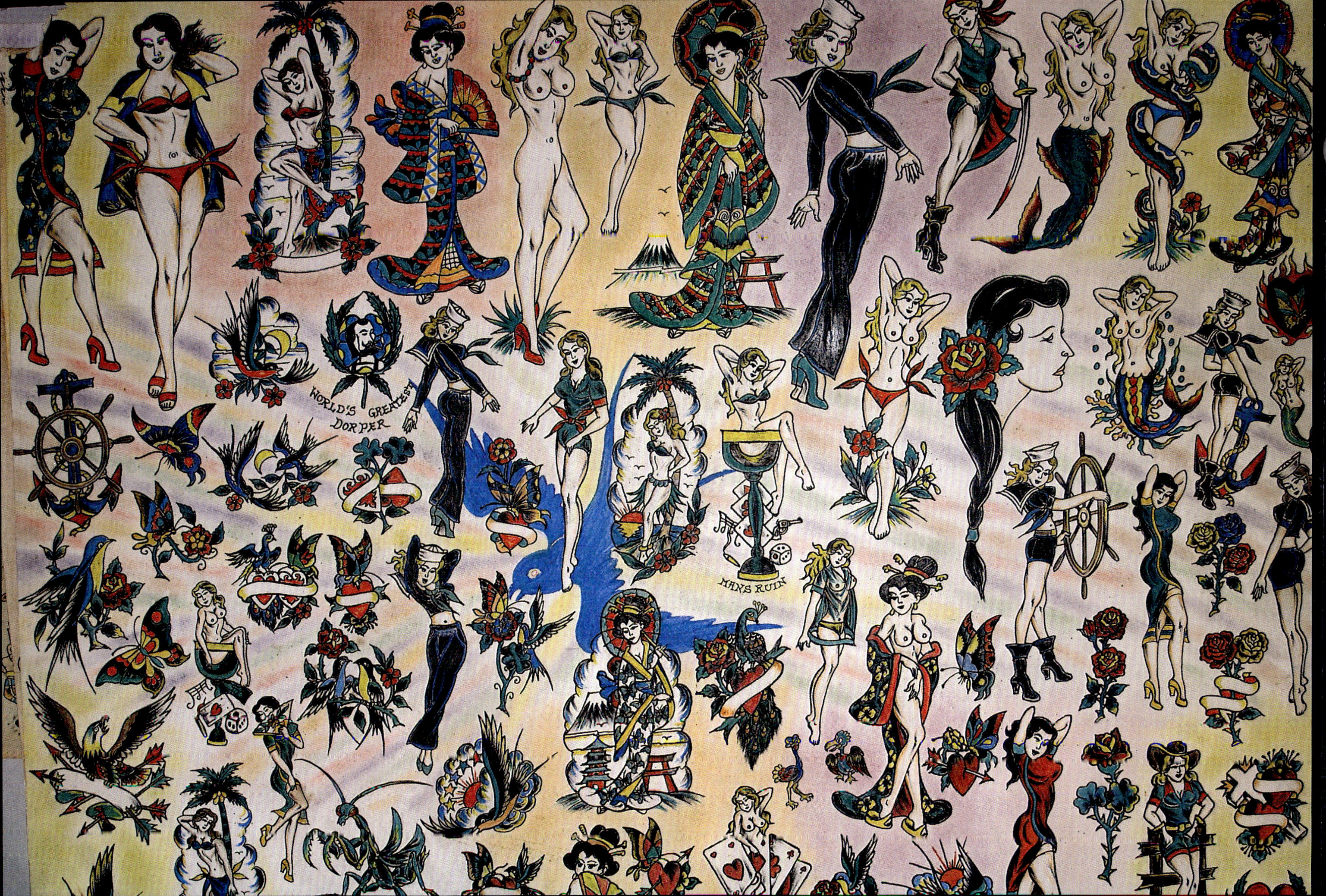
WORLD'S GREATEST
DORPER
MANS RUIN

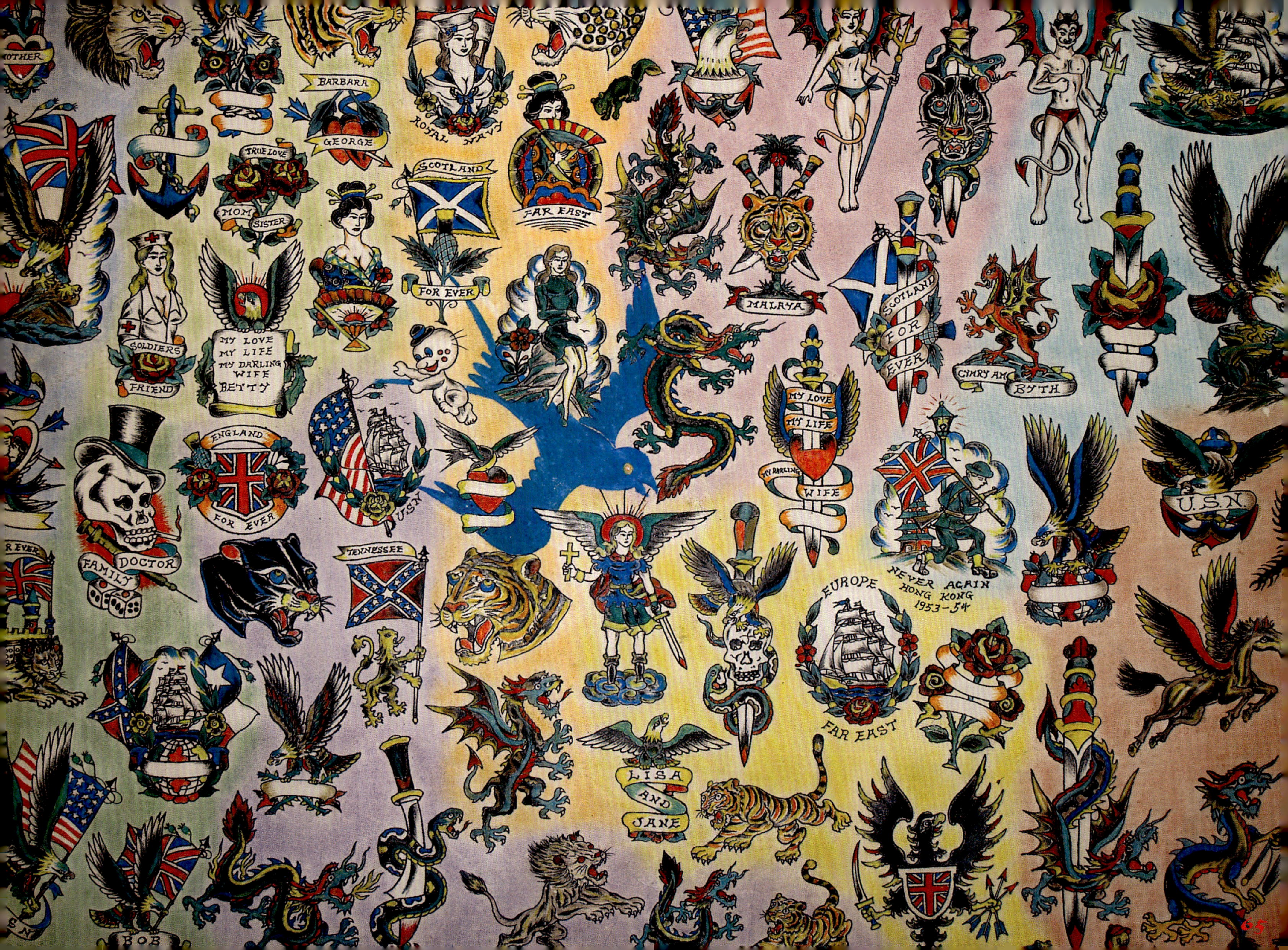
MOTHER
BARBARA
GEORGE
ROYAL NAVY
TRUE LOVE
MOM
SISTER
SCOTLAND
FOR EVER
FAR EAST
MALAYA
SOLDIERS
FRIEND
MY LOVE MY LIFE MY DARLING WIFE BETTY
SCOTLAND FOR EVER
CYMRU AM BYTH
MY LOVE MY LIFE
MY DARLING WIFE
ENGLAND FOR EVER
USN
TENNESSEE
U.S.N.
FAMILY
DOCTOR
EUROPE
NEVER AGAIN
HONG KONG
1953-54
FAR EAST
LISA AND JANE
BOB

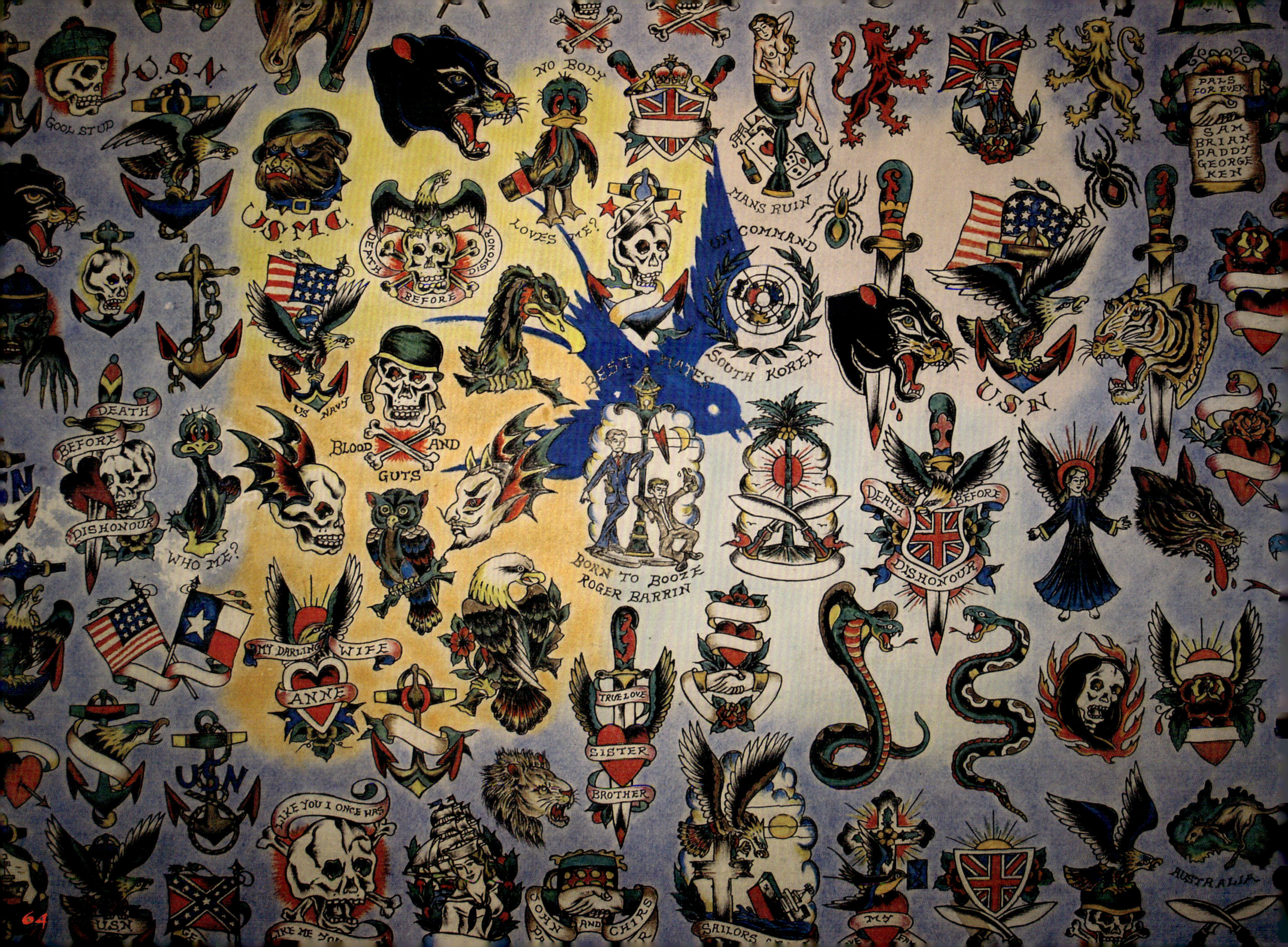

U.S.N.
U.S.M.C.
NO BODY
LOVES ME?
DEATH BEFORE DISHONOR
PALS FOR EVER
SAM
BRIAN
PADDY
GEORGE
KEN
MANS RUIN
UN COMMAND
SOUTH KOREA
BEST MATES
U.S.N.
US NAVY
BLOOD AND GUTS
DEATH BEFORE DISHONOUR
WHO ME?
BORN TO BOOZE
ROGER BARRIN
DEATH BEFORE DISHONOUR
MY DARLING WIFE
ANNE
TRUE LOVE
SISTER
BROTHER
USN
LIKE YOU I ONCE WAS
AUSTRALIA
USN
JOHN AND CHRIS
SAILORS
MY

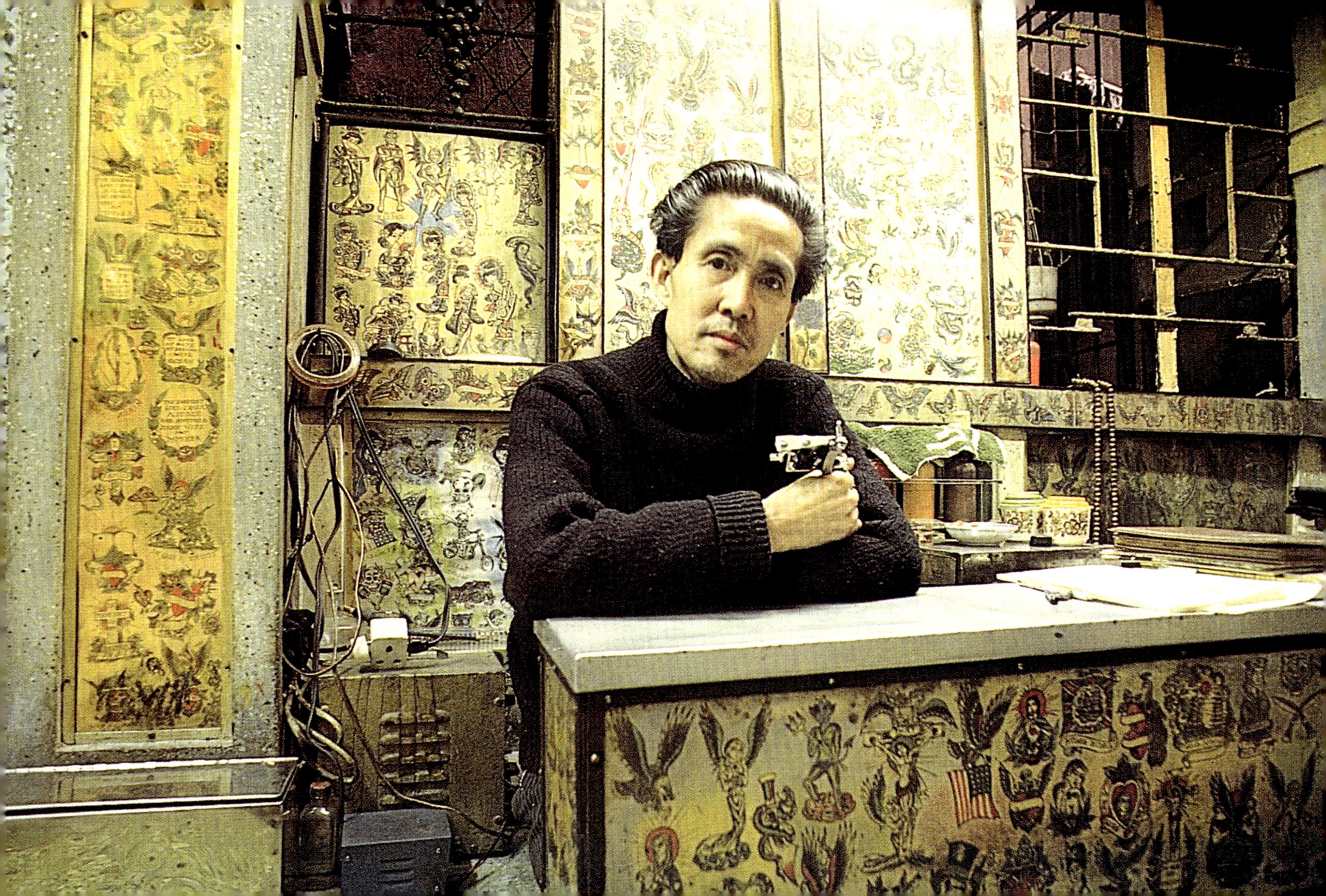

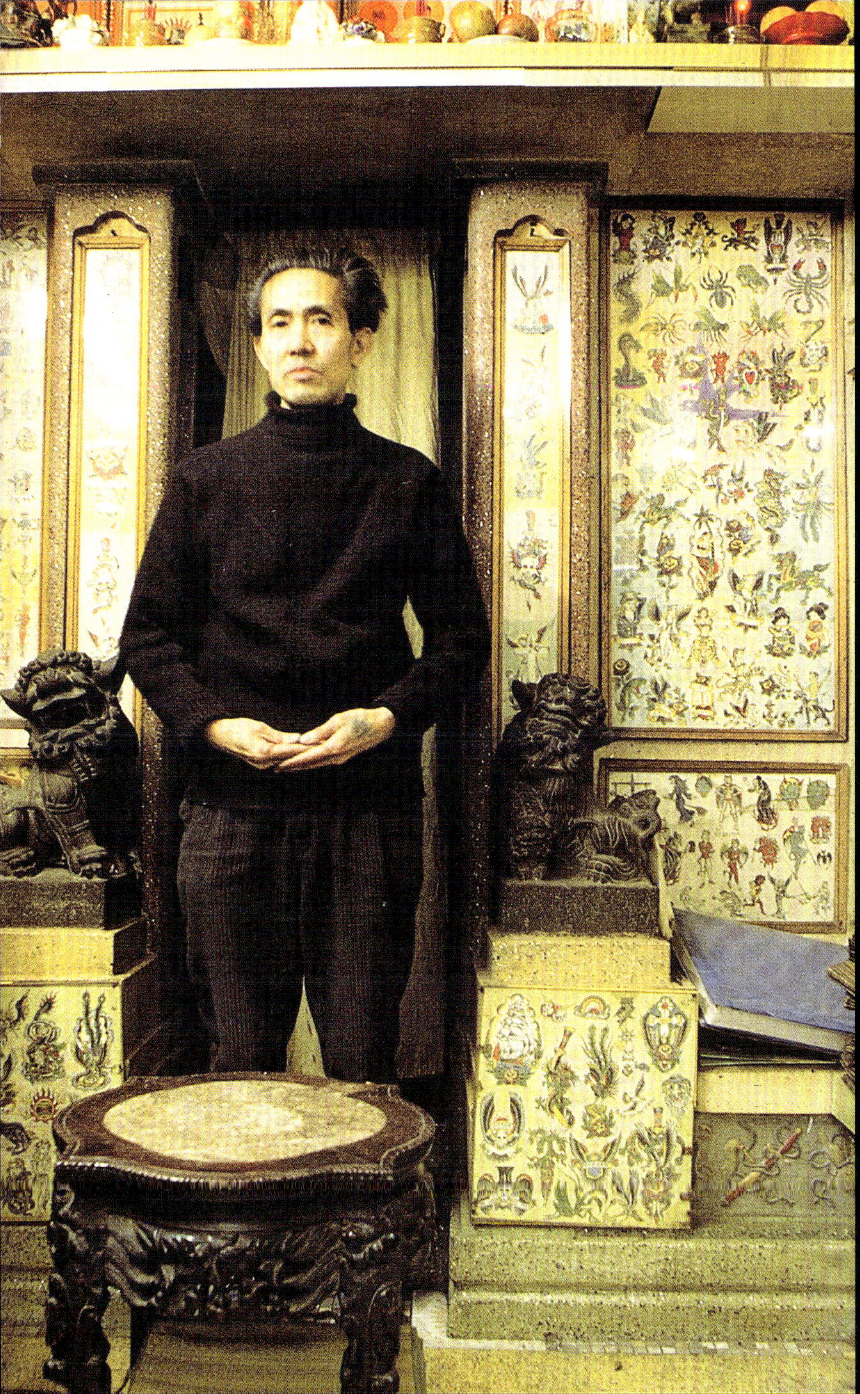

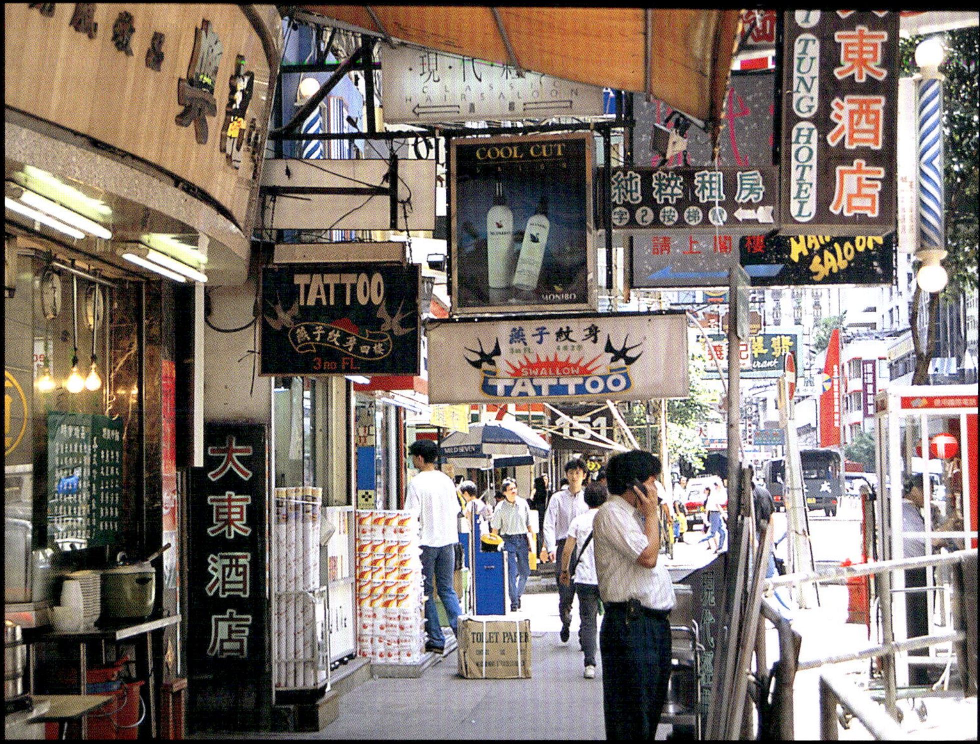

東酒店
TUNG HOTEL
COOL CUT
純粹租房
TATTOO
3rd FL.
燕子紋身
SWALLOW
TATTOO
大東酒店
TOILET PAPER

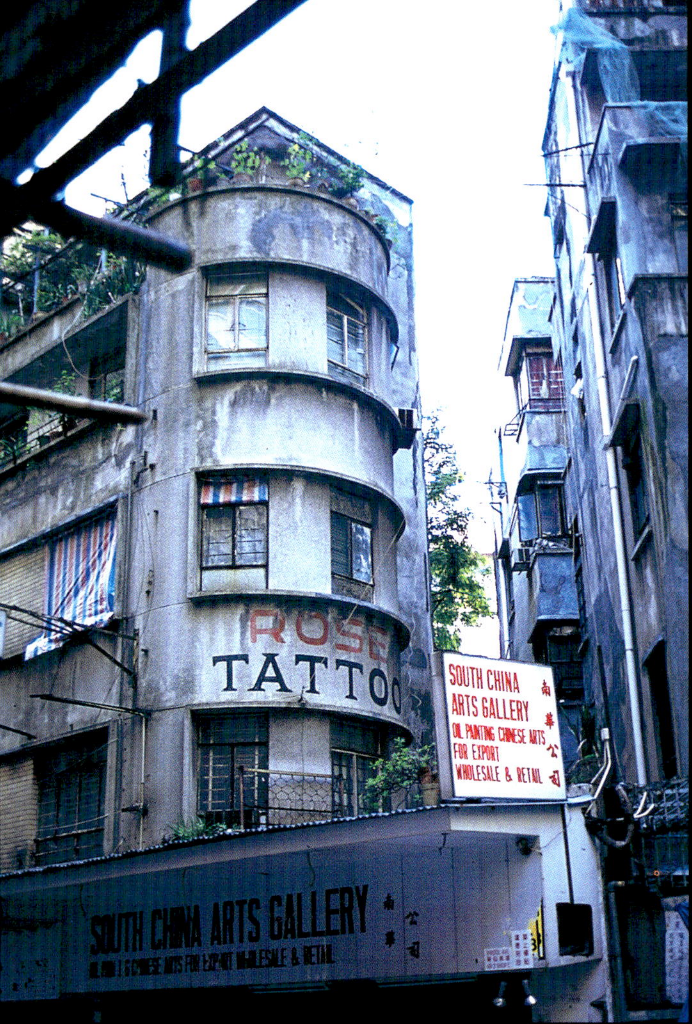
ROSE
TATTOO
SOUTH CHINA
ARTS GALLERY
OIL PAINTING CHINESE ARTS
FOR EXPORT
WHOLESALE & RETAIL
南華公司
SOUTH CHINA ARTS GALLERY

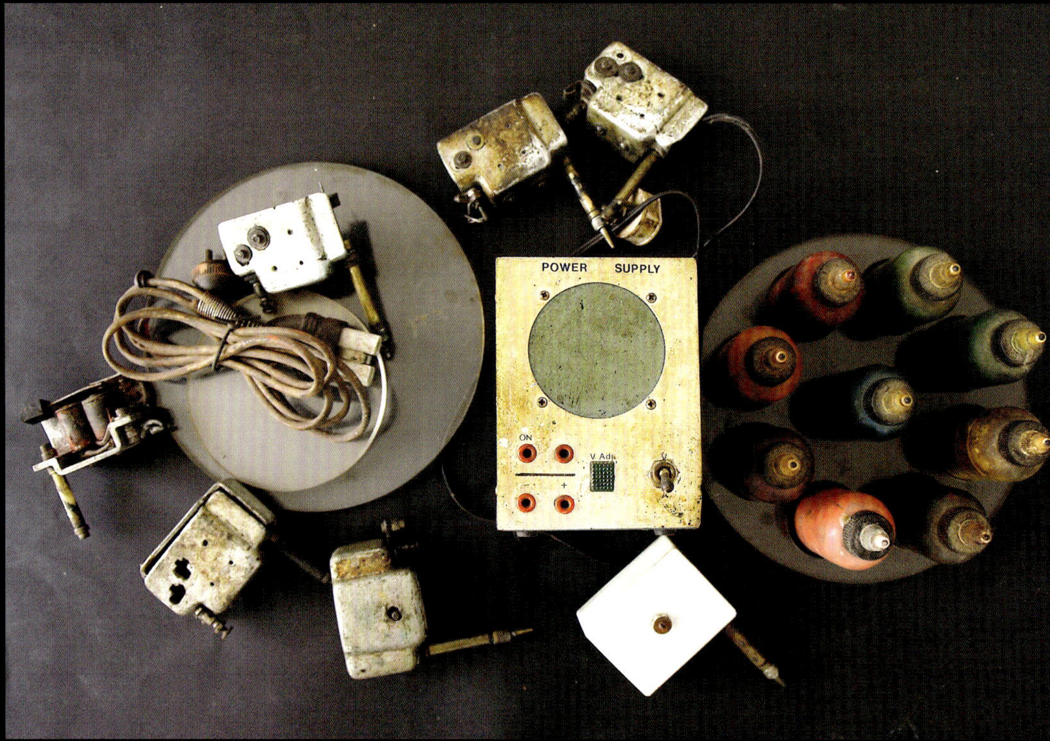
POWER SUPPLY
ON

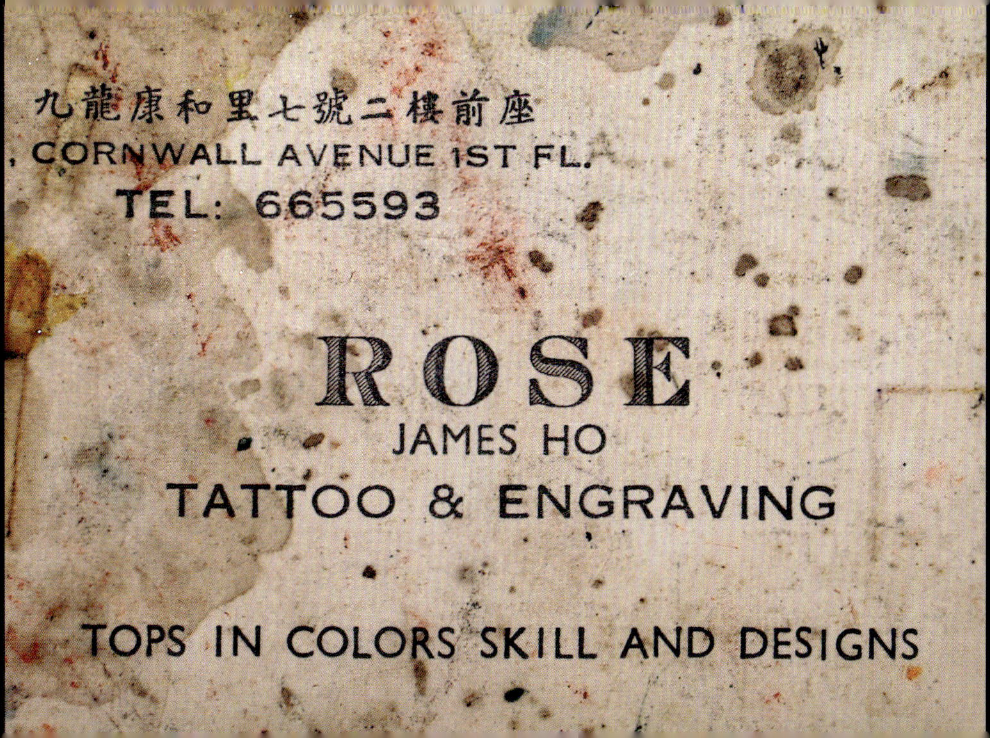
九龍康和里七號二樓前座
, CORNWALL AVENUE 1ST FL.
TEL: 665593

ROSE
JAMES HO
TATTOO & ENGRAVING

TOPS IN COLORS SKILL AND DESIGNS

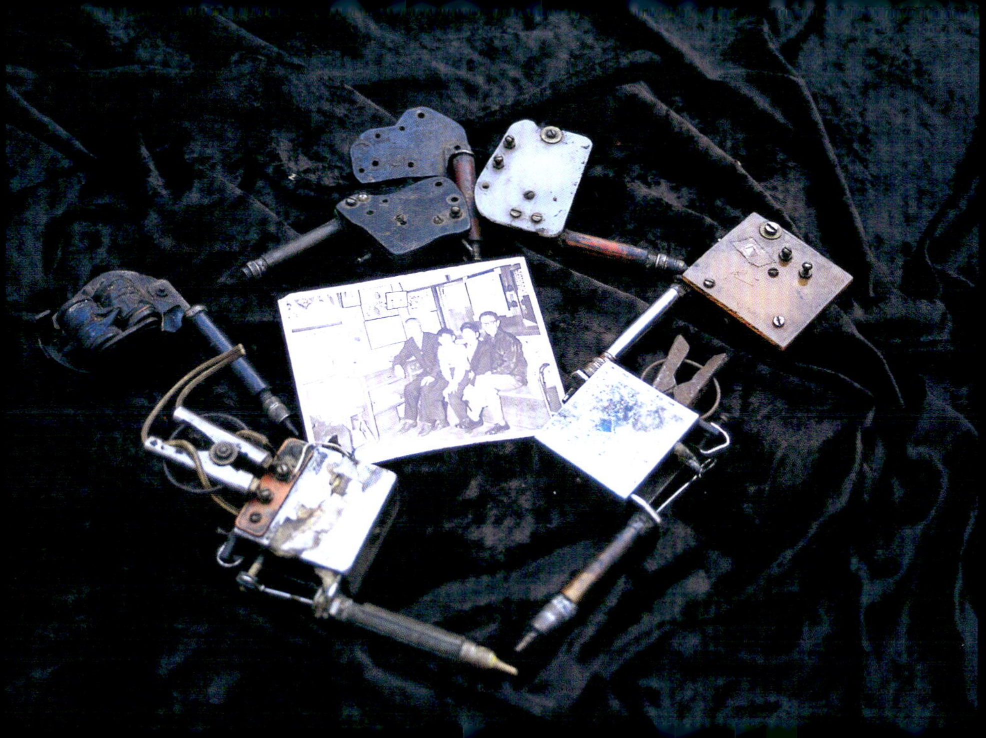

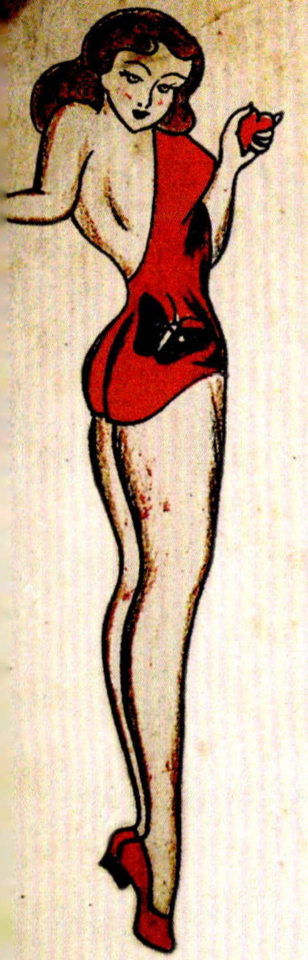

香港纹身

20世纪40年代引进香港的电动纹身，是在一个不同寻常的情况下发生的。在这之前，任何人想纹身都要先找到纹身师的秘密服务地点，他们通常会用竹针或缝衣针手绘出简单的图案。那时候纹身还是一种受黑道分子保护的地下活动 。

不过，当一个年轻的中国水手登上一艘从南中国海出发的商船后，情况很快就发生了变化。

这个人是一位年轻的工程师，名叫 James Ho，1903年出生于上海。在完成学业之后，他决定做一名航海工程师，但是1940年，他所服务的那艘船却被日本的潜艇击沉。

他抓住船的残骸，奇迹般生还了，随后被一艘美国的驱逐舰救起，并被放在印度的加尔各答港。

在康复期间，James对许多水手的纹身着迷。复原后，他找到了这些纹身店，并仔细观察纹身师如何用电木、自行车阀来自制工具，并通过电池驱动来创作纹身。

在获得类似的材料之后，他自己制作了一些纹身机，回国后，他决定对它们做一些改进和完善。这一次他让市电来驱动它们工作。

那时纹身在中国还不是一个有利可图的行当，不过James很快就发现，对成千上万奔赴各个战区的军事人员来说，香港是他们的家，这使得香港成为靠这项手艺赚钱的理想地点。

他离开上海回到香港的家中，并于1946年开设了香港第一家正式的纹身店。他将自己的店命名为“玫瑰纹身”。尽管他是一个经验丰富的工程师，但却缺少艺术细胞，因此他必须找到能工巧匠和他一起打拼。

一天在他去店里的路上，他注意到一个年轻人在街边忙着擦鞋子。他看到旁边的便道被一些粉笔画装饰得很漂亮，于是他就驻足欣赏起来。当他知道这个擦鞋的年轻人便是这些粉笔画的作者时，他毫不迟疑地把这份工作给了他。这个年轻人叫Lai Johnson，刚刚离开大陆的家，到这里来寻找更好的机会。后来当他于1963年开了自己的纹身店时，他为自己赢得了“燕子”这样一个尊号。

James 还找到了其他一些艺术家在玫瑰纹身工作，像Pinky Yan、Ricky和Benny Tsoi 等等。后来他们所有人都开设了自己的纹身店。今天James 的儿子Jimmy Ho在九龙的某处新址延续着父亲开创的传统。而Ricky 过去40年都在湾仔埋头苦干。

今天玫瑰和燕子的纹身店都不复存在，但是燕子的作品全集和其设备如今却在法国的纹身画廊中展出。

一本展示燕子全部纹身设计的画册以及他的自传也很快将要出版。

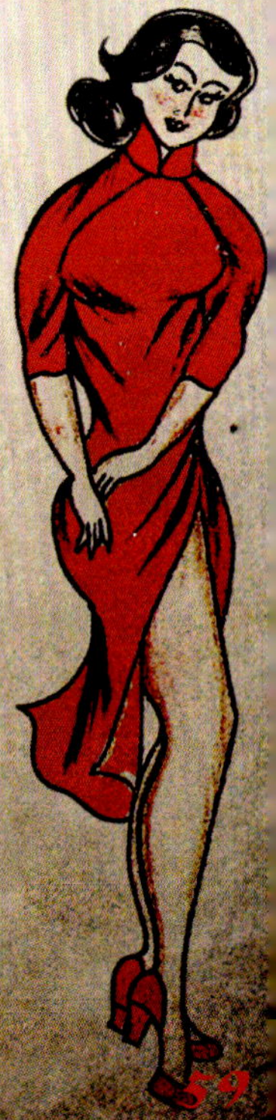

Hong Kong Tattoo

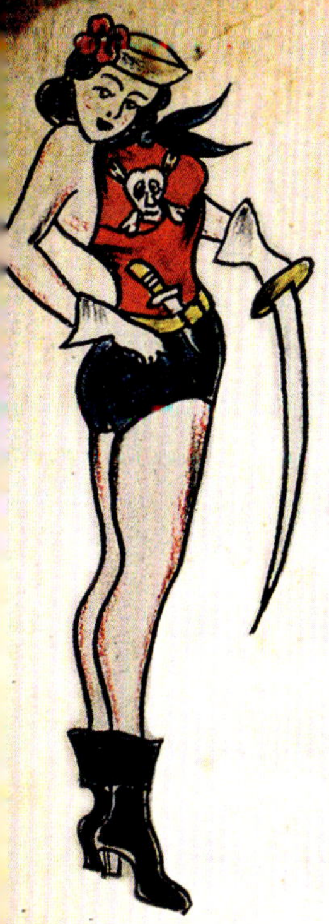

The introduction of electric tattooing to Hong Kong in the 1940's occurred in the most unusual circumstances. Prior to this time anyone wishing to obtain a tattoo would have to seek the clandestine services of a tattooist who would apply simple designs by hand, using a bamboo stick and sewing needles.In those days tattooing was an underground activity, normally patronized by gang members.
All that changed however, when a young Chinese sailor boarded a merchant vessel and set out on the South China Seas. The person in question was a young engineer, named James Ho, who was born in Shanghai, in 1903. After completing his studies, he decided to become a marine engineer, but in 1940, the ship he was sailing on was attacked and sunk by a Japanese submarine.
Miraculously he survived by clinging onto wreckage and was picked up by an American destroyer, which landed him in the port of Calcutta, India.
During his convalescence, James became fascinated by the tattoos that many of the sailors wore. When he recovered, James found his way to the Indian tattoo studios where he observed how tattoos were actually created using simple home made devices constructed from doorbells, bakelite and bicycle valves, and powered by batteries.
After obtaining similar materials, he constructed a number of machines and when he returned to his native land, he decided to improve and refine them. This time they worked using mains electricity.
Since tattooing was not a viable activity in China at that time, James quickly realised that Hong Kong , which was home to thousands of military personnel en route to the continuing war zones, would make an ideal location for a lucrative business. He left Shanghai and arrived with his family in Hong Kong where he opened the first official tattoo studio in 1946. He named it Rose Tattoo. Although he was a skilled engineer, he had little artistic talent, which meant that he had to find more capable people to work alongside him.
One day as he walked to his studio, he noticed a young man busily polishing shoes on a street pavement. He also stopped to admire the chalk illustrations that decorated the sidewalk nearby. Once he discovered that the shoeshine boy was responsible for these drawings, he immediately offered him a job. The boy was named, Lai Johnson who had recently left his home in China to seek more lucrative work. He later became known as Swallow when he opened up his own studio in 1963.
James also found a number of other artists who worked at Rose tattoo: Pinky Yan, Ricky, Benny Tsoi, all of whom later set up their own studios. Today his son Jimmy Ho continues the tradition in a new location in Kowloon, and Ricky has been working in Wan Chai for the past 40 years.
The Rose and Swallow studios no longer exist, but the entire Swallow collection and equipment has now been installed in a tattoo gallery in France.

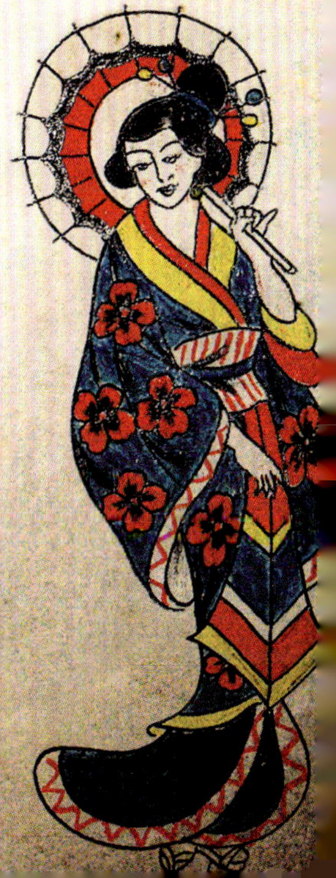

A publication showing the entire range of the designs created by Swallow, together with his biography will be published shortly.

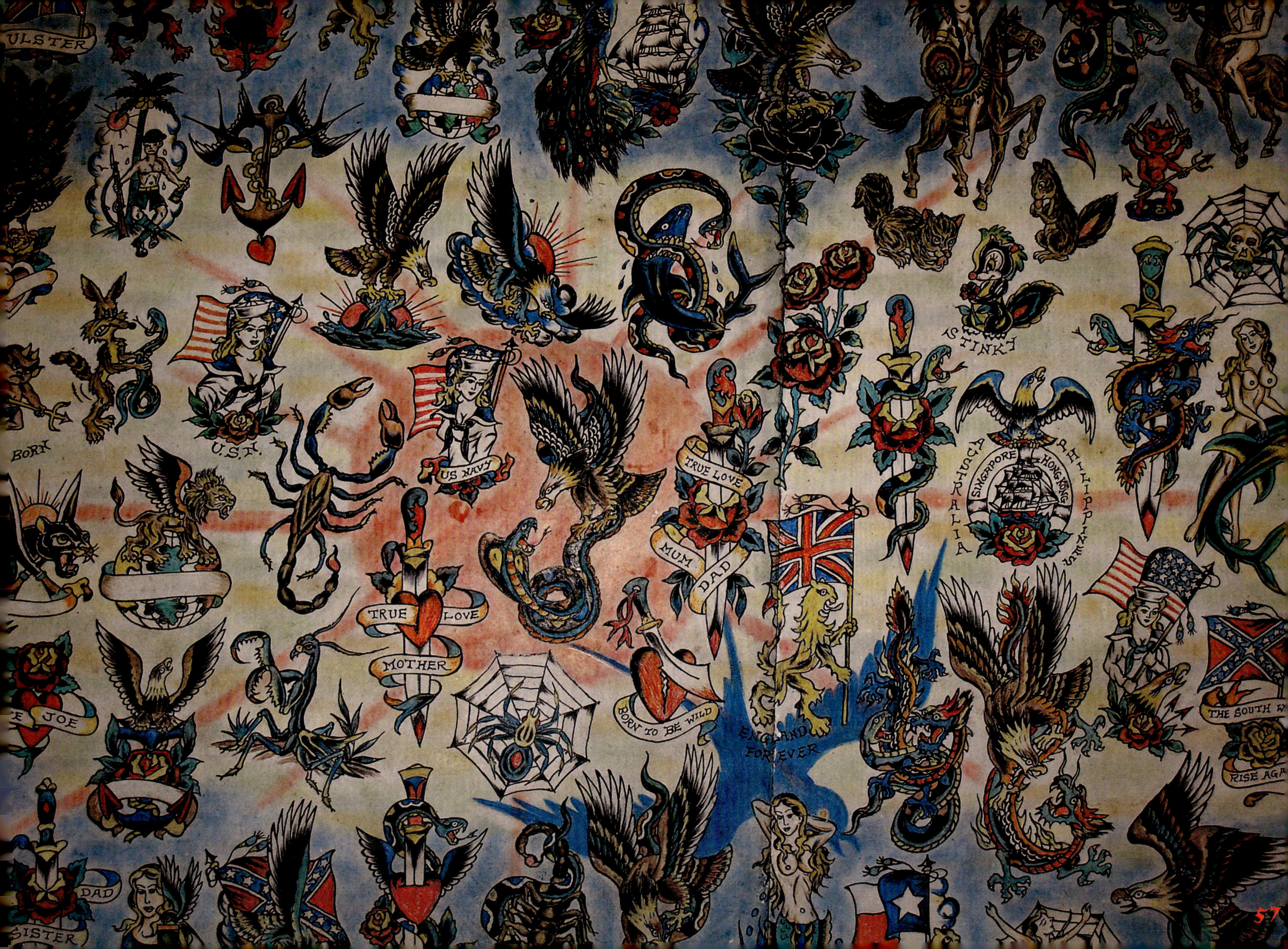
ULSTER
U.S.N.
BORN
US NAVY
TRUE LOVE
MUM
DAD
STINKY
AUSTRALIA
SINGAPORE
HONG KONG
PHILIPPINES
TRUE
LOVE
MOTHER
JOE
BORN TO BE WILD
ENGLAND FOREVER
THE SOUTH W
RISE AGA
DAD
SISTER

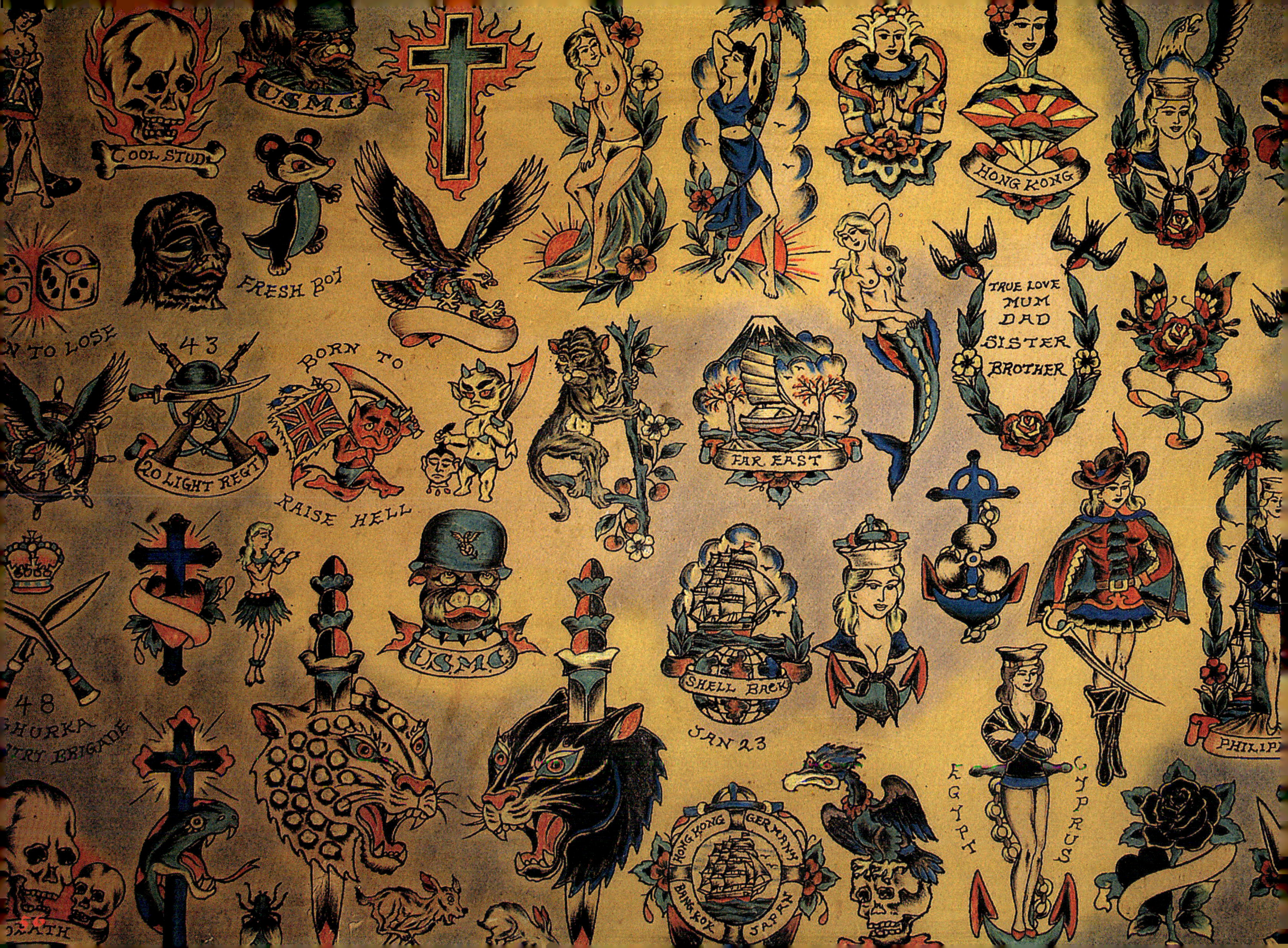

COOL STUD
U.S.M.C.
FRESH BOY
N TO LOSE
43
BORN TO
RAISE HELL
20 LIGHT REGT
TRUE LOVE
MUM
DAD
SISTER
BROTHER
HONG KONG
FAR EAST
U.S.M.C.
SHELL BACK
JAN 23
48
GHURKA
TRY BRIGADE
PHILIP
HONG KONG
GERMANY
BANGKOK
JAPAN
EGYPT
CYPRUS
DEATH

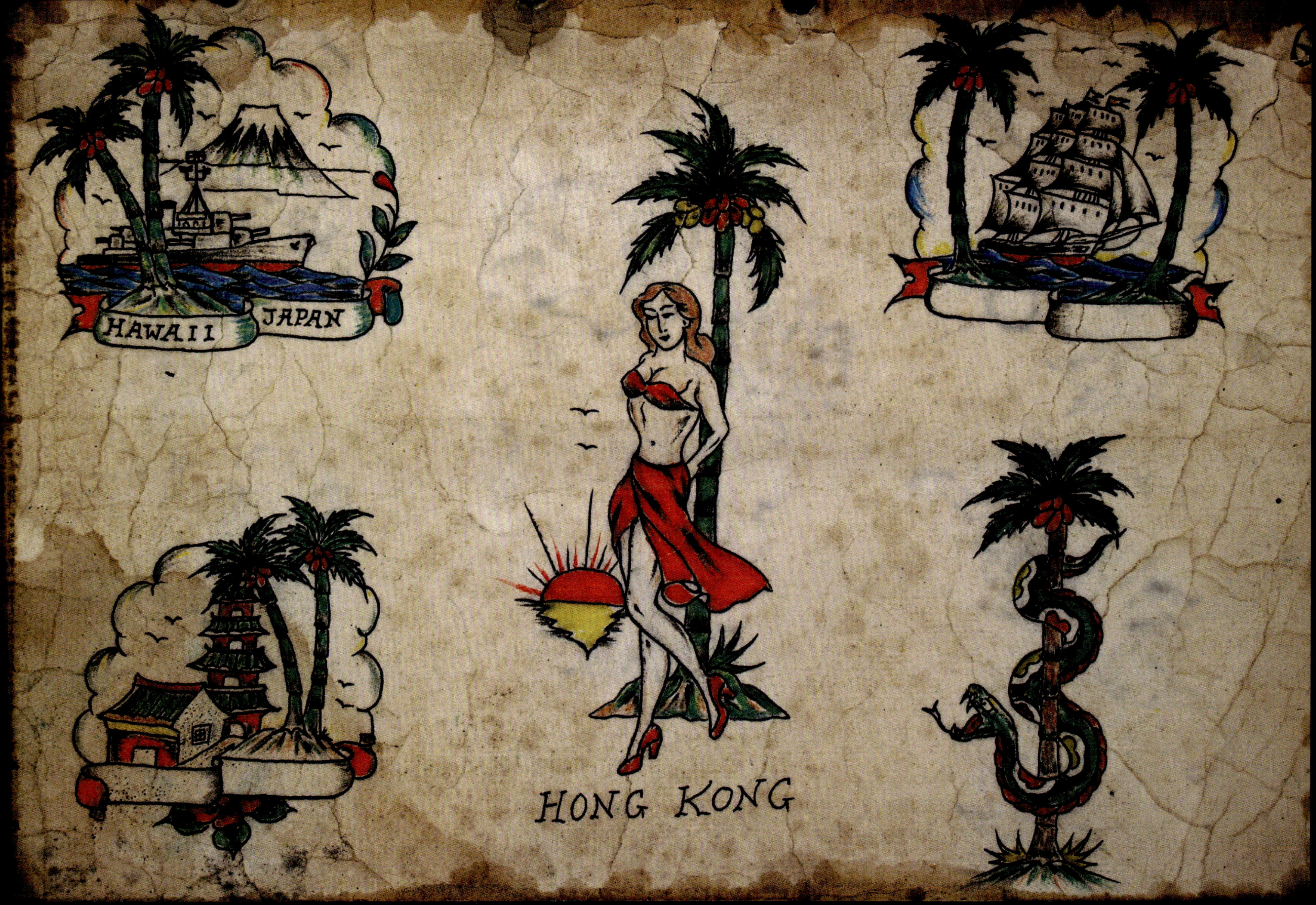
HAWAII
JAPAN
HONG KONG

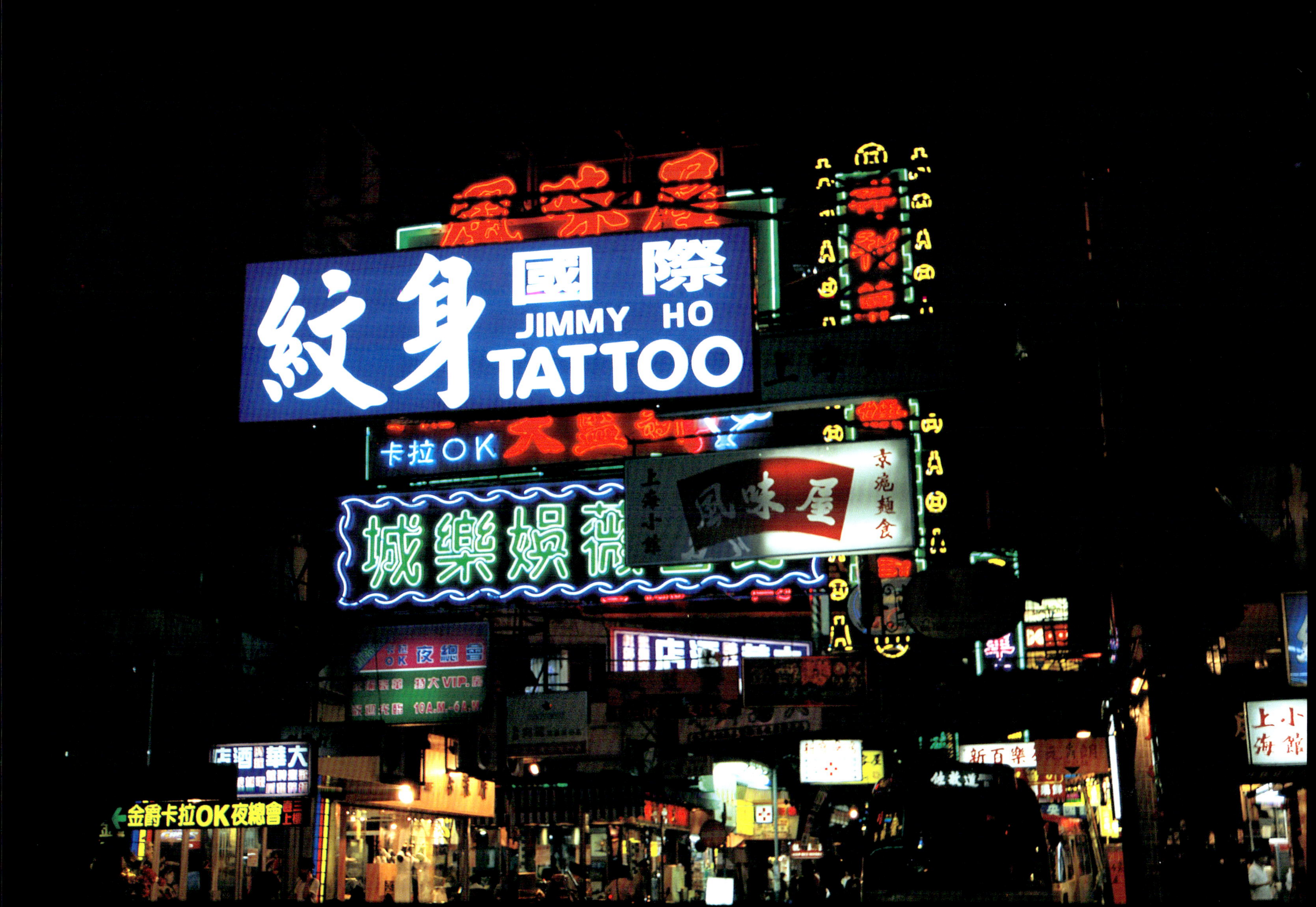

紋身
國際
JIMMY HO
TATTOO
卡拉OK
城樂娛
風味屋
京滬麵食
金爵卡拉OK夜總會

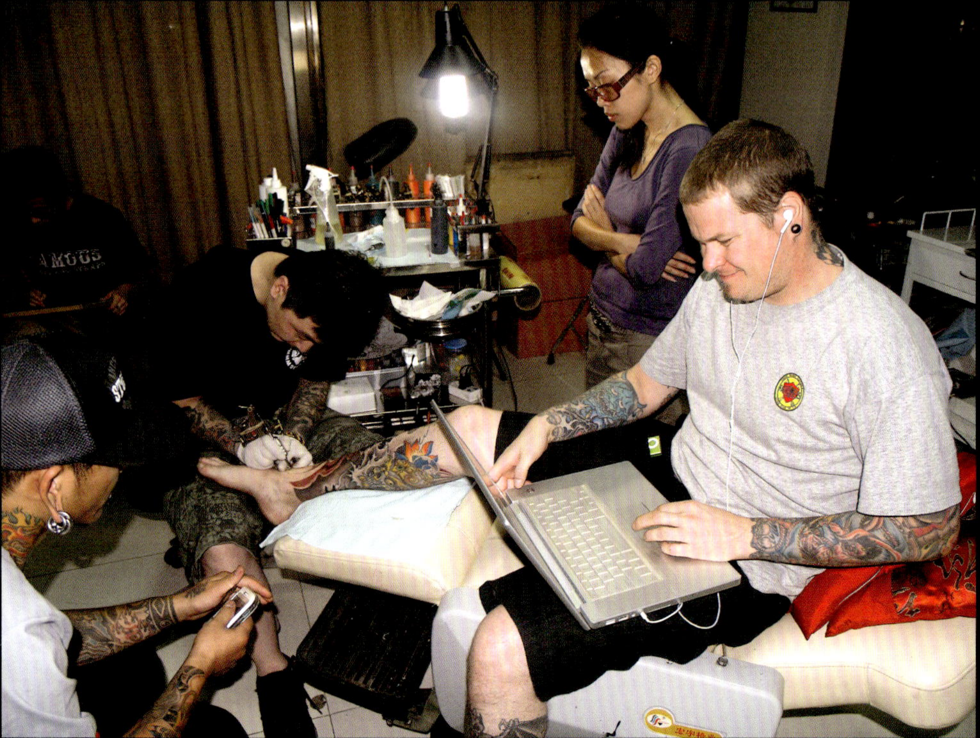

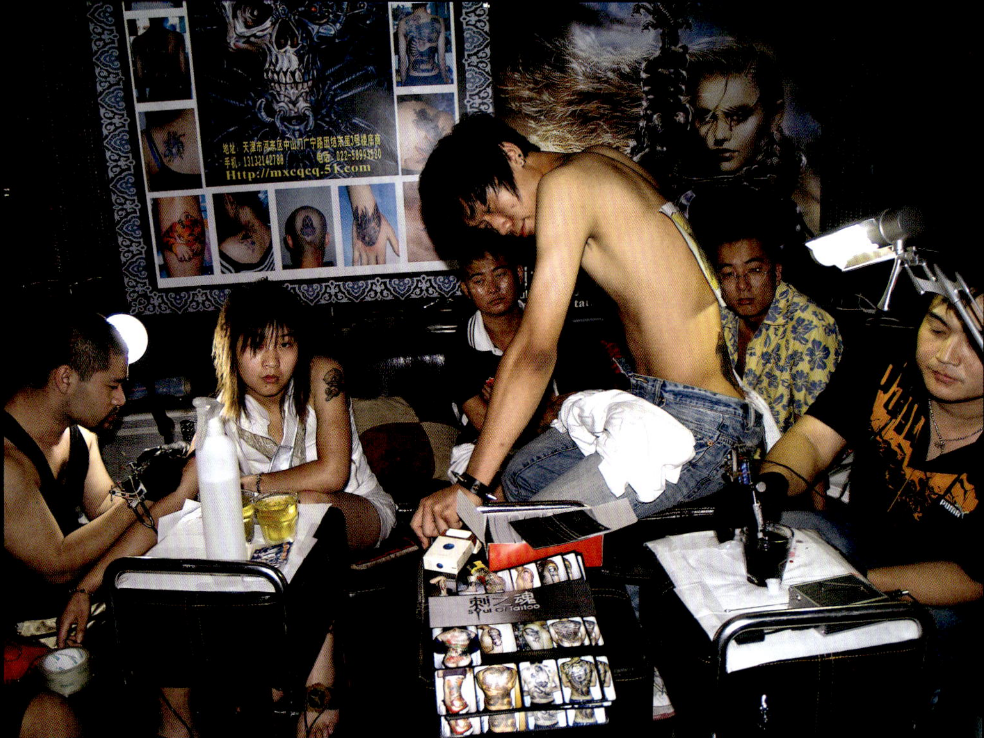
Http://mxcqcq.51.com
刺之魂
Soul Of Tattoo

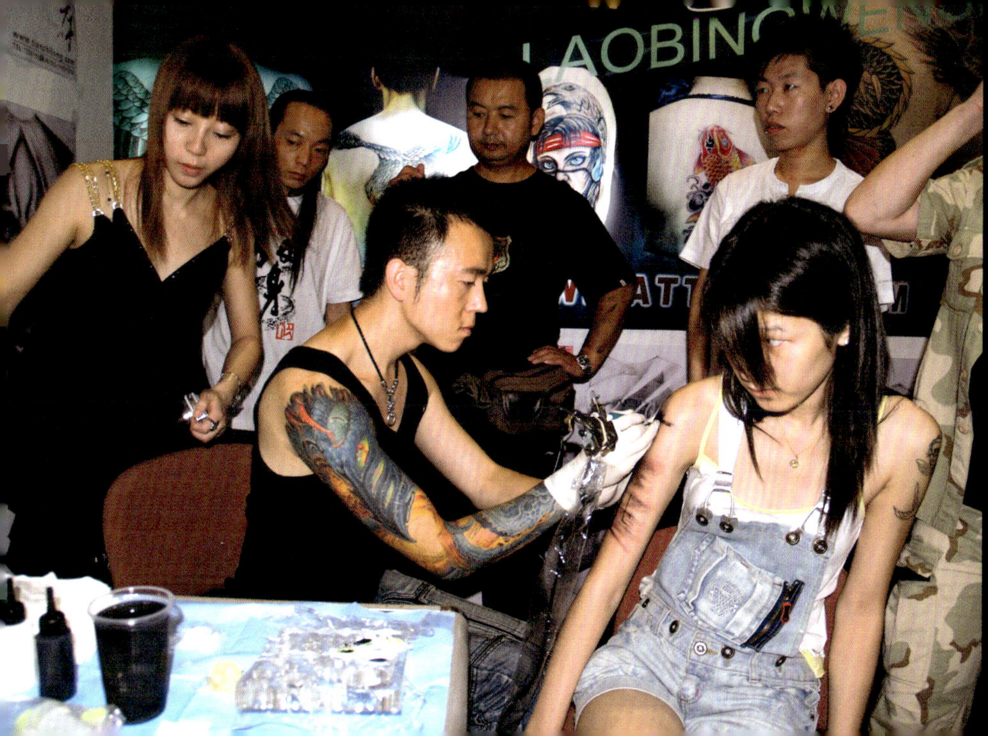
LAOBING

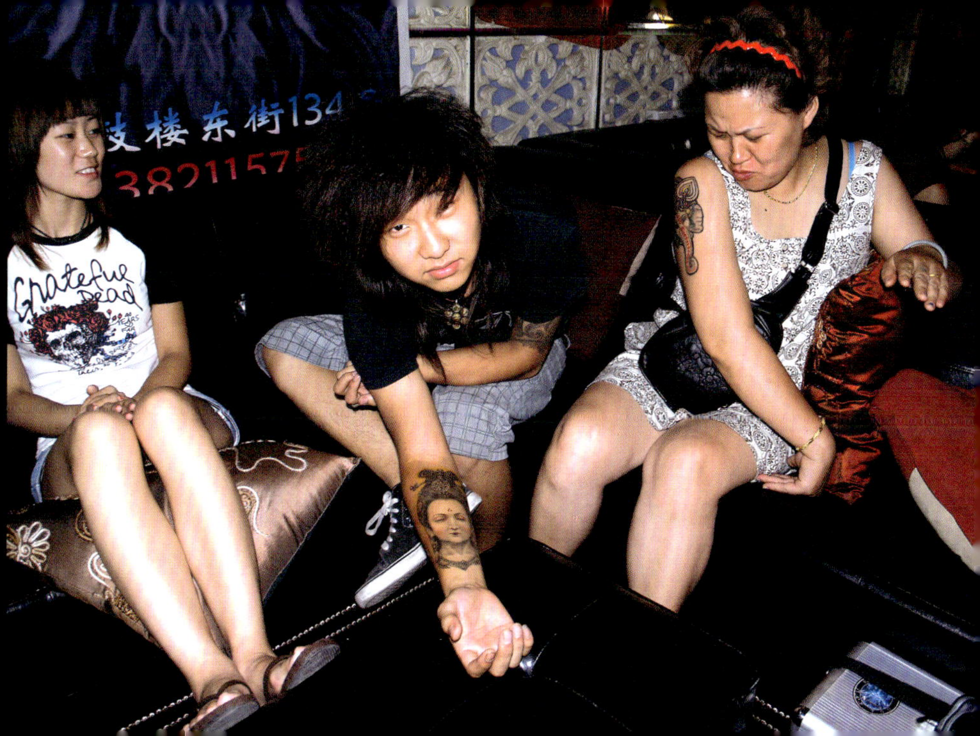
楼东街
Grateful Dead

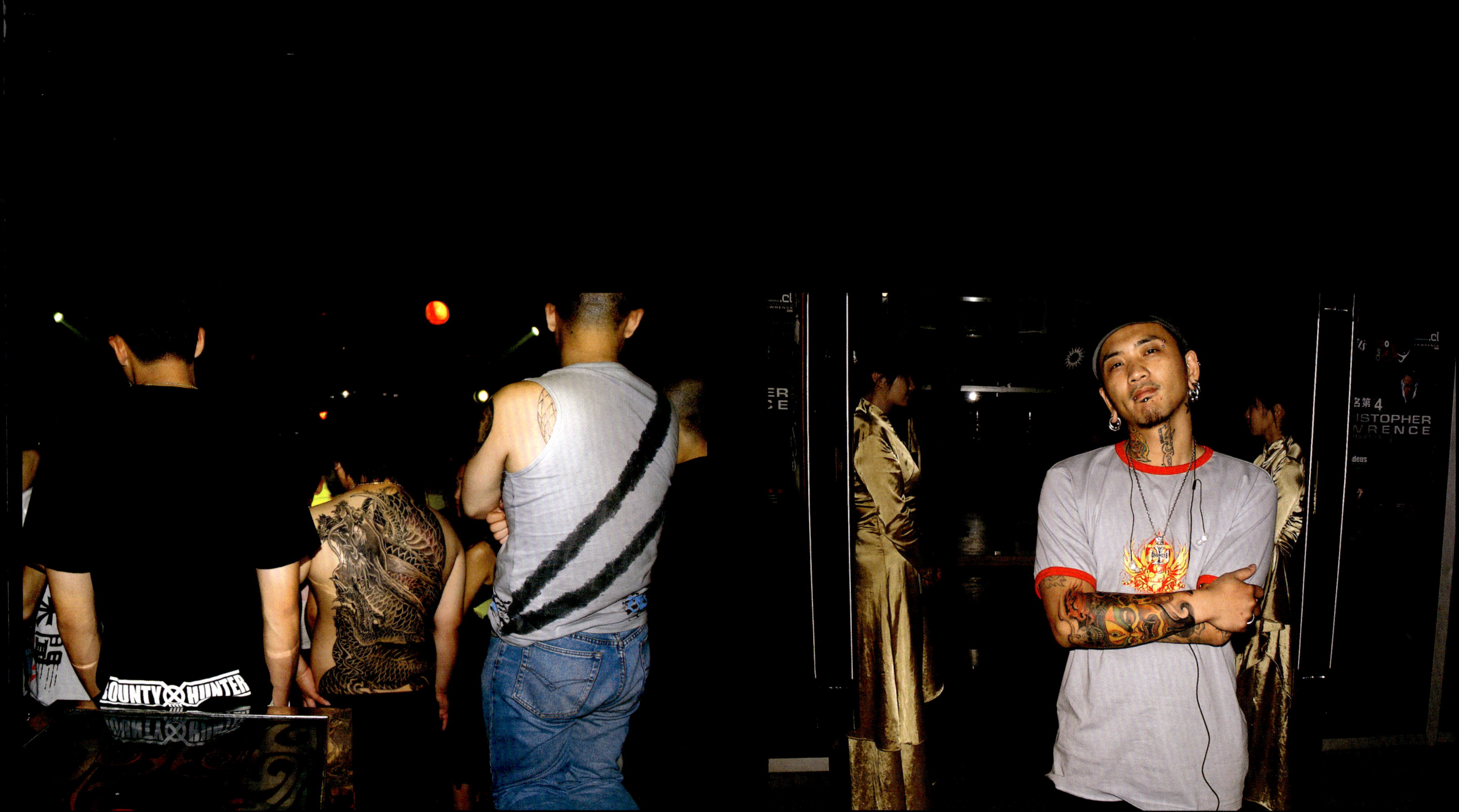

OUNTY HUNTER
ISTOPHER
deus

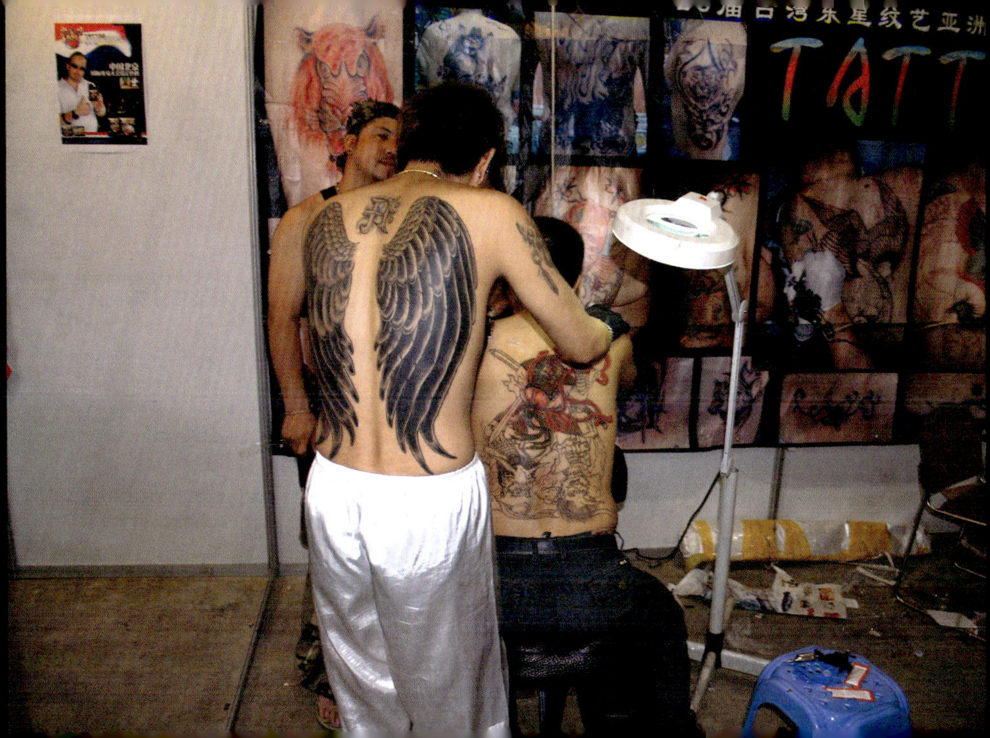
届台湾东星纹艺亚洲
TATT

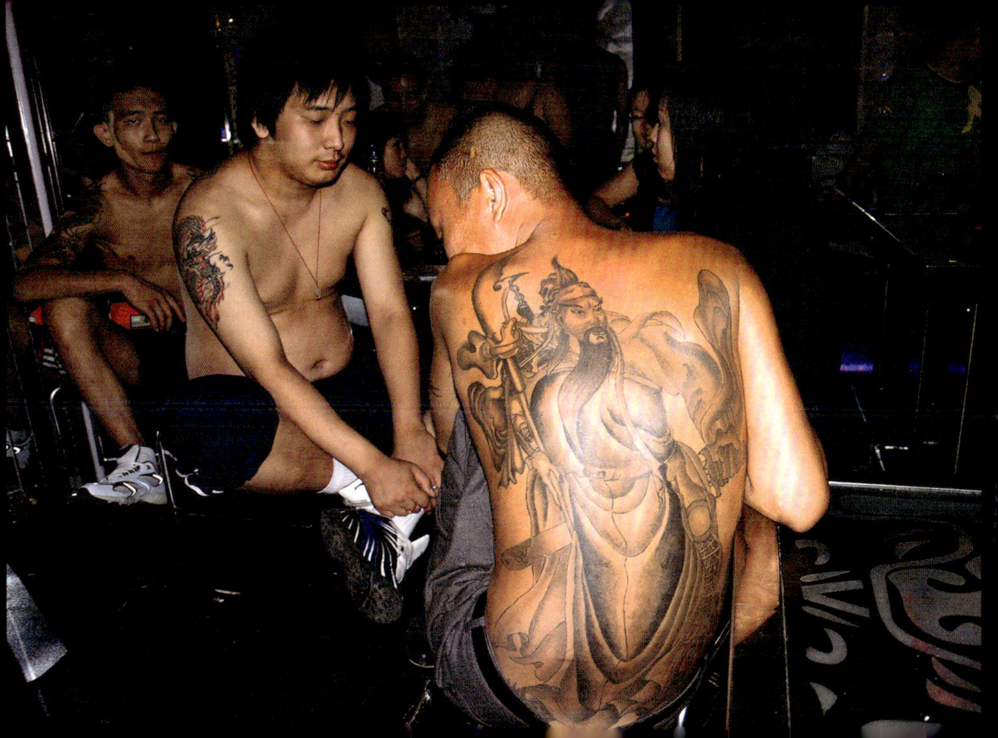

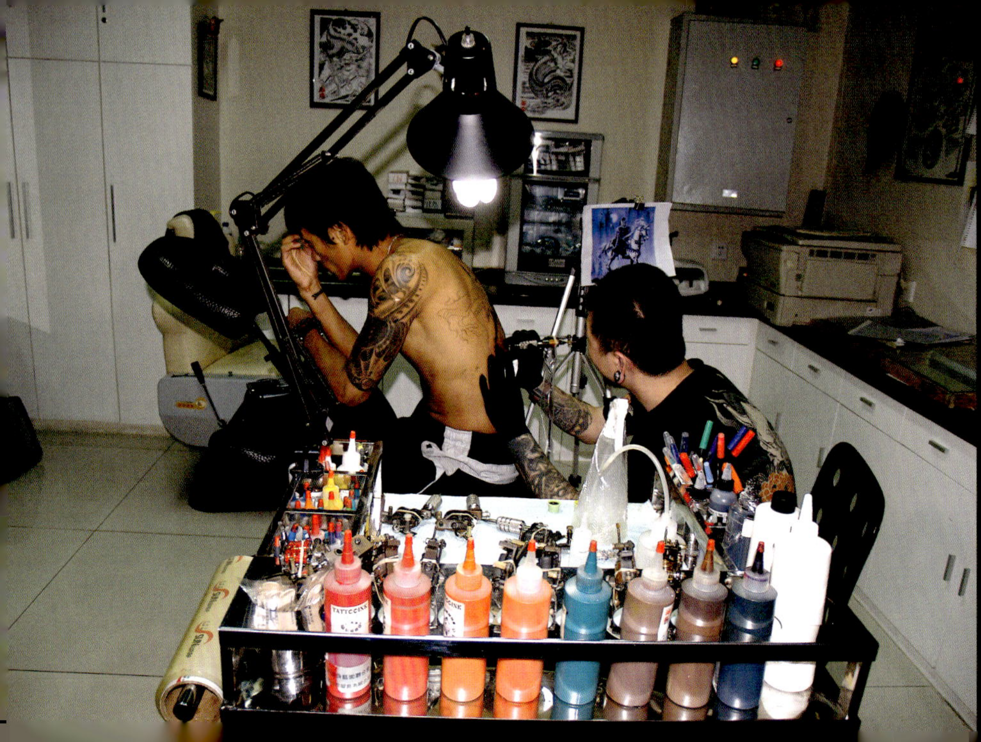

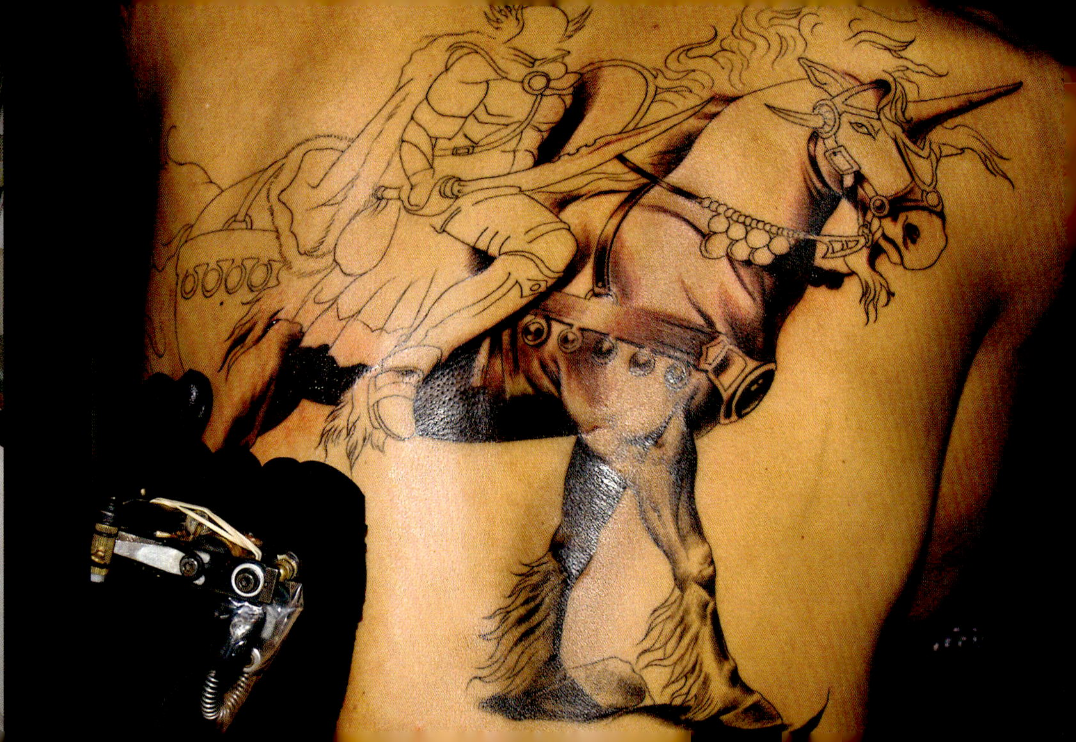

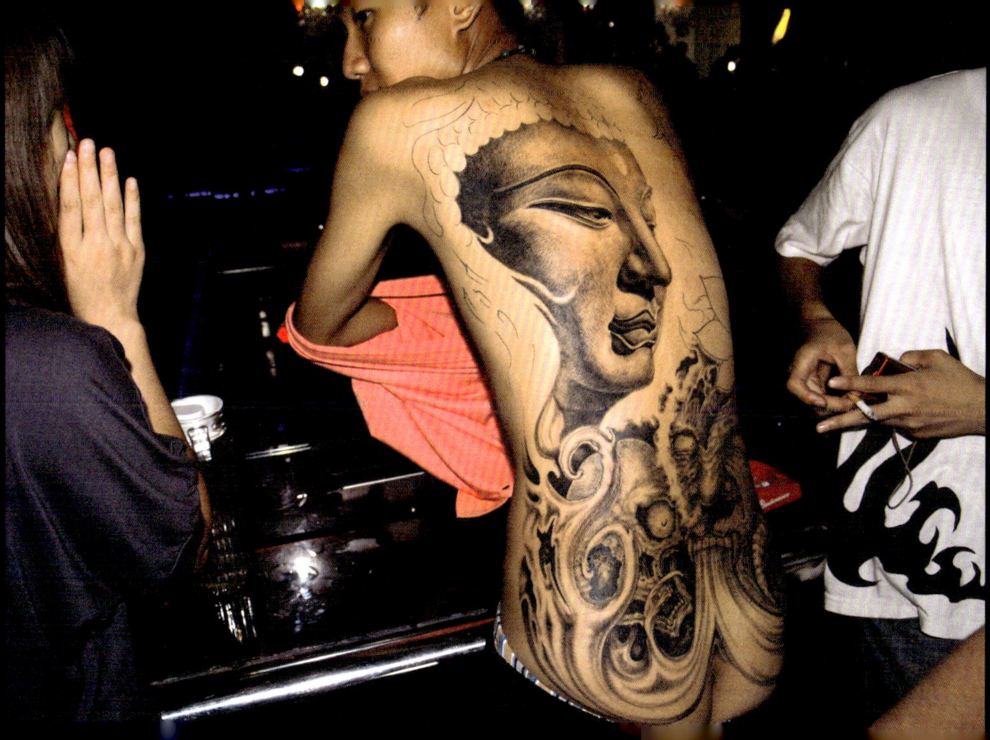
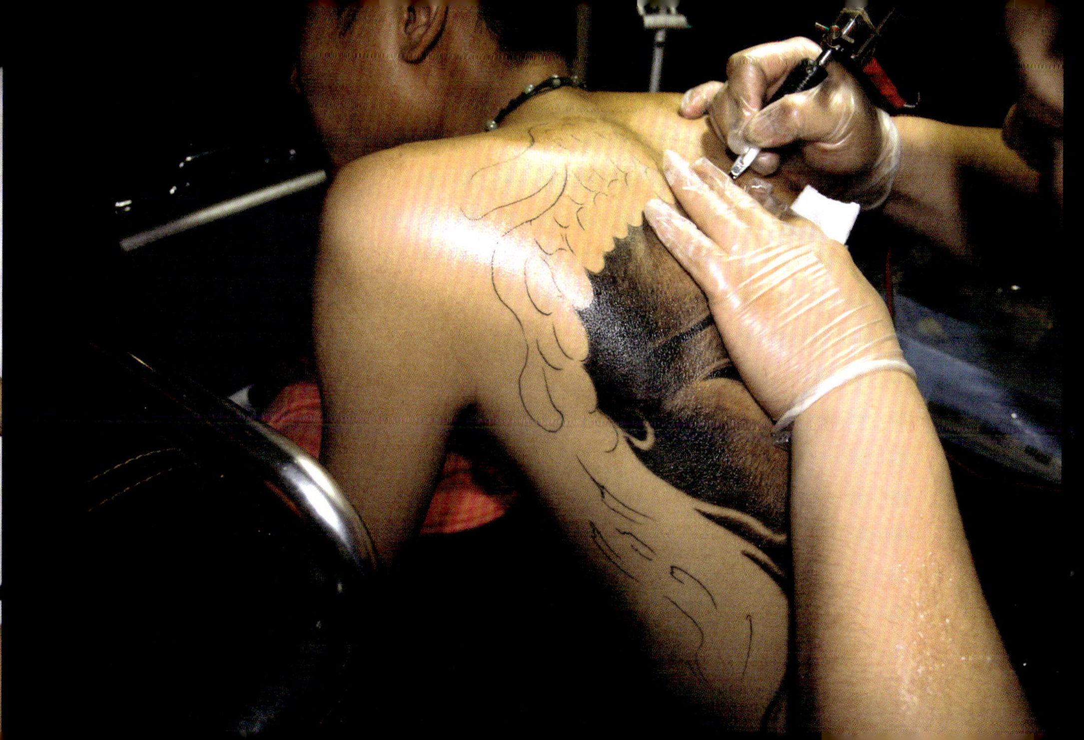

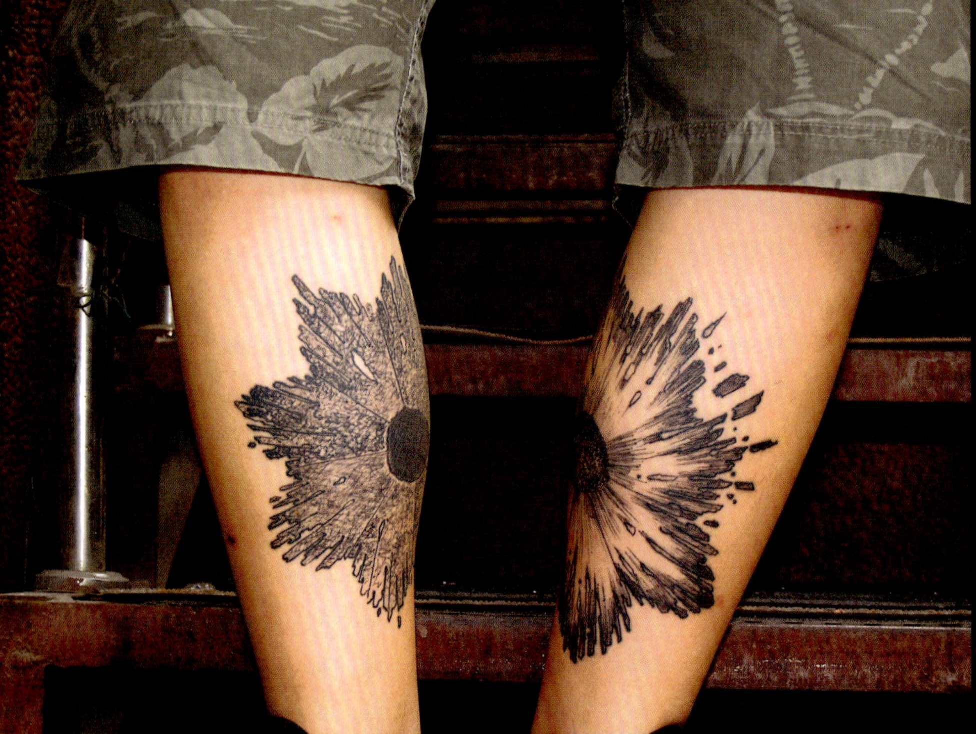

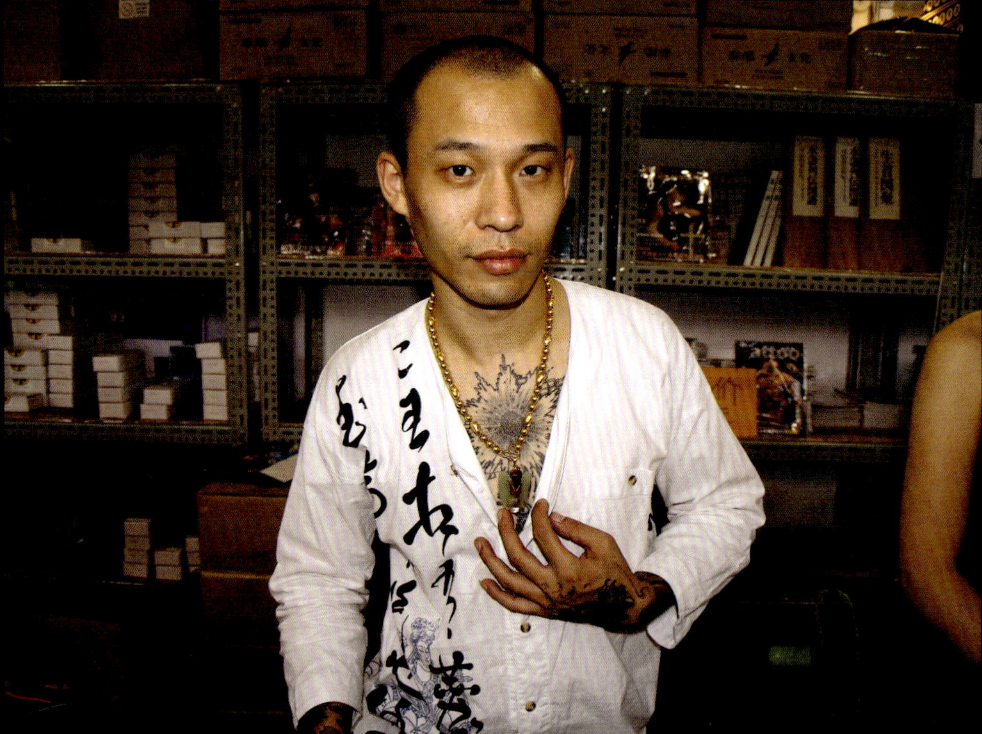

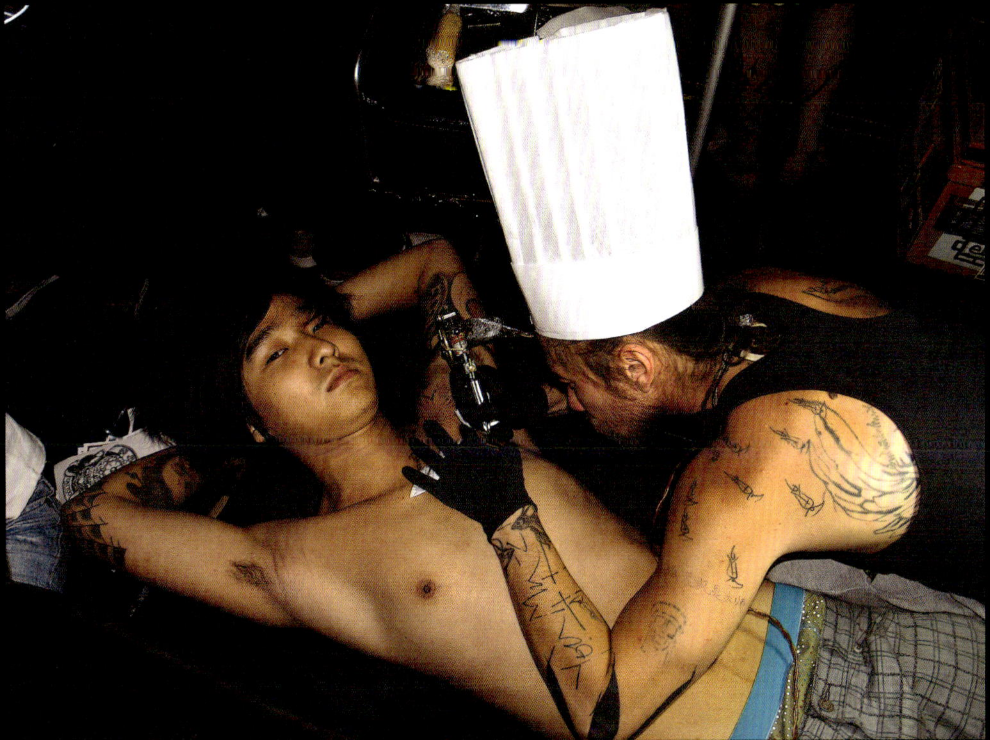

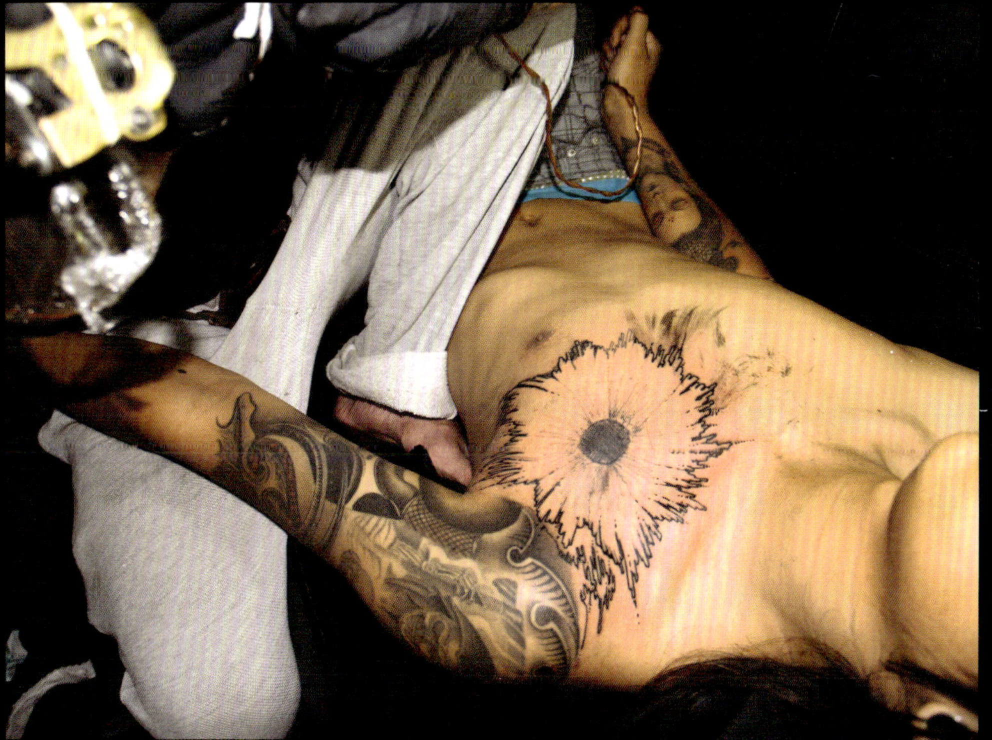

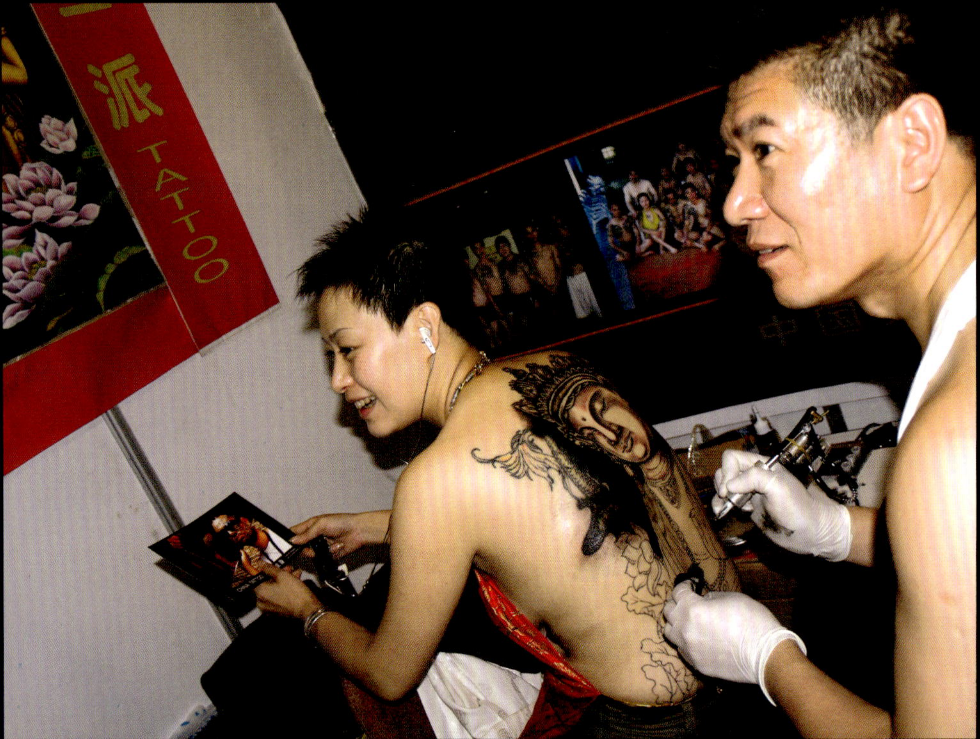
派
TATTOO
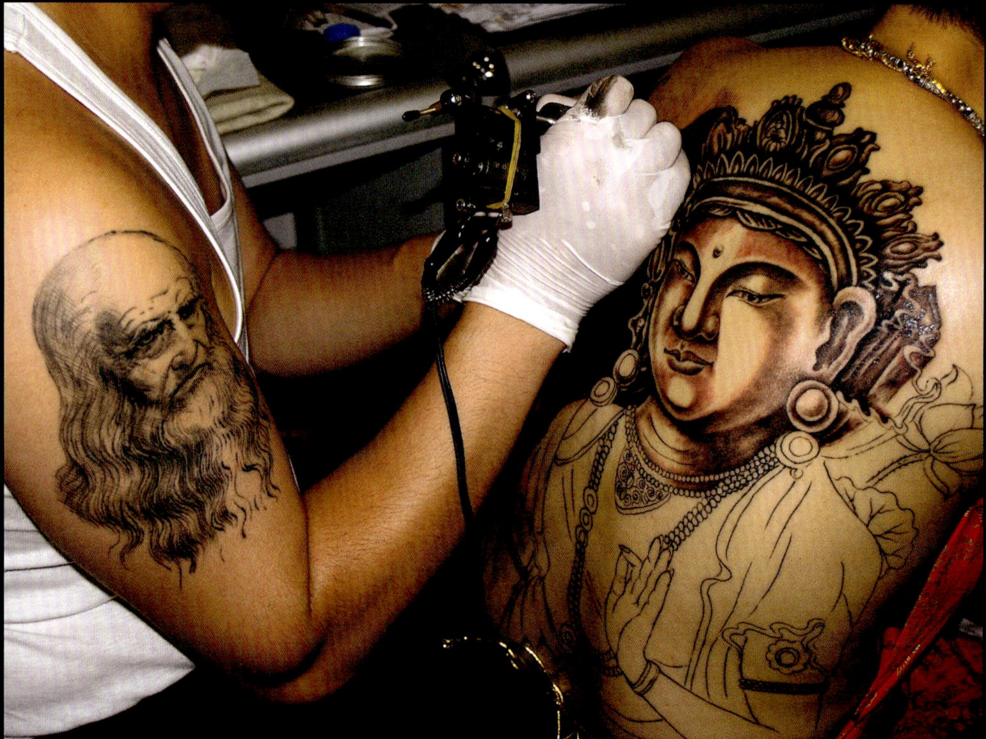

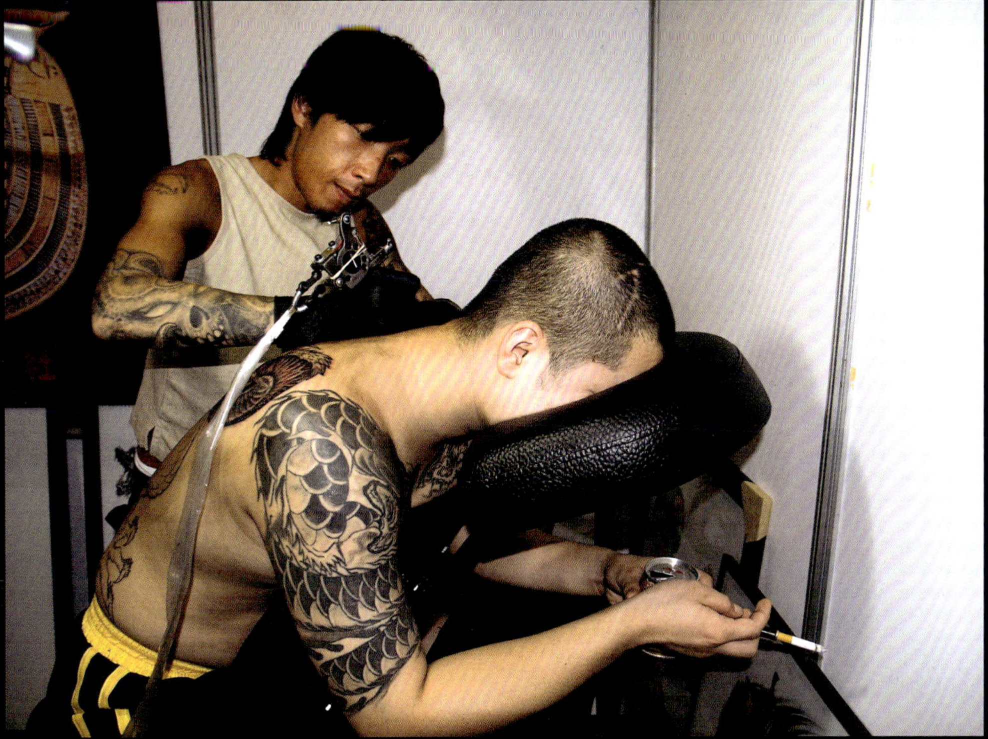

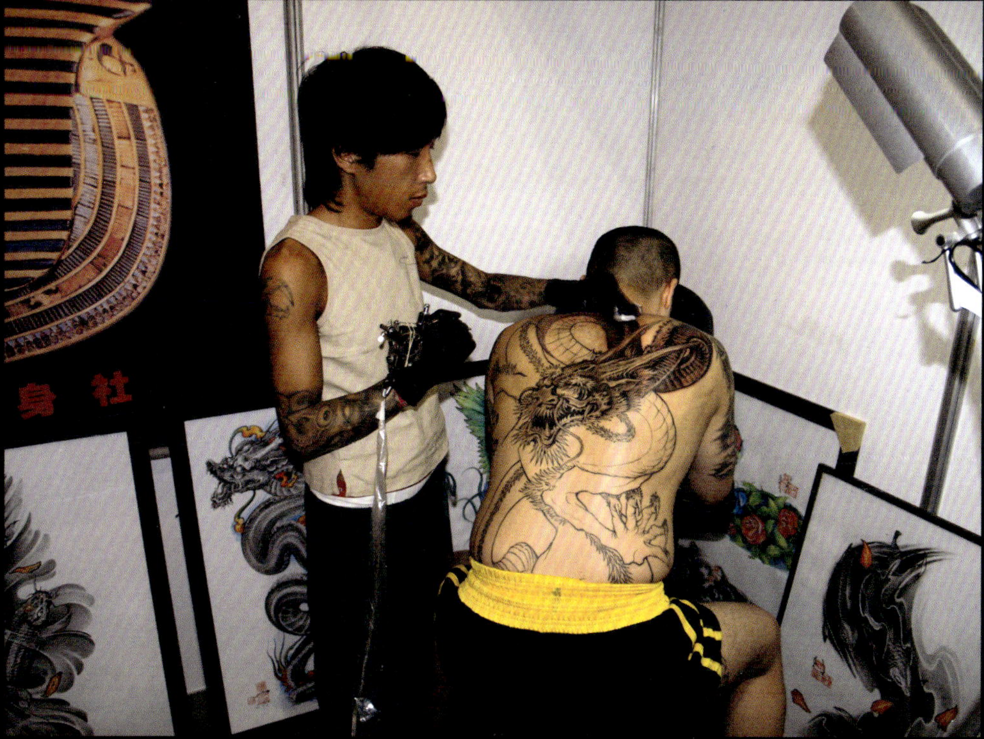

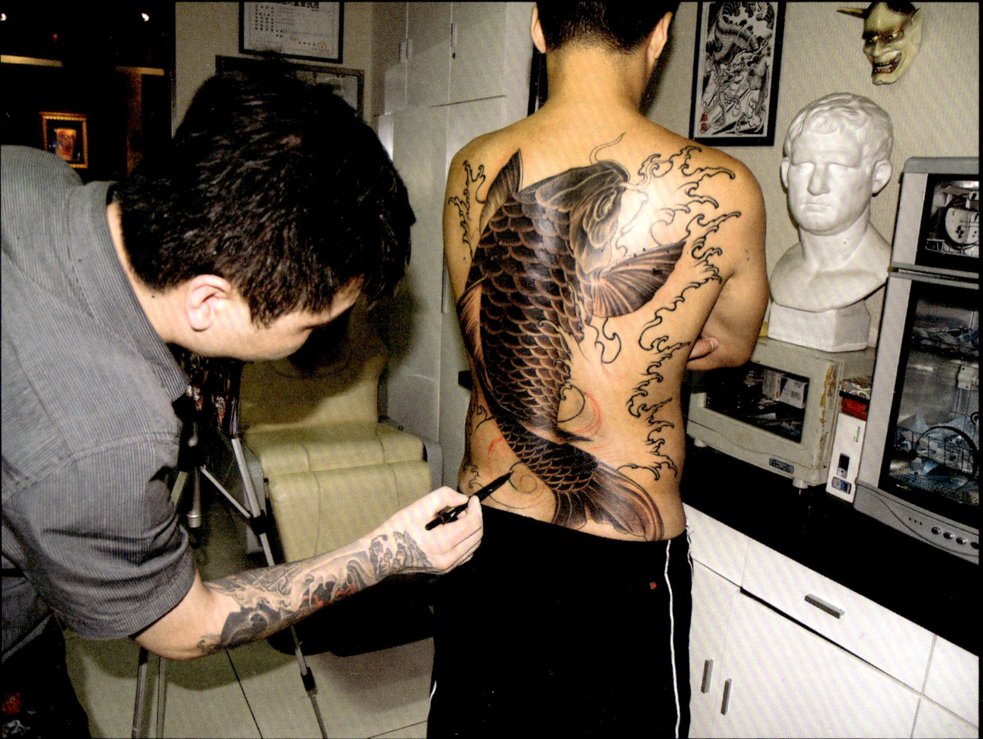

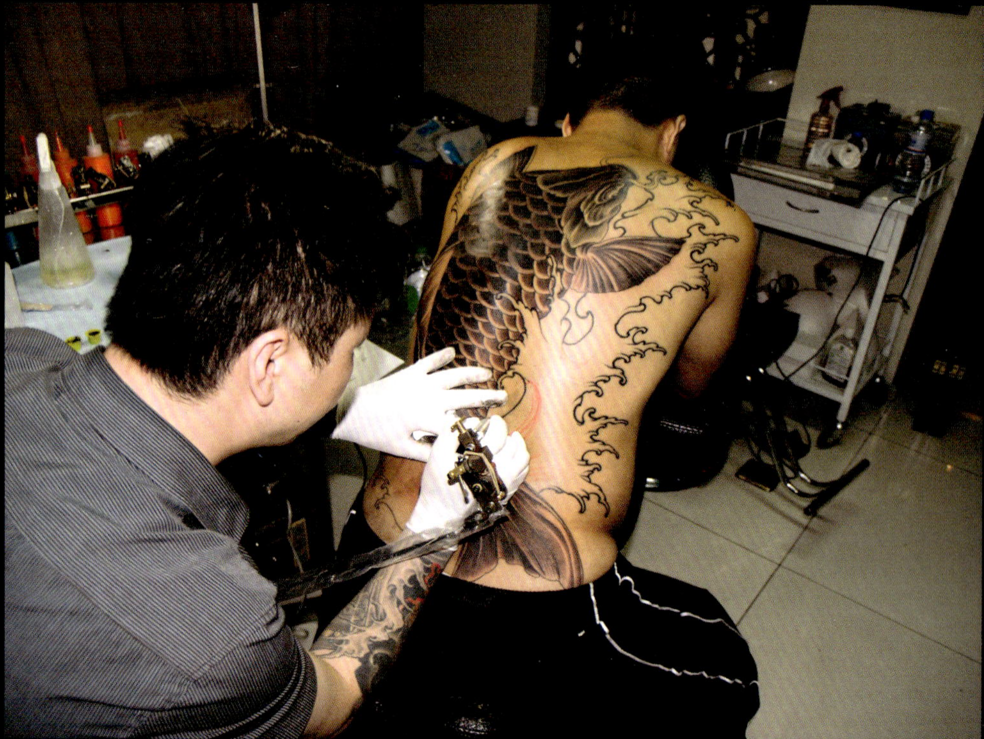